CEMETERY INSCRIPTIONS

of

PUTNAM COUNTY,

NEW YORK

1759-1925

William P. Horton

Including the towns of:

Adams Corners, Carmel, Cold Spring, Doansburg, Farmers Mills, Fredericksburg, Hortontown, Kent, Kent Cliffs, Lake Mahopac, Lake Oscawant, Ludington, Mahopac Falls, Meads Corners, Mekeels Corners, Milltown, Paterson, Secords Corners, Tilley Foster, Towners Corners, and Union Valley

> ## Notice
>
> In many older books, foxing (or discoloration) occurs and, in some instances, print lightens with wear and age. Reprinted books, such as this, often duplicate these flaws, notwithstanding efforts to reduce or eliminate them. The transcript this book was printed from is a carbon copy typed on onion skin paper over 70 years ago, or is a mimeographed edition. The print quality varies throughout the work---this would seem to be due to the wear on the paper. The pages of this reprint have been digitally enhanced and, where possible, the flaws eliminated in order to provide clarity of content and a pleasant reading experience.

Originally published
ca. 1930

Reprinted by:

Janaway Publishing, Inc.
732 Kelsey Ct.
Santa Maria, California 93454
(805) 925-1038
www.JanawayGenealogy.com

2006, 2017

ISBN: 9781596410329

Made in the United States of America

Cemetery
At Adams Corners
Putnam County N. Y.
6 miles N.E. Peekskill

Adams Corners

Adams,	John Adams; died Nov.19,1819-age 55yrs. 8mos. 3days.
"	Charlotte, wife John; died June 7,1847-age 85 years.
"	Eli, son John & Charlotte; died Mar.19,1812- age 17 years, 11 months, 10 days.
"	Catherine, dau.John & Charlotte; died Nov.18,1845- age 37 years.
"	Harvey Adams; died July 24,1880-age 82 years.
"	James S. Adams; died Apr.15,1876-age 64yrs. 11mos. 11day
"	John W. Adams; died July 13,1908-age 71 years.
"	Martha J., wife John W.; died Apr.11,1904-age 63 years.
"	S.Fowler Adams; Oct.30,1813-July 23,1895.
"	Ella L., wife Sanford; Oct.30,1851-Oct.31,1909.
"	Henrietta, dau.Isaac & Henrietta; died Nov.26,1860- age 5 years, 2 months, 23 days.
Armstrong,	Alexander Armstrong; Aug.1,1808--June 23,1898.
"	Sarah Ann Armstrong; died Nov.18,1854-age 44yrs. 15days.
"	Alexander Armstrong,Jr.; died July 13,1856- age 23 years, 1 month, 11 days.
"	Harriet R. Armstrong; died May 7,1863-age 10yrs. 4mos.
"	William Armstrong; died Jan.27,1808-age 35 years.
"	Mary, wife William; died Mar.27,1855-age 77yrs. 6mos.
"	Asbury Armstrong; died Oct.22,1848-age 49yrs. 9mos. 7da.
"	Mary Jane, dau.Asbury & Mary; died Nov.13,1837- age 5 years, 9 months, 13 days.
"	Milton W. Armstrong; Jan.27,1804-Jan.15,1865.
"	Penelope, wife Milton; May 22,1816-Jan.2,1870.
"	Lucinda, wife Milton; died Feb.24,1841-age 30yrs. 5mos.
"	Mary H., dau.Milton & Lucinda; died Aug.2,1866- age 31 years, 8 months, 21 days.

Adams Corners

Armstrong, Milton, son Milton & Lucinda; died Apr.4,1841-age 11mos.

" Elizabeth, dau. Milton & Lucinda; died Aug.11,1837-
age 9 months, 22 days.

" Sela Armstrong; died Sept.5,1827-age 21yrs. 5mos. 29days.

" William Armstrong; died Nov.12,1865-age 42yrs. 1mon. 18da

" Mary Ella, dau. William & Anna; died Sept.11,1850-
age 1 year, 6 months, 3 days.

Avery, John Sela Avery; Feb.3,1834-May 27,1897.

" Solomon Avery; died May 13,1833-age 75yrs. 9mos.

" Sarah H., wife Solomon; died May 12,1828-age 62yrs. 1mon.

" William Avery; Oct.16,1786-Jan.14,1846.

" Sarah, wife William; Sept.29,1801-Nov.15,1869.

" William H. Avery; Sept.7,1820-Aug.16,1904.

" Sarah Jane Avery; Oct.3,1828-Apr.22,1907.

Banker, Orlando Banker; Dec.14,1842-Aug.3,1912.

" Deborah Rundle, wife Orlando Banker;
July 10,1842-April 19,1914.

Barger, Andrew Barger; A native of Germany-age unknown.

" Phebe Lehman, his wife: a Princess; " "

" John, son Andrew & Phebe; died about 1818-

" Martha, wife John Barger, dau. Cornelius Barger; --------

" Phebe, dau. John & Martha; died Sept.9,1830-age 44 years.

" Nathaniel Barger; died Dec.28,1816-age 37 years.

" Daniel Barger; died June 4,1871-age 81yrs. 11mos. 24days.

" Susan, wife Daniel; died Feb.24,1887-age 88yrs. 9mos.

" Daniel Barger, Jr.; died Sept.18,1860-age 24 years.

" Stephen Barger; died Aug.25,1862-age 70yrs. 10mos. 2days

" Chloretta, dau. Stephen & Jane; died Sept.5,1853-
age 4 years, 5 months, 20 days.

Adams Corners

Barger, Washington Barger; son Stephen & Jane; d.Sep.27,1845-5wks.

" Cornelius Barger; died Feb.27,1847-age 77yrs. 3mos. 14da.

" Catherine Ann, wife Cornelius; died Sept.27,1842-
age 45 years, 8 months.

" Rebecca, wife Cornelius; died Aug.31,1862-age 90 years.

" Wright Barger; died Apr.23,1864-age 17yrs. 9mos. 11days.

" William H. Barger; Oct.31,1822-Dec.14,1912.

" Eliza Jane, wife William; died June 2,1869-age 42yrs.10mos

" John Barger; died Dec.24,1856-age 80 years, 5 months.

" Leonard J. Barger; died Apr.18,1877-age 23yrs. 2mos. 3days

" Sarah L. dau.Cornelius & Phebe; died Mar.27,1864-
age 9 years, 2 months, 11 days.

" Henry B., son Cornelius & Phebe; died Mar.27,1864-
age 5 years, 7 months, 3 days.

" Sarah J. dau.David & Susan; died Apr.16,1840-age 13mos.

" Iska, wife Reuben; died May 30,1819-age 27yrs. 9mos. 15da.

" Alfred, son Reuben & Mary; died June 17,1831-age 2yr. 7mo.

Baxter Maria E. Travis, wife Jarvis W. Baxter;
July 19,1844-June 15,1873.

Barrett, Lafayette, son Lawrence & Lucinda; died Dec.8,1853-
age 1 year, 6 months, 11 days.

" Robert C., son Lawrence & Lucinda; d.Sep.26,1855-age 15day

Buckbee, Lewis Buckbee; Nov.25,1811-Aug.19,1883.

" Edward Buckbee; died Dec.19,1839-age 71yrs. 3mos. 10days.

" Elizabeth, wife Edward; died Mar.13,1821-age 49yrs. 9mos.

" Hyatt L. Buckbee; Oct.20,1799-Apr.15,1874.

" Theodore Buckbee; Mar.25,1802-Dec.17,1856.

Bunnell, Elijah Bunnell; died Jan.14,1855-age 84 years, 6 months.

" Mary, wife Elijah; died Apr.23,1866-age 72yrs. 10mos. 17da

" Avis, dau.Elijah & Mary; died Jan.25,1830-age 3yr. 9mo.

Adams Corners

Bunnell,	Lucy Bunnell; died Oct.30,1845-age 21yrs. 10mos. 28days
Chapman,	Jeremiah Chapman; died Dec.9,1831-age 87 years.
"	Leorany, wife Jeremiah; died July 17,1828-age 74 years.
"	Job Chapman; died Dec.25,1844-age 66 years.
"	Mary Chapman; died July 16,1843-age 53 years.
"	Jeremiah Chapman; died Nov.22,1855-age 80yrs. 8mos. 3days
"	Mary, wife Jeremiah; died May 4,1849-age 77yrs. 10days.
"	Emilia, dau.Jeremiah & Mary; died Jan.10,1836- age 15 years, 5 months, 13 days.
"	Sarah Chapman; died Apr.3,1854-age 55yrs. 6mos. 9days.
"	Mary Louise, dau.John & Letitia; died July 30,1852- age 1 year, 5 months, 11 days.
"	Jane, dau.Silas & Hannah; died Jan.19,1836-age 14yr. 7mo.
"	Mary E., dau.Silas & Hannah; died Jan.26,1836- age 4 years, 10 months, 7 days.
"	Ferris, son Silas & Hannah; died Jan.29,1836- age 11 years, 11 months, 6 days.
"	Silas, son James & Katherine; died Mar.2,1849- age 2 years, 11 months, 19 days.
"	William Percival, son James & Katherine; died Sep.29,1852 age 1 year, 7 months, 3 days.
Christian,	Gabriel Christian; died Feb.4,1857-age 84yrs. 4mos. 15day
"	Lurana, wife Gabriel; died Sept.28,1863-age 85yrs. 6mos.
"	Gabriel M. Christian; died Apr.1,1844-age 37yrs. 5mos.
"	Sarah A., wife Gabriel M.; died Nov.6,1853- age 43 years, 9 months, 24 days.
"	Wesley Christian; died June 6,1849-age 50yrs.11mos.11days
"	Eliza J. dau.Samuel & Phebe; died May 7,1846-age 3yr. 7mo.
"	Clarence, son George W. & Eliza A.; died July 29,1861- age 9 years, 8 months, 22 days.
"	Emeline, dau.George W. & Eliza A.; died Dec.4,1861-2mos.

Adams Corners

Cole,	Ebenezer Cole; Dec.27,1786-June 2,1855.
"	Elizabeth, wife Ebenezer; July 18,1792-May 26,1876.
"	James Cole; died Jan.26,1869-age 61yrs. 2mos. 4days.
"	Ann Elizabeth, dau.James & Sarah; died Aug.4,1862-age 13 years, 10 months, 24 days.
Colegrove,	William Colegrove; died Nov.13,1811-age 75yrs. 5mos.
"	Mary Wheeler, wife William Colegrove; died Oct.3,1795-age 60 years, 4 months, 6 days.
"	John Colegrove; died Dec.17,1841-age 74yrs. 5mos. 12day
"	Susannah, wife John; died Mar.31,1842-age 70yrs. 1mon.
Crawford,	Nathaniel Crawford; died Feb.7,1858-age 71yrs. 2mos.
"	Hannah, wife Nathaniel; died Jan.12,1854-age 63yr. 10mo.
"	Jane E, dau.Cornelius & Sarah; died May 12,1845-age 4 years, 11 months, 11 days.
"	Arza B., son Alfred & Betsey; died Feb.14,1868-age 22 years, 11 months, 9 days.
"	Amza R., son Alfred & Betsey; died Feb.22,1865-age 27 years, 1 month, 24 days.
Cummins,	George W., son L.W.& M.A.; died May 22,1855-age 2 years.
Curry,	Frederick Curry; died July 20,1850-age 35 years.
Denny,	William John Denny; Jan.5,1819-Jan.21,1864.
Dusenberry,	Charles Dusenberry; died Oct.28,1839-age 70 years.
"	Elizabeth, wife Charles; died June 14,1863-age 77 years.
"	William Dusenberry; died Nov.7,1815-age 84 years.
"	Sarah, wife William; died May 3,1821-age 88 years.
"	John C., son Charles & Elizabeth; died June 10,1831-age 8 years, 6 days.
Gilbert,	John Gilbert; Apr.11,1817-Aug.14,1891.
"	Sarah, wife John; July 7,1818-Nov.23,1899.
"	Burr, son John & Sarah; died Feb.4,1848-age 2yr. 5mo.

Adams Corners

Gillett,	Henry Gillett; died Aug.3,1858-age 70yrs. 6mos. 11days
"	Mary Mead, wife Henry Gillett; died Apr.12,1848-age 62 years, 1 month, 27 days.
"	William H. Gillett; died Dec.18,1878-age 69yrs. 11mos.
"	Melancthon Gillett; died June 5,1871-age 56yrs. 5mos.
Hadden,	Mary J. wife Gilbert; died May 1,1851-age 39yrs. 11mos
"	Edith H. Hadden; died June 30,1862-age 2years, 1month.
"	Amelia A. Hadden; died Mar.24,1863-age 32yrs. 1mon.
Hills,	Ann Hills; died Jan.30,1794-age 52yrs. 6mos. 23days.
Hopkins,	Mary A., wife James; died July 5,1865-age 31 years.
"	John B., son James & Mary; died Sep.18,1865-age 7yrs.
Horton,	John L. Horton; died Dec.4,1829-age 83yrs. 6mos.
"	Sarah, wife John L.; died Oct.14,1827-age 75yrs.10mos.
"	Lee Horton; died Apr.5,1847-age 61yrs. 8mos. 25days.
"	Mary, wife Lee; died May 22,1862-age 66yrs. 7mos. 3days
Lee,	Margaret Lee; died June 1847-age 79yrs. 8 mos.
Lickley,	Mary J., wife James; died Dec.9,1851-age 26yrs. 11mos.
"	Emeline, dau.James & Mary; died Jan.21,1853-age 3 years, 11 months, 21 days.
"	Phebe A., dau.Absalom & Sarah; died May 12,1852-age 18 years, 5 months, 4 days.
Loveless,	William H., son William & Sarah A.; died Feb.26,1849-age 8 months, 26 days.
McCabe,	Stephen McCabe; Jan.12,1788-Dec.17,1866.
McCastline,	Andrew McCastline; died July 29,1849-age 89 years.
Odell,	John Odell; died July 1,1855-age 54yrs. 10mos. 8days.
"	Naomi, wife John; died Sept.1,1880-age 79yrs. 9mos.
"	John Odell; died Nov.25,1851-age 95yrs. 5mos. 25days.
"	Susannah, wife John; died June 25,1842-age 86 years.

Adams Corners

Odell, James Odell; died May 24,1880-age 59yrs. 8mos. 20days.

" Mary, wife James; died July 18,1862-age 37yrs. 5mos. 8days

" Tamar A. wife James; died Aug.9,1872-age 43yrs. 2mos. 22da

" Charles C., son James & Mary; died Apr.28,1865-age 18yrs.

" Naomi, dau. James & Mary; died Dec.25,1849-age 11mos. 25da.

" John W., son James & Mary; died Oct.15,1864-age 18yr. 9mo.

" Mary M., dau. James & Mary; died Feb.20,1857-age 5yrs. 4mos

" Sarah A. dau. James & Mary; died June 21,1862-age 1yr. 5mo.

" Mary Ann Odell; died Sept.2,1857-age 46yrs. 5mos.

" Charles H., son Charles G.& Martha; died Oct.20,1863-
age 2 years, 2 months, 25 days.

" Alice L., dau. Charles & Martha; died Jan.13,1869-age 23mos

Owen, Jehiel Owen; died Apr.10,1865-age 61 years, 1 month.

" Elizabeth, wife Jehiel; died Mar.13,1855-age 43yrs. 6mos.

" Wilbur Fiske, son Jehiel & Elizabeth; died Dec.14,1847-
age 6 years, 5 months, 28 days.

Pierce, Cornelius P. Pierce; died July 19,1880-age 53yrs. 10mos.

" Minerva A., wife Cornelius; died Apr.5,1868-age 48yr. 2mo.

" Elvira, dau. Cornelius & Minerva; died Feb.15,1849-age 7mos

" Samuel Pierce; Aug.26,1822-Aug.19,1909.

" Margaret, wife Samuel; died Apr.15,1849-age 69 years.

" Phebe M. dau. Samuel & Margaret; died Aug.15,1848-age 28yrs

" Martha W., dau. Stephen & Rachel; died Nov.14,1848-
age 13 years, 29 days.

" Ebenezer, son Aaron & Fanny; died Nov.4,1847-age 15yr. 7mo

" William H. Pierce; Dec.30,1850-Dec.27,1873.

" M. Curtis Pierce; Apr.26,1854-Sept.23,1868.

" Theodore T. Pierce; Aug.8,1858-Dec.11,1861.

Adams Corners

Post, James K., son Theodore & Hester; died Jan.14,1847-
　　　　　　age 1 year, 2 months, 7 days.

"　　　Isaac Post; died July 3,1812-age 80 years.

"　　　Sarah Post; died May 15,1858-age 81yrs. 7mos. 15days.

"　　　Robert Post; died Dec.20,1853-age 76yrs. 9mos. 16days.

"　　　Mary, wife Robert; died Sept.15,1865-age 89yrs. 7mos.

"　　　Sarah A., dau.Robert & Mary; died Jan.5,1867-
　　　　　　age 50 years, 6 months, 17 days.

"　　　John W. Post; died May 2,1879-age 65 years.

"　　　Hester A., dau.John W. & Phebe; died Feb.1,1860-age 10yrs.

"　　　Charles Wilbur, son John W.& Phebe; died Feb.17,1860-
　　　　　　age 2 years, 4 months, 28 days.

Robinson. Elizabeth, wife John; died Feb.20,1840-age 57 years.

Shelley, John W., son Moses & Mary; died May 25,1872-age 34yrs.

Smith, William C. Smith; died June 21,1862-age 41yrs. 2mos.

"　　　Emeline, wife William; died Nov.3,1848-age 22yrs. 2mos.

"　　　Alexander Smith; "Co.F. 6th.N.Y. H.A."
　　　　　　died Feb.15,1878-age 55 years.

Tompkins, Nathaniel Tompkins; died Dec.6,1811-age 81yrs. 8mos.

"　　　Elizabeth, wife Nathaniel; died June 1824-age 94yrs.

"　　　William H. Tompkins; died Oct.10,1895-age 62 years.

"　　　Isaac S. Tompkins; May 13,1826-May 24,1897.

"　　　Hannah H. Robertson, wife Isaac S. Tompkins;
　　　　　　May 22,1833-Oct.25,1908.

"　　　Susan M., dau.Isaac & Hannah; died Dec.23,1863-age 9yrs.

"　　　James F. Tompkins; July 29,1865-Jan.10,1893.

"　　　Mary E., wife James F.; Apr.8,1835-Jan.5,1914.

"　　　Joshua Lee, son Andrew J.& Phebe A.; died May 24,1844-
　　　　　　age 1 month, 24 days.

"　　　Phebe, wife Robert; died Aug.2,1807-age 26yrs. 5mos. 12da.

Adams Corners

Tompkins, Elijah, son Jonas & Jane; Oct.18,1824- ------

" Johnathan Tompkins; Dec.4,1819-Nov.2,1903.

" Mary J. Christian, wife Johnathan Tompkins;
March 11,1820-April 18,1907.

" Joshua Tompkins; died Apr.20,1856-age 65yrs. 9 mos. 15 day

" Hannah, wife Joshua; died May 4,1869-age 79yrs. 4mos.

" Morris B. Tompkins; Feb.23,1852-Feb.17,1857.

" Frances J. Tompkins; died Dec.18,1878-age 49yrs. 8mos.

" Daniel D. Tompkins; died Feb.11,1858-age 72yrs. 11mos.

" Phebe, wife Daniel; died Nov.4,1867-age 79yrs. 3mos. 24da.

" Elizabeth Tompkins; died Aug.31,1860-age 52yrs. 6mos. 9da.

" John Tompkins; died Feb.13,1882-age 30 years, 14 days.

" Julia A., wife Daniel; died Nov.17,1890-age 71yrs. 10mos.

" Cyrus, son Jackson & Phebe; died Mar.30,1876-
age 6 years, 2 months, 17 days.

" Ida May, dau.Joshua & Sarah; died Aug.16,1879-age 1 year.

" Cornelius Tompkins; died Jan.30,1826-age 69yrs. 6mos.

" Tamar, wife Cornelius; died Feb.13,1826-age 28yrs. 9mos.

" Abby J. wife Cornelius; died Sept.20,1872-age 45yrs. 10mos

" Asbury, son Cornelius & Abby; died Feb.20,1857-age 11mos.

" Jane, dau.Elijah & Mary; died June 2,1833-age 19 years.

" Ella Tompkins; died Oct.18,1885-age 20 years.

" Amanda J. wife Joseph; died Nov.10,1877-age 39yrs. 4mos.

" Polly, wife N.M.; died Oct.30,1848-age 16 years, 6 months.

" Nathaniel Tompkins; died Aug.3,1865-age 68yrs. 7mos. 8day

" Monmouth, son Nathaniel & M.A.; died Mar.5,1862-
age 2 years, 6 months, 27 days.

Travis, Daniel D. Travis; died Oct.3,1852-age 66yrs. 4mos. 21days

" Phebe A. wife Daniel; died Sept.2,1875-age 78yrs. 4mos.

Adams Corners

Travis,	Henry Travis; July 26,1820-Oct.20,1910.
"	Sarah E., wife Henry; died Apr.20,1908-age 79 years.
"	Charlotte Travis; ------
"	Henry M. Travis; died Oct.3,1847-age 19yrs. 3mos. 23da.
"	Jasper W. Travis; Oct.28,1857-June 17,1912.
"	Olive A., wife Stephen; died Apr.29,1883-age 74yrs.8mos
"	Chloretta, dau.Ebenezer & Phebe J.; died Jan.27,1865-age 7 years, 8 months, 21 days.
"	George W., son George W.& Adah; died Apr.30,1855-age 19 years, 10 months, 4 days.
"	Jeremiah, son George W.& Adah; died Oct.24,1846-age 20 years, 5 months, 22 days.
Vail,	Hamline, son Rev.Adee & Harriet O.; died Aug.12,1848-age 10 months.
Vredenburg,	Willie, son William & Susan; died June 22,1863-age 1 year, 6 months.
"	Our Mary Elizabeth; --------

Some old markers in
the Baptist Church ground
at Carmel, Putnam Co.
New York.

Baptist, Carmel

Baker,	Jesse Baker; died Jan.26,1853-age 47yrs. 2mos. 20days.
Bailey,	Hannah, wife Samuel; died Oct.26,1848- age 81 years, 6 months, 2 days.
Barnes,	Laura, wife A.J.; died Dec.8,1853-age 52 years.
Baxter,	Thomas Baxter; died Nov.17,1884-age 78yrs. 6mos. 19days.
"	Uretta, wife Thomas; died Aug.27,1867- age 56 years, 11 months, 13 days.
Brooks,	Mitchell W.Brooks; died Feb.15,1863-age 32 years.
Brown,	Ferris H.Brown; died March 13,1849- age 50 years, 9 months, 17 days.
"	Daniel Brown; died Mar.6,1813-age 43 years.
"	Phebe, wife Daniel; died Feb.2,1848-age 83 years.
Clapp,	Rev.William S.Clapp; Nov.2,1822-Mar.4,1869.
Coldwell,	Rebecca Coldwell; died Aug.9,1869-age 79 years.
"	Susan G., dau.John & Mary; died Oct.3,1836- age 6 years, 7 months, 19 days.
Cole,	Capt.Reuben Cole; died Oct.30,1910-age 75years.
"	Elizabeth, wife Capt.Reuben; died Dec.26,1858- age 91 years, 3 months, 26 days.
"	Antha J., wife Thomas O.; died Sept.13,1840-age 27yrs.
"	Sarah Cole-Rhodes;
"	Joseph Cole; died Jan.28,1843-age 53 years, 11 months.
"	Betsey, wife Joseph; died May 5,1871-age 75 years.
"	Mary E., dau.Joseph & Betsey; died Feb.7,1845- age 16 years, 9 months, 12 days.
"	Jarvis W.Cole; died Apr.9,1868-age 48yrs. 11mos. 10days.
"	Henry Cole; died Nov.15,1838-age 21 years, 6 months.
"	Betsey, wid.Eleazer & former wife John Cole; died May 3,1857-age 71 years.
"	Catherine, dau.Joseph & Adah; died Dec.2,1843- age 13 years, 10 months, 20 days.

Bap. Carmel

Cole, Sarah Cole-Knox;

" Betsey Cole-Kelley;

Crosby, Enoch Crosby; died Sept.1,1862-age 80 years.

" Jane, wife Enoch; died Nov.10,1867-age 83 years.

Dean, Cloe Wilson, wife Amos Dean; died July 20,1851-
age 71 years, 6 months, 7 days.

Downes, Mary, wife Sturgis; Mar.1,1791-Feb.27,1850.

Eames, Amanda, wife Thomas; died Nov.7,1843-age 34yrs. 2mos.

Ferris, Laurette Ferris; died May 27,1851-age 46 years, 6 months.

" Andrew Ferris; died June 15,1839-age 64yrs. 11mos. 26days

" Aner, wife Andrew; died Feb.8,1837-age 61 years, 2 months.

" Angeline Ferris; died Feb.17,1851-age 47yrs. 10mos. 27da.

Fisher, John Fisher; died Mar.25,1881-age 80 years, 3 months.

" Mary, wife John; died Feb.22,1869-age 44 years.

" Sarah, wife John; died Feb.2,1844-age 38yrs. 6mos. 12days

" Jane A., wife John T.; died Jan.2,1859-
age 18 years, 11 months, 2 days.

Foshay, Mary, wife James E.; died Sept.27,1866-age 28 years.

Frost, James Frost; died July 30,1836-age 39 years, 4 months.

Ganong, Alexander Ganong; died Aug.4,1842-age 62 years.

" Elizabeth, wife Alexander; died Aug.16,1861-
age 78 years, 1 month, 1day.

" Josiah Ganong; died Sept.22,1848-age 49yrs. 2mos. 8days.

Ganoung, Horton Ganoung; May 8,1836--------

GaNun, Caroline, wife Arza; died Feb.1,1845-age 23yrs. 11mos.

Gay, Sally Gay; died Sept.12,1862-age 82 years.

" Lucinda Gay; died Feb.23,1838-age 27 years.

" Phebe, wife Daniel; died May 6,1846-age 61 years.

" Cyrus Gay; died Dec.18,1862-age 79 years.

Bap.Carmel

Gay,	Ebenezer Gay; died Feb.19,1868-age 79 years, 7 months.
Gimbert,	Francis Gimbert; died Mar.8,1876-age 52 years, 2 months.
"	Maria, wife Francis; died Apr.1,1881-age 60 years.
Gregory,	Elizabeth, wife Alvah; died Apr.8,1840-age 43yrs. 11mos.
"	Catherine Gregory-Sloat;
Haines,	Aaron Haines; died Apr.15,1842-age 81 years, 8 months.
"	Miriam, wife Aaron; died Oct.16,1840-age 82 years.
"	Horace Haines; April 7,1790-April 12,1847.
"	Jane Haines; April 28,1798-September 14,1888.
Holmes,	Elizabeth Holmes-Kelley;
Hyatt,	James Hyatt; died Apr.1,1836-age 57 years, 8 months.
"	Mary, wife James; died Apr.26,1860-age 78yrs. 4mos.
Jones,	- - - - -
Kelley,	Celeria, wife Selah; died Apr.13,1826-age 21 years.
"	Betsey, wife David Kelley, former wife George E.Cole; died Sept.29,1841-age 41yrs. 4mos.
"	Levi Kelley; died Aug.26,1859-age 62 years.
"	Mary, wife Levi; died Dec.10,1863-age 72 years.
"	Elizabeth, wife Judah; --------
Kelly,	Eli, son Jesse & Eleanor; --------
Knapp,	William Knapp; died Apr.10,1852-age 53yrs. 5mos. 16days.
"	William H.Knapp; died Sept.30,1853-age 27 years, 4 months
"	Betsey, wife William H.; Jan.5,1805-Dec.9,1887.
Kniffen,	James H.Kniffen; died Sept.9,1881-age 69yrs. 10mos. 12da.
"	James Kniffen; died Jan.3,1853-age 73yrs. 6mos. 20days.
"	Eliza, wife James; died Oct.26,1840-age 58yrs. 10mos.
Knox,	Sarah Cole, wife Frederick Knox; died Nov.10,1834-age 64 years.

Bap.Carmel

Latham,   James Latham; died July 18,1872-age 61 years, 3 months.

Lawrence, Charles Lawdence; died Sept.18,1858-age 61yrs. 7mos.

"   Mary, wife Charles; died Jan.3,1881-age 85 years.

Light,   Alzada, wife Belden; died Aug.16,1847-age 26 years.

"   Georgianna, dau.Belden & Alzada; died May 26,1861-
                        age 15 years, 9 months, 1 day

Lockwood, William R.Lockwood; died Mar.7,1841-age 31yrs. 6mos.

Mead,   John W.Mead; died Apr.10,1836-age 39 years.

"   Benjamin Mead; died Dec.15,1850-age 24 years, 6 months.

Merrick,   David Merrick; died Nov.22,1863-age 95 years.

"   Mary, wife David; died Mar.19,1857-age 83 years, 11 months

Merritt,   Nathan Merritt; died Feb.27,1870-age 70yrs. 3mos. 14days

"   Eliza Merritt; died June 1,1857-age 51yrs. 11mos. 22days.

"   Elisha Merritt; died Aug.17,1841-age 73 years.

"   Deziah, wife Elisha; died Nov.23,1857-age 82 years.

Nichols,   Henry Nichols; died Feb.10,1849-age 79yrs. 1mon. 14days.

"   Susannah, wife Henry; died Oct.2,1856-
                        age 83 years, 2 months, 10 days.

Northrup, Jesse Northrup; died Oct.10,1838-age 32 years.

"   Joseph, son Jesse & Malinda; died Jan.10,1839-
                        age 4 years, 8 months, 5 days.

"   Hannah, wife John; died Oct.25,1843-age 63yrs. 1mon.

"   James M., son John & Hannah; died June 30,1837-a
                        age 21 years, 5 months, 26 days.

Onoon,   Mary Onion; drowned June 22,1849-age 27 years.

Pierce,   Betsey Pierce; -----

"   Mary J., dau.Edmond H.& Betsey; died Aug.16,1835-
                        age 2 years, 7 months, 2 days.

"   Jane E.Pierce; died Aug.27,1841-age 2 years.

Raymond, William Raymond; died Apr.18,1833-age 57yrs. 8mos. 3days.

Bap. Carmel

Raymond, Hannah, wife William; died Jan.9,1841-
age 66 years, 11 months, 17 days.

Rhodes, Samuel C. Rhodes; died April 16,1888-
age 64 years, 10 months, 9 days.

Seymour, Elijah Seymour; died Mar.15,1851-age 65 years.

" Deborah, wife Alexander; died Aug.25,1851-
age 20 years, 6 months.

" Adeline, wife Alexander; died Aug.1,1858-age 29 years.

Shear, Hezekiah Shear; died Nov.4,1839-age 24 years, 1 month.

" Julia M., wife John C.; died Mar.30,1852-
age 34 years, 10 months, 10 days.

" Rufus, son John C.& Julia M.; died Apr.18,1852-
age 11 years, 7 months, 5 days.

Shenton, John Shenton; Nov.27,1821-Apr.16,1896.

" Annis, wife John; July 5,1828-Mar.28,1910.

Sloat, Martha Sloat; died Sept.15,1876-age 70 years.

" Catherine, wife Mitchell Sloat, former wife Lewis Gregory
died March 17,1848-age 56 years.

Smalley, Zacharia Smalley; died Feb.24,1864-age 59 years.

" Louisa, wife Zacharia; died May 9,1840-age 43 years.

" Esther, wife Zacharia; died Mar.2,1864-age 58 years.

Smith, Horace Smith; died Jan.7,1860-age 58 years.

" Ruth, wife Horace; Jan.21,1800-Sept.20,1866.

Taylor, Francis T., son Thomas & Nancy; died Nov.18,1857-
age 11 years, 10 months, 14 days.

" Thomas W., son Thomas & Nancy; died Mar.31,1857-
age 19 years, 7 months, 24 days.

" John W., son J.C.& Adelaide; d.Aug.12,1839-age 1 month.

" Adelaide, dau.J.C.& Adelaide; d.July 22,1858-age 4 mos.

Tillott, James Tillott; died Jan.6,1846-age 35 years.

" Sarah I., wife James; died Mar.5,1838-age 25 years.

Bap. Carmel

Tompkins,	Julia A., wife Howard; died May 7, 1861-age 42 years.
Townsend,	Samuel R., son W.R.; died May 30, 1844-age 9 years.
"	Uriah Townsend; died Feb.1, 1864-age 80 years, 11 months
"	Sally, wife Uriah; died Sept.14, 1843- age 57 years, 11 months, 26 days.
"	Abijah Townsend; died Nov.5, 1838-age 78 years.
"	Esther, wife Abijah; died Feb.4, 1844-age 85 years.
Vredenburg,	Samuel Vredenburg; died July 29, 1863-age 85yrs. 2mos.
"	Polly, wife Samuel; died May 13, 1844-age 68yrs. 6mos.
"	Elisa Vredenburg; died July 25, 1836-age 32yrs. 9mos.
Warren,	Rev. John Warren; died July 21, 1863-age 83yrs. 1mon.
"	Desire Warren; died Mar.31, 1869-age 76yrs. 2mos. 8days
Washburn,	Laura R. dau. Johnathan & Naomi; d. Nov.7, 1866-age 35yrs
"	Samuel Washburn; July 2, 1773-Aug.1, 1847.
"	Phebe, wife Samuel; May 4, 1776-Feb.20, 1870.
Whitbeck,	Jane Whitbeck; Apr.13, 1803-June 15, 1861.
Wilson,	Thomas Wilson; died Nov.6, 1841-age 63yrs. 9mos. 24days
"	Harvey N. Wilson; died Mar.9, 1863 from wounds received at Antietam; age 22yrs. 4mos.
"	Sarah Wilson; died Jan.16, 1844-age 87 years.
"	Martin Wilson; died June 25, 1851-age 33yrs. 7mos. 29da.
"	Lana, wife Martin; died May 2, 1854-age 34yrs. 3mos.
"	Cloe Wilson;
Yeamans,	Epenetus Yeamens; died Aug.19, 1850-age 75 years.
"	Amplias Yeamans; died Mar.3, 1873-age 72 years.
"	Eliza, wife Amplias; died Sept.3, 1855- age 49 years, 5 months, 19 days.

Mt. Gilead Cemetery

one mile south of Carmel -

Putnam County, N.Y.

1924

Index

Badeau,	11.	Mc Mahon,	12.
Bailey,	3, 8.	Marick,	4.
Baker,	3, 7.	Merrick,	6.
Beale,	6.	Myrick,	6.
Belden,	9, 10.	Markham,	12.
Bundige,	1.	Marvin,	3.
		Mead,	2.
Christie,	7.	Mens,	2.
Cole,	3.	Miles,	10.
Coldwell,	5.	Moore,	6, 7.
Colwell,	5.	Munger,	8.
Crain,	8.		
Crane,	2.	Nickerson,	9.
Crosby,	1, 2, 6.		
		Pearce,	8.
Dean,	3.	Pierce,	8.
Delavan,	11.	Phillips,	6.
De LaLuz,	10.		
Drew,	8.	Rundle,	2, 6.
Duel,	9.		
		Seeley,	7.
Everett,	7.	Shaw,	12.
		Sloat,	2.
Ferris,	2, 4.	Sloot,	7.
Foster,	6, 11.	Smalley,	12.
Fowler,	2, 3, 4, 6, 9, 11.	Smith,	6, 10.
Frost,	4, 7, 8, 9, 10.	St. John,	10.
		Strang,	2.
Ganong,	2, 7, 11.		
Garrison,	2, 5.	Thorn,	10.
Gregory,	4.	Tillotson,	8.
		Tompkins,	2.
Haines,	3.	Travis,	9, 12.
Halcomb,	9.	Trowbridge,	3.
Hamilton,	5.		
Hazen,	5, 6, 10.	Vail,	12.
Hitchcock,	7.		
Hooker,	10.	Washburn,	3.
Hopkins,	5, 9, 11.	Watts,	8.
Hughson,	3.	Williams,	8.
		Willson,	3.
Kelly,	5.	Wilson,	3.
Kemper,	12.	Wood,	3.
King,	2.		
Kniffin,	7, 8, 12.	Yeamans,	3, 8.

Mount Gilead

Crosby,   Enoch Crosby (Harvey Birch) "Patriot Spy of the
           American Revolution"
           born June 5, 1750--died June 26, 1835.

   "He braved danger and death that this land
   might be free. To the cause of Liberty he offer-
   ed his all without hope of reward. Honored by
   Washington, Revered by his Countrymen, We who
   inherit the freedom for which he died raise this
   Monument to his glorious Memory.

   "Erected 1914 by Ferdinand Hopkins."

"   Sarah, wife Enoch Crosby; died September 4, 1811
          aged 56 years.

"   Rebecca, daut. Enoch & Sarah; died Mar. 17, 1814-
          aged 21 years.

"   Betsey, daut. Enoch & Sarah; died Oct. 16, 1806 -
          aged 21 years.

"   Edward Crosby, M.D. June 22, 1812 - Oct. 30, 1890.

"   Lewis Crosby; died April 30, 1836 -
               aged 46 years, 6 days.

"   Cornelia, wife Lewis; died Dec. 3, 1857 -
               aged 64 years, 2 months, 2 days.

"   Rachel Duel, wife Edward Crosby, M.D.
               died April 7, 1871 - aged 53 years.

"   Hancie Bundige, wife Edward Crosby, M.D.
               Feb. 14, 1820 - July 12, 1903.

"   Charles, son Lewis & Cornelia; died June 8, 1849-
          aged 20 years, 8 months, 22 days.

"   Enoch R., son Lewis & Cornelia; died May 15, 1826-
          aged 6 years, 3 months, 19 days.

"   Thomas, son Lewis & Cornelia; died Mar. 24, 1819 -
          aged 1 month, 22 days.

"   Elizabeth, dau. Lewis & Cornelia;
               died Feb. 17, 1825 - aged 16 days.

"   Joseph Crosby; died Jan. 13, 1869 -
               aged 54 years, 4 months, 4 days.

"   Zilla Crosby; died July 23, 1863 -
               aged 46 years, 10 months.

Mt. Gilead.

Rundle,   Hannah Crosby, wife Philip Rundle;
                    died Apr. 16, 1871 - aged 71 years.

Sloat,   Abigail, wife James; died May 15, 1825 aged 69 years

Ganong,   Eli Ganong; died Feb. 3, 1827 -
                    aged 40 years, 9 months, 12 days.

"   Fanny, wife Eli; died Oct. 26, 1865 -
                    aged 83 years, 2 months, 15 days.

"   Theron, son Eli & Fanny; died Aug. 1, 1823 -
                    aged 14 years, 1 month, 22 days.

"   Reuben Ganong; died Dec. 29, 1886 -
                    aged 79 years, 3 months, 23 days.

"   Lewis Ganong; died Mar. 28, 1812 - aged 14 years.

"   James M. Ganong; died Oct. 15, 1814 - aged 21 years.

Ferris,   Nancy, wife Andrew; died May 26, 1792 - aged 20 yrs.

"   Alvah, son Andrew & Nancy; died Aug. 9, 1825 -
                    aged 18 years, 9 months.

Crane,   Jesse, son Samuel & Polly; died Oct. 1, 1828 -
                    aged 21 years.

Tompkins,   Abby Jane, wife Dilazon; died Jan. 17, 1845 -
                    aged 30 years.

"   Mary Esther, dau. Dilazon & Abby; d. Feb. 14, 1843 -
                    aged 1 year, 1 month.

Mead,   Elizabeth, wife Ethan; died Apr. 4, 1812 - aged 63 yrs.

Fowler,   Harvey, son Moses & Adah; died Sept. 22, 1805 -
                    aged 41 years, 8 months.

Garrison,   James Garrison; died Jan. 18, 1881 - aged 80 years.

"   Mary, wife James; died May 6, 1874 - aged 65 years.

"   Cornwell, son James & Mary; June 1, 1877 - aged 43 yrs.

Mens,   Cornelius Mens; died July 28, 1886 - aged 70 years.

Strang,   Theda, wife Charles H.; died April 19, 1866 -
                    aged 60 years, 24 days.

King,   Andrew, son Levi & Adah Zillah; d. June 27, 1822 -
                    aged 2 years, 6 months.

Mount Gilead

55

Washburn,	Zebulon Washburn; died Nov.12,1833 -aged 86 years
"	Phebe, wife Zebulon; D. May 23,1846-aged 80 years.
Trowbridge,	Alvah Trowbridge; died June 10,1856 - aged 76 years, 8 months, 6 days.
"	Sally, wife Alvah; died April 6,1833 - aged 52 years, 9 months, 9 days.
Fowler,	John Fowler; died Aug.23,1827 - aged 30 years, 1 month, 2 days.
Bailey,	Rosalinda, wife William H.; died Aug.20,1848 - aged 28 years, 3 months, 13 days.
Fowler,	Chlorinda Jane, dau. William & Catherine; died Jan. 8,1834 -aged 1yr. 10mo. 10days
"	Edwin Fowler; died Jan. 2,1870 - aged 48 years, 8 months.
"	Martha Marvin, wife Edwin Fowler; died Apr. 3,1879 -aged 59yrs. 1mon. 24days
Dean,	Rhoda, wife Amos; died Dec.28,1818 -aged 41yrs.
Haines,	Elihu Haines; died March 25,1850 - aged 72 years, 9 months, 14 days.
"	Hester, wife Elihu; died June 11,1833-age 56yrs.
Yeamans,	Sarah, wife Epenetus; died Oct. 2,1818 - aged 42 years.
Hughson,	Jeremiah Hughson; died Apr.12,1812 - aged 63 years, 1 day.
"	Rebecca, wife Jeremiah; died April 7,1812 - aged 61 years, 10 months, 9 days.
Willson,	Jesse Willson; died Sep.21,1805 -aged 22 years.
Wilson,	Thomas Wilson; died Oct.7,1805 - aged 49 years.
"	Mary Cole, wife Thos. Wilson; died April 16,1825- aged 62 years, 11 months, 27 days.
"	Wallace, son Daniel & June; died May 31,1831 - aged 20 years, 8 months, 5 days.
Baker,	Abigail Baker; died Oct. 3,1805 - aged 80 years.
Wood,	John Wood; died Dec.17,1808 - aged 34 years.

Mount Gilead

Fowler,   Irene, dau. Edwin & Martha; died Oct.21,1857 -
                               aged 1 month, 11 days.

Frost,   Munson Frost; died Sep.26,1823 -
                               aged 24 years, 9 months, 3 days.

"   John Frost; died Mar.27,1831 -aged 91 yrs. 9 mon.

"   Huldah, wife John; died Oct.13,1802 aged 60 years.

"   Mehetable, dau. John & Huldah;
                               May 10,1783 - June 6,1856.

Ferris,   Clarissa, wife Samuel; died Dec.20,1818-age 20yrs.

"   Sally, dau. Samuel & Clarissa;
                               died Jan.12,1824 -aged 8 years

Gregory,   Hart Gregory; died Apr.9,1844 -
                               aged 20 years, 6 months, 16 days.

"   John Gregory; died April 13,1839 -
                               aged 70 years, 7 months, 12 days.

"   Polly, wife John; died Nov.12,1831 -
                               aged 52 years, 5 months, 2 days.

"   Lauretta, dau. John & Polly; died Feb.8,1833 -
                               aged 23 years, 3 months, 8 days.

"   Hanny Gregory; died Sep.25,1819 - aged 22 days.

"   ARminda Gregory; Sep.19,1819 -aged 5 years, 7 mon.

"   Clarinda Gregory; died Sep.4,1819 -
                               aged 5 years, 6 months, 16 days.

"   Lucy Ann Gregory; died Nov. 5,1855 -
                               aged 48 years, 4 months, 26 days.

Marick,   David Marick; died May 8,1806 - aged 69 years.

"   Hannah, wife David; died Feb.24,1807-aged 77 years.

Fowler,   Solomon Fowler; died Oct.21,1828 -
                               aged 61 years, 4 months, 14 days.

"   Hannah, wife Solomon; died July 1,1849 -
                               aged 73 years, 11 months.

Gregory,   Doct. Ebenezer G. Gregory; died Jan.23,1832 -
                               aged 26 years, 6 months, 15 days.

Mount Gilead

Coldwell,	Hannah Coldwell; died Oct. 4,1847 -aged 49 years.
"	Elizabeth Coldwell; died August 10,1851 - aged 50 years, 3 months, 1 day.
"	Joseph Coldwell; died May 14,1804 -aged 65 years.
"	Elizabeth Coldwell; died Apr.20,1794 - ----
Colwell,	Thomas Colwell; died Sep.20,1813 - aged 35 years.
"	William Colwell; died Sep.13,1825 -aged 84 years.
"	Phebe, wife William; died Mar.25,1818-aged 81 yrs.
"	James Colwell; died July 4,1837 - aged 76 years.
"	Phebe, wife James; -----------
"	Phebe, dau. Jas. & Phebe; d.Mar.27,1844 -age 39yrs.
"	Jane Colwell; died Jan.19,1846 - aged 54 years.
Garrison,	Ichabod Garrison; Dec.12,1841 - Feb. 9,1910.
Kelly,	Ella E. Kelly; Jan.13,1870 - --------
"	Alexander, son Levi & Mary; died Nov. 2,1846 - aged 18 years, 4 months, 11 days.
Hazen,	Caleb Hazen; April 4,1720 - March 5,1777.
"	Sarah Hamilton; wife Caleb Hazen; Mar.1721-Dec.1814
"	Capt. Eleazer Hazen; "Soldier of the Revolution" died Sep.20,1793 - aged 38 years
"	Col. Caleb Hazen; " Soldier of the Revolution" died Mar.31,1806 - aged 56 years
"	Ruth, wife Col.Caleb; died Dec.18,1828 -aged 77yrs.
Hopkins,	Capt. Solomon Hopkins; " Soldier of the Revolution" died Sep.22,1792 - aged 54 years.
"	Elizabeth, wife Capt. Solomon; died Jan. 6,1804- aged 62 years.
"	Reuben Hopkins; died July 22,1798 -aged 31 years.
"	Elenor, wife Thatcher; died Mar.24,1786-aged 30yrs.
"	Rebeckah, wife Johnathan; Jan.15,1801 - --------

Mount Gilead

Phillips,	Rev. Ebenezer Phillips; died Feb.15,1834-aged 48yrs
"	Mary, wife Rev. Ebenezer; died October 15, 1837 - aged 46 years, 13 days.
"	Esther Ann, dau. Ebenezer & Esther; died May 8,1832 - aged 17 years.
"	Nancy, dau. Philetus & Esther; died Mar.10,1792 - aged 4 years, 1 month, 6 days.
"	Daniel B., son Philetus & Esther;died Mar.20,1792- aged 2 years, 4 days.
Myrick,	John Myrick; died May 14,1812 - aged 42 years.
Merrick,	E. Merrick; ————————
Fowler,	Caleb Fowler; died Aug. 6,1805 - aged 72 years.
"	Elizabeth, wife Caleb; died Jan.8,1807-aged 80yrs.
Rundle,	Lewis, son Ezra & Hannah; died Oct.5,1804 - aged 2 years, 11 days.
Smith,	Sarah, wife Jesse; died Nov.17,1766 -aged 62 years.
Foster,	Isaac Foster; died Nov. 2,1813 - aged 28 years.
"	Betsey, wife Thomas; died June 17,182- aged 27 years, 1 month, 17 days.
"	Huldah, wife Seth; died Oct.20,1797 -aged 40 years.
Cresby,	Elizabeth, wid. Thomas; died Aug. 6,1801-age 92yrs.
Beale,	Lois, wife Matthew; died July 14,1785-aged 27 years
"	Sarah, wife George; died Jan.13,1790 - aged 37yrs.
Hazen,	John Hazen; 1773 - 1813.
Beale,	Mercey, wife George; died Mar.28,1845-aged 54 years
"	Hannah, dau. George & Mercey; died Apr.12,1808 - aged 22 years.
Merrick,	Letitia, wife Samuel; died Jan.25,1831 - aged 48 years, 7 months, 15 days.
Moore,	Moses Moore; died May 21,1869 -aged 67 years, 6 mon.
"	Ann, wife Moses; died Nov.18,1877 -aged 83 years.

Mount Gilead

Everett,   Abraham Everett; died Mar. 5,1858 - aged 69 years.

"   Jane, relict Abraham; died Jan.31,1755 -
           aged 89 years, 5 months, 20 days

Sloot,   Abigail, wife James; died May 15,1825 -aged 69 years

Ganong,   Theron, son Eli & Fanny; died Aug. 1,1823 -
           aged 14 years, 1 month, 22 days.

"   Lewis Ganong; died Mar.28,1812 -aged 14 years.

"   James M. Ganong; died Oct.15,1814-aged 21 years.

"   Thomas, son Samuel & Elizabeth; died Dec.10,1814-
           aged 24 years.

Moore,   James Moore; died Mar.19,1879 - aged 75 years.

Christie,   Lizzie, wife James; Feb. 9,1834 - July 13,1888.

Baker,   Saloma, wife Josiah; died Dec.26,1845 -
           aged 71 years, 1 month, 26 days.

Frost,   Herbert C. Frost; Sept.21,1843 - Jan.23,1911.

"   Munson Frost; died Sep.24,1848 -
           aged 43 years, 8 months, 24 days.

"   Mary L. Hitchcock, wife Munson Frost;
           Feb.14,1819 - July 4,1891.

"   John Frost; died May 11,1862 -
           aged 88 years, 6 months, 16 days.

"   Cornelia, wife John; died April 14,1844 -
           aged 61 years, 11 months, 27 days.

"   Cornelia, dau. John & Cornelia; died July 22,1822-
           aged 6 years, 9 months, 18 days.

"   Benaiah Y., son Floyd T. & Sophia O.;
           died Nov.3,1834 -aged 25 days.

"   Margaret M., dau. Floyd T. & Sophia O.; --------------

Seeley,   William H. Seeley; died Mar.11,1828 -
           aged 53 years, 3 months, 11 days.

"   Mary, dau. William & Mary; died Sept. 9,1820 -
           aged 1 year, 3 months, 26 days.

Kniffin,   Amos Kniffin; died Feb.5,1842 -aged 84yrs. 10mon.

"   Clarinda Kniffin; died Apr.28,1834-age 67yr.11mo.24 days.

Mount Gilead

Kniffin,   Chlorinda, dau. Amos & Clarinda; died July 28,1815-
                       aged 11 years.

Bailey,   Daniel D. Bailey; died May 24,1861 -
                       aged 51 years, 4 months, 25 days.

"   William Bailey; died July 13,1842 -
                       aged 59 years, 11 months, 19 days.

"   Mary, wife William; died Feb. 9,1842 -
                       aged 59 years, 7 months, 18 days.

Williams,   Harriet, dau. Wright & Elizabeth; died May 13,1852-
                       aged 4 years, 4 months, 12 days.

Tillotson,   Coles W., son Eleazer & Sarah; d.Feb.22,1795-11yrs.

"   William, son Eleazer & Sarah; d.June 9,1791- 10yrs.

Watts,   Elizabeth, wife Robt.; died Apr.11,1836-age 91 years

Frost,   Mary S. & John M.; children Floyd & Sophia; ————

"   Emily Frances, dau. Floyd & Sophia; died Sep.23,1842
                       aged 1 year, 5 months, 13 days.

Yeamans,   Amplias Yeamans; died Feb.22,1853-aged 74yrs. 9days

"   Abigail, wife Amplias; died March 10,1848 -
                       aged 63 years, 8 months, 9 days.

Pierce,   Isaac Pierce; died Dec.17,1863 -
                       aged 73 years, 3 months, 26 days.

"   Arminda Craig, wife Isaac Pierce; died June 7,1883-
                       aged 88 years, 3 months, 19 days.

Pearce,   Isaac Pearce; died May 15,1835 -aged 77yrs. 7mon.

"   Elizabeth Pearce; died Sep.9,1817 -aged 22 years.

"   Elizabeth, wife Isaac; died Sep.28,1815-age 53yrs.

Drew,   Ann Drew; died Apr.23,1848 -aged 47yrs. 9mo.13da.

"   Phebe Drew; died Jan.13,1820 - aged 22 years.

"   William Drew; died Sep.11,1857-aged 32yrs.3mo.20da.

"   Jane, wife William; died Dec. 6,1828 -aged 70 years

Munger,   Joel Munger; died Mar.25,1807 - aged 72 years.

Mount Gilead

Fowler,	Susan Fowler; died Oct.1,1847 -aged 80yrs.7mo.21da.
"	Phebe Fowler; died Sep.23,1847 -aged 83 yrs. 11 days
Halcomb,	Catherine Duel, wife Milo Halcomb; died Apr.28,1871- aged 62 years, 8 months, 24 days.
Travis,	Joseph Travis; died Mar.1,1841 - aged 75 years, 1 month, 24 days.
"	Deborah, wife Joseph; died June 12,1845-aged 77yrs.
Nickerson,	Tartullas Nickerson; died May 4,1841 - aged 66 years, 1 month, 4 days.
Frost,	Hulda, dau. Ezra & Mary; died Aug.12,1833 - aged 19 years, 6 months, 20 days.
Hopkins,	Arvah, son Thatcher & Mary; died Aug.25,1812 - aged 16 years.
Travis,	David Travis; died Feb.11,1823 - aged 30 years.
"	Hannah, wife Gilbert H.; died June 19,1833 - aged 36 years, 11 months, 19 days.
"	Elizabeth, dau. Gilbert & Sally; died Jan. 1,1835- aged 8 years, 11 months, 22 days.
"	Gilbert Travis; died Sep. 3,1814 -aged 74 years.
"	Jemima, wife Gilbert; died Oct.30,1833 - aged 92 years, 7 months.
"	Sarah, dau. Joseph & Deborah; died Jan.24,1852 - aged 56 years, 6 months, 13 days.
Belden,	Amos Belden; died May 4,1830 - aged 66 years.
"	Elizabeth, wife Amos; died Dec.27,1851-aged 82 years
"	Charlotte, dau. Amos & Elizabeth; died Sep.26,1827- aged 28 years, 9 months.
"	Trim, a servant of Amos Belden; d. May 26,1817-8yrs.
"	Benjamin L. Belden; died June 12,1858 - aged 48 years, 11 months.
"	George Belden; died Jan.14,1855 - aged 60 years.
"	Sophia Louise, wife George; died Apr.3,1873-age 72yr.
"	George M. Belden; died Oct.7,1873 - aged 46 years, 11 months.

Mount Gilead,-

Belden,	John Belden; died Aug. 17, 1882 - aged 77 years, 6 months, 22 days.
"	Maria De LaLuz, wife John Belden; died Jan. 9, 1900 - aged 82 years.
"	Charles Belden; died Feb. 22, 1858 - aged 65 years.
"	Helen E.R., wife Charles; died May 29, 1842 - aged 39 years.
"	Helen Elizabeth, dau. Chas. & Helen E.R.; died Sep. 9, 1846 - aged 8 years.
"	Augustus Bartlett, son Amos & Elizabeth; died July 19, 1815 - aged 8 months, 9 days
Hooker, St.John,	- - - - - - - Julia, wife Hooker St.John; dau. Amos & Eliz. Belden died Sep. 14, 1817 - aged 26 years, 3 mon.
"	Frederick Agustus, son Hooker & Julia; died June 2, 1839 - aged 22 years.
Miles,	William Miles; died May 18, 1830 - aged 61 years.
"	Sarah, wife William; died Aug. 22, 1844 - aged 60 yrs.
Smith,	Thomas Smith; died Sep. 16, 1825 - aged 49 yrs. 7 mon.
"	Philip Smith; died Jan. 1, 1828 - aged 73 years, 9 months, 18 days.
"	Elizabeth, wife Philip; died Jan. 30, 1829 - aged 69 years, 10 months, 21 days.
"	Sarah Ophelia, dau. Geo. & Julia; died Dec. 10, 1840 - aged 5 years, 1 month, 21 days.
Hazen,	Julia, dau. Caleb & Laura; died Dec. 25, 1840 - aged 4 years, 5 months, 20 days.
Smith,	Hannah, wife Alfred H.; died Aug. 15, 1847 - aged 25 years, 10 months, 18 days.
Thorn,	Nancy Thorn; died June 14, 1879; aged 82 years, 8 months, 24 days.
Frost,	Hon. Joel Frost; died Sept. 11, 1827 - aged 62 years.
"	Martha, wife Hon. Joel; died Oct. 21, 1860 - aged 88 years, 2 months, 29 days.

Mount Gilead

Foster,	Tilly Foster; died April 4, 1842 - aged 49 years, 16 days.
"	Sally, wife Tilly; died April 8, 1836 - aged 40 years, 6 months, 14 days.
"	Emily, dau. Tilly & Sally; died April 6, 1844 - aged 14 years, 3 months, 4 days.
"	Laura A. Foster; died Nov. 30, 1847 - aged 43 years.
"	Thomas Foster; died Sept. 22, 1840 - aged 45 years.
"	Isaac E. Foster; died Sept. 22, 1847 - aged 26 years, 11 months, 10 days.
"	Seth Foster; died Sept. 15, 1837 - aged 76 years, 4 months, 5 days.
"	Elizabeth, wife Seth; died Jan. 28, 1848 - aged 86 years, 14 days.
Delavan,	Agnes, wife Samuel; died Aug. 26, 1832 - aged 78 years.
Ganong,	Joseph Ganong; died May 24, 1836 - aged 58 years.
"	Susannah, wife Joseph; died Aug. 19, 1848 - age 69 yrs.
"	Jacob Ganong; died Dec. 22, 1834 - aged 86 years.
"	Hannah, wife Jacob; died May 22, 1845 - aged 92 years, 2 months, 6 days.
Fowler,	Johnathan Fowler; died Oct. 26, 1848 - aged 79 years, 1 month, 15 days.
"	Mary, wife Johnathan; died April 16, 1835 - aged 59 years, 1 month, 27 days.
"	Mary, dau. Johnathan & Mary; died Feb. 17, 1823 - aged 17 years, 7 months, 1 day.
Badeau,	James Badeau; died Aug. 20, 1851 - aged 46 years, 3 months, 24 days.
"	Malinda, dau. James & Sally; died June 4, 1845 - aged 1 year, 10 months, 5 days.
Hopkins,	Jeremiah Hopkins; died Oct. 17, 1829 - aged 67 years, 2 months, 1 day.
"	Thankful, wife Jeremiah; died April 13, 1833 - aged 70 years, 7 months, 14 days.

Mount Gilead

Kniffin, Capt. Samuel Kniffin; "Soldier of the Revolution"
died March 9, 1828 -
aged 77 years, 11 months, 9 days.

" Jane, wife Samuel; died Feb. 21, 1844 aged 86 years.

" Zillah, dau. James & Eliza; died Oct. 24, 1833 -
aged 25 years, 7 months, 18 days.

" Clarissa, dau. James & Eliza; died July 10, 1834 -
aged 15 years, 8 months, 12 days.

Vail, William Francis, son James S. & Phebe Ann;
died Apr. 6, 1848 -aged 1 year, 5 months, 18da.

McMahon, James Mc,Mahon; Aug. 1, 1838 - May 6, 1879.

" Jennie Markham, wife James Mc Mahon;
Aug. 7, 1852 - Jan. 9, 1888.

" Florence, dau. James & Jennie;
Oct. 4, 1884 - Jan. 29, 1888.

Travis, Johnathan Travis; died Feb. 1, 1845 -aged 85 years.

" Elizabeth, wife Johnathan;
died Feb. 28, 1840 -aged 88 years.

" Infant son, Henry & Emeline; born May 7, 1841 - -----

" Richard Travis; died Oct. 25, 1844 -
aged 56 years, 6 months, 18 days.

Shaw, Edward Marcellin Shaw; Sep. 19, 1839 - Oct. 13, 1906.

" Julia Ann Smalley, wife Edward M. Shaw;
Dec. 14, 1837 - May 3, 1904.

" Adelaide Morris, dau. Edward M. & Julia A.;
June 27, 1871 - Apr. 30, 1893.

"
Kemper, Edith Emma, dau. Edward M. & Julia A. Shaw, and
wife Edward S. Kemper;
Mar. 27, 1867 - Apr. 26, 1894.

Marcellin E., son Edward S. & Edith Emma;
Feb. 17, 1893 - Sep. 10, 1893.

A Burying ground

Back of village Fire House.

Carmel, Putnam Co. N.Y.

copied in 1925

W.P.Horton.

Carmel, N.Y.

Agor,	Charles Agor; died Dec.7,1819 - age 95 years.
	Mehetible Agor; died May 14,1822 - age 31 years, 8 months, 13 days.
Armstrong,	Noble H., son Orrin M.& Bulia M.; drowned Jan.16,1818 -age 10yrs. 10mos. 21day
Ballard,	Tracy Ballard; died Jan.1,1829 -age 72 years.
"	Mercy, wife Tracy; died Feb.8,1826 -age 69 years.
"	Joseph Ballard; died Mar.11,1810 -age 27 years.
"	Benjamin Ballard; died Aug.22,1823 -age 39 years.
"	Naomi, wife Benjamin; died May 1,1881 -age 95yrs.
"	Alanson Ballard; died Sept.12,1831 - age 23 years, 6 months, 7 days.
"	Rachel Wood, wife Joseph Ballard: Nov.22,1788 - Mae.27,1876.
Birdsall,	Betsey, wife Ezra; died Feb.20,1819 -age 20 years.
"	Christana Roberts, late Birdsall; died Apr.24,1848- age 86 years, 5 months, 11 days.
Brown,	Lewis L., son Morris & Sally; died Aug.29,1834 - age 6 years, 5 months, 6 days.
Chase,	Obadiah Chase; "7th.Regt. Dutchess Co. N.Y.S.Mil." died July 4,1799 - age 56 years.
"	Ruth, wife Alvin; died Apr.17,1832 - age 49 years.
Cole,	John Cole; died Mar.24,1828 - age 30 years.
"	Zillah Cole; died Feb.21,1813 - age 22 years.
"	Rachel, wife Elisha J.; died Jan.1,1815 -age 20yrs.
"	Eliza, dau.Reuben & Elizabeth; died May 6,1815 -age 9 years.
"	Ansel, son Obed & Liddy; died Aug.20,1808-ae.1yr.
"	Eleazor Cole; died May 29,1858 -age 68yrs. 11days.
"	Sarah, wife Eleazor; died Aug.30,1826 - age 53 years, 4 months.
"	Eleazor H. Cole; died Apr.13,1834-age 29yr. 10mo.

Carmel

Cole, Berry Cole; died May 29,1835 -age 66yrs. 4mos. 5days

" Hannah, wife Berry; died Dec.23,1821 -
age 47 years, 11 months, 2 days.

" Alveson, son Berry & Hannah; died Apr.9,1811 -
age 13 years, 5 months, 15 days.

" Amanda, dau. Berry & Hannah; died Nov.13,1835 -
age ----

" Amanda J., dau. Ormond H. & Mary; died Sept.3,1834 -
age 1 month, 20 days.

" Antoinette, dau. Elisha J.& Eliza; died May 23,1837-
age 2 years, 9 months, 7 days.

" Zillah, dau. Elisha J.& Lydia; died Nov.10,1821-2yrs.

" Nathan Cole; died Feb.6,1803 -age 59 years.

" Mehitabel, wife Nathan; died Aug.1807 -age 59 years.

" Ebenezer Cole; died Aug.18,1815 -age 61 years.

" Mary, wife Ebenezer; died Aug.30,1806 -age 44 years.

" David Cole; died Dec.10,1834 -age 85yrs. 1mon. 14days

" Susannah, wife David; died Nov.3,1857 -
age 102 years, 4 months, 8 days.

" Mary, wife Hiram; died April 14,1839 -
age 24 years, 4 months, 27 days.

Colwell, Charlotte, wife Thomas; died May 28,1820 -age 40 year

Cronk, Adolphus J., son Abram & Bellecha; died Mar.21,1832-
age 4 years, 5 months.

Crosby, Nathan Crosby; died Oct.27,1805 -age 72 years.

" Eunice, wife Nathan; died Jan.17,1821 -age 73 years.

" Julia, dau. Enoch & Jane; died Nov.2,1805 -
age 2 years, 4 months.

" Ira J., son Enoch & Jane;died Sept.18,1819 -
age 6 years, 4 months, 14 days.

" Juliaett, dau. Enoch & Jane; died Feb.14,1830 -
age 6 years, 26 days.

Crane, Susannah Chase, wife Noah H. Crane & former wife of
Stephen Waring; died June 4,1828 -age 46yr. 1mo. 11da

Carmel

Curtis,	Dorcas, wife Eder; died Jan.26,1826 -age 55 years.
Dean,	David Dean; died Apr.24,1860 -age 92yrs.4mos.21days
"	Deborah, wife David; died May 22,1827 - age 58 years, 5 months, 10 days.
"	David Dean Jr.; died Feb.11,1819 - age 20 years.
Disbrow,	Lydia, wife Solomon; --------
Ferguson,	Tamer, wife Isaac; died Sept.27,1819 -age 35 years.
Frost,	David Frost; died Jan.8,1818 - age 51 years.
"	Lydia, wife David; died Dec.11,1815 -age 47 years.
"	Daniel Frost; died Apr.8,1847 - age 82 years.
"	George Frost; died June 28,1815 - age 43 years.
"	Harrison, son George & Polly; died Dec.29,1815-2yrs.
Fuller,	Nathan Fuller; died Dec.12,1811 - age 44 years.
"	Temperance Fuller; died Sept.6,1813 -age 48 years.
"	Elijah Fuller; died June 9,1821 -age 77 years.
"	Martha, wife Elijah; died May 14,1818 -age 76 years.
"	Martha, dau.Eleazar & Sally; died Aug.27,1818 - age 2 years, 2 months.
Ganong,	Rachel, dau.Jeremiah & Hannah; d.Oct.11,1814-18mos.
Griffin,	John Griffin; died July 31,1842 - age 69 years, 6 months, 12 days.
"	Mary, wife John; died Feb.12,1859 - age 88 years, 10 months.
"	Morrice Griffin; died May 31,1841 - age 37 years, 11 months, 9 days.
"	Jane, dau.John & Mary; died Nov.2,1837 - age 26 years, 4 months, 10 days.
Hazelton,	Amanda, dau.Augustus W.& Polly; died Dec.1,1816 -age 5 years.
Hill,	Abraham Hill; died May 1,1817 - age 70 years.
	Hannah, wife Abraham; died July 5,1818 -age 70 years.

Carmel

Hopkins, Elizabeth, wife Jeremiah: --------

" Joseph Hopkins; died Jan.31,1833 -
age 81 years, 9 months, 14 days.

" Elizabeth, wife Joseph; died Dec.16,1837-age 82yrs.

" Egbert J., son Reuben & Manery; died July 21,1841 -
age 5 months, 7 days.

" Theron, son Reuben & Manery; died Mar.27,1843 -
age 5 months, 24 days.

Hughson, James Hughson; died Dec.22,1834 -
age 54 years, 7 months, 2 days.

" Abigail, wife James; died Mar.8,1843 -
age 59 years, 3 months, 18 days.

" James, 2nd.son James & Abigail; died Mar.28,1841-
age 20 years, 6 months, 29 days.

" Laura, wife Russel; died Aug.8,1832 -age 47 years.

Jones, Abby, wife Joshua S.; died Dec.7,1857 -
age 33 years, 10 months, 8 days.

Kelley, John, son Worden & Betsey; died Sept.13,1827 -
age 6 years, 2 months, 7 days.

" Eliza Ann, dau.Worden & Betsey; died Aug.11,1827-
age 2 years, 11 months, 8 days.

" Judah Kelley; died Sep.17,1837 - age 80 years.

" Lydia, wife Judah; died May 21,1818 -age 58 years.

" Naomi, wife Judah, & former wife Doct.Weeks;
died Sept.20,1820 -age 40 years.

" Judah, son Jesse & Eleanor; died Sept.23,1820 -
age 10 years, 4 months, 11 days.

" Deborah, dau.M.& Chloe; died May 19,1814 -age 15yrs.

Kelly, John Kelly; died May 7,1826 - age 82 years.

" Elizabeth, wife John; died Jan.27,1830 -age 81 years.

" John Kelly; died June 27,1817 - age 45 years.

Killey, Elizabeth Killey; Feb.1803 - --------

" Joseph E., son Ezra & Eliza; died July 4,1821-25da.

" Almira, dau.Ezra & Eliza; d.Aug.25,1820 -age 1yr.6mo.

Carmel

Lawrence,	Mary E. Mead Lawrence; 1794 - 1866.
Mabie,	Abraham Mabie; died Aug. 7, 1817 - age 90 years.
"	Sarah, wife Abraham; died Aug. 12, 1816 - age 87 years.
Mead,	Lydia, dau. Tartulus & Elizabeth; died Jan. 3, 1805 - age 1 year, 5 months.
"	Elizabeth, wife Tartulus; died Dec. 16, 1820 - age 43yrs.
"	James Mead; died April 5, 1830 - age 58 years.
Merritt,	Gilbert Merritt; died Mar. 4, 1824 - age 70 years.
Munson,	William H., son Ira & Elizabeth of New York. died Oct. 22, 1822 - age 19 years.
Nichols,	Susannah, dau. Henry & Susannah; died July 14, 1818 - age 8 years, 1 month, 16 days.
"	Sarah H., dau. Henry B. & Julianne; died June 30, 1835 - age 1 year, 8 months.
"	William H., son Joseph & Levetta; died Dec. 22, 1824 - age 1 year.
Northrop,	John Northrop; died Aug. 30, 1829 - age 55 years, 9 months, 11 days.
Northrup,	Patty, wife Joseph; died Jan. 9, 1835 - age 93 years, 6 months, 20 days.
Organ,	Cornelius Organ; died Oct. 3, 1818 - age 57 years.
"	Rachel, wife Cornelius; died Sept. 18, 1836 - age 73 years, 3 months.
Parce,	Orpha, dau. Abizer & Jane; died Aug. 8, 1809 - age 8 months, 6 days.
Rider,	John, son William & Zillah; d. Feb. 9, 183-, ae. 5mos.
Robinson,	Lewis Robinson; killed by lightning May 27, 1810 - age 53 years.
"	Mary, wife Lewis; died May 8, 1838 - age 81yrs, 22days
Sharp,	Julia, wife Robert; Mar. 11, 1810 - July 28, 1851.
Sprague,	Martha, dau. John & Lydia; died June 24, 1814 - 24 years.
Stephens,	Henry S., son Herman R. & Harriet; died May 9, 1819 - age 1 year, 7 months, 8 days.

Carmel

Stephens, Mary Ann, dau.Herman R. & Harriet; died June 22,1832-
age 19 years, 6 months.

Tillott, Richard Tillott; Apr.--,1823 - --------

" Josephus Tillott-Rulla; died Apr.24,1818 -age 52yrs.

" Nancy, dau.Josephus & -------; d.July 5,1821 -ae.18yrs.

Townsend, Ardalis Townsend; died Oct.29,1824 -age 24yrs. 4days.

" Gen.James Townsend; "A soldier of the Am.Revolution"
died Mar.13,1832 - age 76 years.

" Priscilla, wife Gen.James; died June 11,1839 -83yrs.

" Almira, dau.James & Priscilla; died Dec.10,1811 -age ?

" Jackson, son James,Jr. & Betsey; died Sept.20,1820 -
age 10 months, 11 days.

" Deborah Townsend; died Jan.23,1821 -age 39 years.

" Hannah Townsend; died Dec.27,1803 - age 18 years.

" Amanda, dau.Frederick & Hannah; died Aug.3,1807 -
age 2 years, 1 month, 20 days.

" Ruth, dau.Fredk.& Hannah; died May 1,1805 -age 3yrs.

" Elizabeth, dau.Fredk.& Hannah; d.Oct.8,1805-age 8yrs.

" Armina, dau.Fredk.& Hannah; died Oct.6,1805-age 5yrs.

" Huldah, dau.Fredk.& Hannah; died Oct.4,1805-age 13yrs.

" Hosea Townsend; died June 24,1833 - age 48 years.

" Evah, consort Hosea; died Apr.10,1838 -
age 49 years, 7 months, 6 days.

Meeks, Doct.Robert Meeks; died May 14,1816 -age 44 years.

Yeamans, Rachel, wid.John Kelly & wife Eppinetus Yeamans;
died March 4,1850 -
age 72 years, 8 months, 7 days.

An Old Cemetery

on Cedar Street,

Cold Spring,

Putnam County, N.Y.

Index

Adams,	5.	Haacke,	3.
Alexander,	7.	Haight,	1,11,12.
Allis,	4.	Hamilton,	7,12.
Angyvine,	4.	Harper,	3.
Annin,	8.	Hart,	4.
Anthony,	7.	Henyan,	1, 3.
		Higgins,	10.
Bailey,	8, 9.	Hill,	11.
Ball,	6.	Nines,	13.
Barton,	13.	Hitchcock,	1.
Basker,	3.	Horton,	4.
Baxter,	6.	Huestis,	8.
Bell,	8.	Hustis,	3, 8,10.
Blakly,	14.	Hyde,	5.
Bloomer,	7.		
Bogart,	6.	Ireland,	6,14.
Booth,	3, 5.	Isham,	2.
Boyce,	11.		
Boyd,	6.	Jaycox,	1, 4, 8,10.
Briggs,	10.	Jefferds,	12.
Brunker,	12.		
Bunnell,	13.	Kleinklaus,	4.
Butler,	13.		
Butterfass,	7.	Ladue,	6, 8,11.
		LaForge,	9.
Christian,	9.	Lawrence,	1, 2, 9.
Conklin,	1, 4, 8.	Lawson,	5.
Connor,	6.	Ledwick,	5.
Crawford,	9.	Lemmon,	5.
Croft,	12.	Lent,	10.
Cronk,	5, 9.	Lipsey,	5.
		Lounsbury,	12.
Davenport,	3, 4, 7, 9.		
Davis,	9,14.	McCaffray,	12.
Depew,	1.	McCoy,	3, 9.
Disbrow,	9.	McDonnell,	2.
Dougherty,	2.	McGovern,	9.
Dykeman,	13.	McIlravy,	3.
		McLean,	5.
Eityengn,	12.	Mahan,	1.
Emerson,	7.	Marquis,	6.
Ett,	11.	Marrian,	7.
		Marshall,	12.
Ferris,	12.	Mekeel,	9,13.
Fisher,	14.	Merrick,	4.
Foreman,	4.	Merritt,	9.
		Miller,	8,11,14.
Garrison,	6, 7.	Monroe,	8.
Gaudineer,	7.	Mosher,	9.
Gibson,	9.	Mosier,	8.
Gower,	3.	Mulholland,	9.
Gray,	3,10.		
Green,	10.	Nagle,	12.
Grey,	3.	Nelson,	3,11.
Griffin,	3,10.	Newhinnie,	3.
Groundwater,	4.		

Index

Odell,	11,14.
Osborn,	10.
Parker,	7.
Parsons,	9.
Patterson,	3.
Penny,	2.
Pleaven,	6.
Post,	10.
Reynolds,	12.
Riggs,	10,11.
Robinson,	3, 7.
Rogers,	8.
Rose,	10.
Rumpf,	6.
Schedule,	9.
Schenk,	1.
Scholefield,	9.
Secor,	8.
Sheldon,	9.
Skedgel,	13.
Slater,	7.
Sloan,	13.
Smith,	7,10.
Spalding,	10.
Speedling,	2.
Spellman,	12.
Squires,	5.
Stevenson,	7.
Stillwell,	12.
Tate,	11.
Taylor,	11.
Travis,	8.
Truesdell,	12.
Truman,	10.
Turner	11.
VanVoorhis,	2.
Walsh,	1.
Warren,	3,11.
Weitz,	3.
White,	8,13.
Wiltsie,	1,10.
Windberg,	10.
Winning,	2.
Wise,	11.
Wood,	1, 2, 5, 6,10,13.
Woolsey,	2.
Wright,	6.
Yeomans,	12.

Cedar Street

Lawrence, Willice A., son John W. & Elizabeth; died Dec.3,1858- age 2 years, 2 months, 23 days.

Henyan, Jeremiah, son Elias & Mary F.; died Sept.15,1865- age 6 years, 4 months, 25 days.

" Sarah E. dau.Elias & Mary F.; d.Dec.14,1865-age 1mo.17da.

Wiltse, Joseph Wiltse; died Dec.11,1866-age 76 years.

Schenck, August, son Gottlieb & Barbara; died Mar.2,1859- age 3 years, 4 months, 11 days.

" William, son Gottlieb & Barbara; died Feb.26,1862- age 7 years, 5 months, 19 days.

" Anna, dau.Gottlieb & Barbara; died Aug.6,1868- age 4 years, 10 months, 19 days.

Jaycox, Marion, dau.John & Angeline; d.Mar.27,1863-age 3yr. 6mo.

Conklin, Isaac S.Conklin; died Aug.14,1863-age 50 years.

Woods, Robert Woods; died Aug.10,1867-age 63 years.

" Jane, wife Robert; died Mar.27,1866-age 57 years.

" Sarah J.Woods; died Jan.11,1893-age 58 years.

" James T.Woods; died Dec.25,1892-age 44 years.

" Thomas S.Woods; died ------1850-age 2 years.

Mahan, Nancy Woods, wife George E.Mahan; died Sept.18,1877- age 32 years,

Haight, Jane, wife Clarkson; died July 23,1859- age 25 years, 2 months, 5 days.

Walsh, Deborah Ann, dau.William & Georgiana; died Aug.12,1867- age 1 year, 3 months, 25 days.

Hitchcock, Charles Edward, son Felix & Maria; June 30,1858-Jan.25,1859.

Depew, Emma Teresa, dau.John P.& Ann E.; died Nov.1,1858- age 2 years, 5 months, 12 days.

Jaycox, Mary Elizabeth, dau.William & Jane; d.Nov.2,1839-age 6yr.

" Mary Emma, dau.Henry & Juliette; died Nov.3,1852; age 3 years, 5 months, 16 days.

Cedar st.

McDonnell, Charles A. McDonnell; died July 17, 1865—age 1yr. 3mo.

Penny,   William Penny; died Mar. 26, 1866—age 75 years.

"   Mary Woolsey, wife William Penny; d. Dec. 4, 1866—age 70yr.

"   John W., son William & Mary; died Aug. 15, 1858—age 24yrs.

"   Elizabeth, dau. William & Mary; died March 30, 1847—
           age 16 years, 1 month, 27 days.

"   John, son William & Mary; died Nov. 7, 1834—age 2 years.

"   Elijah, son William & Mary; died Sep. 2, 1829—age 14 days.

"   Stephen, son William & Mary; died Oct. 11, 1839—
           age 1 year, 2 months, 25 days.

Woolsey,   Josiah Woolsey; died Nov. 24, 1874—age 84 years.

"   Deborah Penny, wife Josiah Woolsey;
           died Mar. 2, 1882—age 84 years.

Lawrence, Enoch Lawrence; died May 31, 1879—age 88 years, 22 days

"   Martha Wood, wife Enoch Lawrence; died Dec. 6, 1868—
           age 72 years, 7 months, 17 days.

Wood,   Cornelius Wood; died Sept. 7, 1863—age 32yrs. 5mos. 5days

"   Martha, wife Cornelius; died Oct. 3, 1861—age 21yrs. 9mos.

Dougherty, James V. son William & Mariam; died Nov. 27, 1862—
           age 5 years, 6 months, 10 days.

Speedling, William A. J. Speedling; died Dec. 19, 1860—age 42yrs. 28da.

"   Deborah A., dau. William A. & Eliza; died Feb. 7, 1871—
           age 14 years, 6 months, 13 days.

VanVoorhis, John A. VanVoorhis; "Corp. Co. I. 19th. Regt. N.Y. State Mil."

"   Joshua VanVoorhis; died July 26, 1861—age 46yrs. 2mos.

Winning,   Mary Louise, dau. George W. & Sarah; died June 12, 1865—
           age 6 years, 6 months.

"   William E., son George & Sarah; died June 20, 1865—
           age 4 years, 2 months.

Isham,   Elizabeth, wife Charles; died Mar. 5, 1857—age 37 years.

"   Mary Eliza, dau. Charles & Elizabeth;
           died May 19, 1858—age 15 years.

Cedar St.

Newhinnie,	John Newhinnie; died May 9,1857-age 56yrs. 5mos. 19days
Henyan,	Eugene A., son James & Susan; died June 5,1863-age 5yrs
McIlravy,	Hugh McIlravy; Oct.14,1867-
"	Jane, wife Hugh; died Nov.29,1862-age 68 years.
"	Mary F., dau.Hugh & Eliza; died June 12,1865-age 18mos.
Haacke,	Mary Henrietta, dau.Charles & Bertha; died Feb.15,1861-age 2 years, 11 months.
Grey,	Hiram J.Grey; died Aug.29,1874-age 45 years.
"	Alanson Grey; died Nov.21,1857-age 73yrs. 6mos. 6days.
"	Jemima, wife Alanson; died Sept.2,1858-age 63yrs. 23da.
Davenport,	Isaac John Davenport; Sept.26,1815-Sept.18,1860.
"	F.R.Davenport; ------
Gray,	Albert Gray; died June 8,1866-age 44 years.
Warren,	Nelson Warren; died Jan.8,1871-age 71 years.
"	Mary Gower, wife Nelson Warren; died Jan.24,1878-82yrs.
"	Frederick, son Nelson & Mary; Mar.22,1846-Sep.28,1853.
Booth,	Robert, son William & Elizabeth; -----
Nelson,	Davenport Nelson; Apr.14,1814-Feb.10,1862.
"	Esther Hustis, wife Davenport Nelson; May 20,1820-September 6,1891.
McCoy,	James McCoy; died Nov.25,1865-age 11yrs. 4mos. 21days.
Griffin,	Florence, dau.Eli K.& Phebe J.; d.July 24,1860-age 5mo.
Weitz,	Catherine Weitz; died July 12,1872-age 77yrs. 6mos.
Patterson,	James Patterson; died Jan.22,1864-age 36 years, 10 mos.
Basker,	Abby A.Basker; died Sept.13,1860-age 23yrs. 3mos. 24da.
Harper,	Mary Ann, wife James; died Oct.23,1863-age 30yrs. 4mos.
"	Lizzie, dau.Andrew & Julia; died Oct.23,1870-age 8yr.8mo.
Robinson,	David Robinson; died Sept.9,1855-age 73 years, 4 months

Cedar street

Groundwater, Sarah, wife John; died Nov.14,1862-age 44 years.
" Mary Emma, dau.John & Sarah; died Sept.27,1860- age 7 years, 1 month, 24 days.

Kleinklaus, August Kleinklaus; ------
" Maggie Kleinklaus; ------

Allis, Frances, wife S.B.; died Sept.9,1863-age 30 years.
" A dau.S.B.& Frances; Sept.6,1858-----

Horton, Elizabeth Horton; died Sept.29,1874-age 71yr. 3mo. 28da
" Phebe Jane Horton; died Sept.18,1864-age 30yrs. 3mos.

Conklin, Catherine Conklin; died Jan.5,1873-age 44yrs. 3mos.

Davenport, Benjamin Davenport; died Apr.3,1863-age 64yrs. 8mos.
" Catherine, wife Benjamin; died Dec.31,1871- age 73 years, 5 months, 28 days.
" Martha J., dau.Benjamin & Catherine; died July 2,1835- age 6 months, 18 days.

Merrick, Issacher Merrick; died Sept.29,1854-age 76 years.
" Mercy, wife Issacher; died Dec.17,1854-age 70 years.
" Maria Herrick; died Apr.19,1878-age 72yrs. 1mon. 28da.
" Addison Merrick; died Jan.13,1880-age 59yrs. 4mos. 26d
" John Merrick; died Apr.28,1880-age 69yrs. 11days.
" Jennie Merrick; ----

Jaycox, Eunice Jaycox; died June 13,1859-age 67yrs. 8mos.
" Amelia, wife James E.; died Sept.15,1855-age 21yr. 11mo

Angyvine, Lavinia Angyvine; died Nov.8,1873-age 90yrs. 5mos. 3da.

Foreman, Benjamin Foreman; died Mar.6,1873-age 80yrs. 3mos. 4day
" Rebecca, wife Benjamin; died Nov.8,1867-age 69yrs. 6mos
" Catherine A., dau.Benjamin & Rebecca; died Apr.30,1863- age 27 years, 21 days.

Hart, Martin, son Martin & Mary; died July 28,1882-age 7yrs.

Cedar st.

Adams,   Mary, dau. John & Eliza; died July 30, 1869-age 1yr. 3mo.

McLean, Elias C. McLean; died May 28, 1870-age 74 years.

"   Tamar, wife Elias; died Oct. 14, 1858-age 61yrs. 8mos.

"   Elizabeth A., wife Elias; Mar. 15, 1808-Oct. 3, 1871.

"   Joseph B. McLean; died Sept. 1, 1864-age 37yrs. 6mos. 19days.

Squires, John J. Squires; died Apr. 5, 1854-age 38yrs. 11mos. 10days.

"   Susan Margaret, wife John J. Squires;
        August 15, 1819-January 9, 1896.

"   Martha E., dau. John & Susan; died Apr. 10, 1863-age 10yr. 6mo

Booth,   Zilpha, wife George; died March 1, 1866-age 86 years.

Wood,   Samuel, son Samuel & Sarah; died Aug. 22, 1847-age 6mos. 4day

"   Sarah, dau. Samuel & Sarah; died Aug. 22, 1849-age 11 weeks.

Hyde,   William Hyde; born 1819-died May 11, 1884.

"   Mary, wife William; born 1820-died Sept. 4, 1883.

"   Mary Martha, dau. William & Mary; 13 years.

"   William, Isabella, Addie, children William & Mary; ----

Cronk,   William Cronk; died Feb. 12, 1854-age 49yrs. 6mos. 25days.

"   Hannah, dau. John & Lydia; died May 30, 1855-age 21yrs. 6mos.

Lipsey, John Lipsey; died Nov. 16, 1861-age 71 years.

"   Robert Lipsey; died Mar. 11, 1862-age 33 years.

"   James Lipsey; died Jan. 24, 1853-age 35yrs. 1mon. 16days.

"   John Lipsey; died Aug. 28, 1854-age 33yrs. 4mos. 13days.

"   Francis Lipsey; died Jan. 29, 1857-age 27yrs. 6mos. 29days.

Ledwick, Mary, wife John Ledwick, dau. John & Sarah Lipsey;
        died Sept. 10, 1856-age 29 years.

Lawson, Samuel Lawson; died June 3, 1861-age 63 years.

"   Jane Lawson; died Nov. 25, 1847-age 44 years.

Lemmon, Hannah, wife William; died Apr. 8, 1861-age 52yrs. 2mos. 6da.

Cedar st.

Ireland, Patience, wife Isaac; died Apr.29,1852-age 44yrs. 6mos.

" Sarah A., dau.Isaac & Patience; died Apr.27,1841-
age 2 years, 6 months, 16 days.

" Harriet T. dau.Isaac & Patience; died April 5,1845-
age 7 years, 6 months, 14 days.

" Catherine Ann, dau.Isaac & Patience; died Nov.2,1853-
age 21 years, 5 months, 2 days.

Ladue, John P.Ladue; died Apr.27,1854-age 34yrs. 6mos. 20days.

" Tamar, dau.John P.& Nancy; died Sept.11,1847-age 1yr. 20da

Baxter, Solomon Baxter; died Oct.9,1861-age 52 years.

" Phebe. wife Solomon; died Sept.2,1863-age 57 years.

Wood, Phebe, wife William F.Wood; died Apr.20,1864-age 29 years.

Marquis, James L., son David & Anne; died Sep.7,1854-age 4yr. 4mo.

Pleaven, Charlotte Maria, dau.Hugh & Charlotte; d.Aug.9,1852-2 mos.

Boyd, Doct.William D.Boyd; died Sept.11,1842-age 54yrs. 1mon.

" Harriet, wife Doct.W.D.; died Sept.3,1856-age 77yrs. 10mos

Rumpf, Charley Rumpf; -----

" Louisa Rumpf; -----

Ball, Leander Ball; died July 17,1873-age 26 years, 2 months.

" James A.Ball; died Nov.19,1880-age 61 years, 8 months.

" Ida, dau.James A.& Catherine; died Sept.19,1851-age 17mos.

Connor, Catherine Bogart, wife William Conner; died May 7,1865-
age 80 years, 8 months.

Wright, Augusta, wife George; died Mar.15,1865-age 39yrs. 8days.

" Charles E., son George & Augusta; died Apr.19,1863-
age 17 years, 10 months, 8 days.

Garrison, Martin Garrison; died Dec.3,1858-age 85yrs. 6mos. 2days.

" Amy, wife Martin; died Sept.3,1856-age 58 years.

" Martin, son Martin & Amy; died Oct.5,1852-age 32 years.

" William Garrison; died Mar.10,1863-age 67yrs. 3mos. 13day

Cedar st.

Butterfass, Theador, son F. & C.; died Mar. 30, 1864-age 2yrs. 8mos.

Garrison, Mary Jane, dau. George & Charlotte; died Aug. 21, 1846-age 11 months, 28 days.

Anthony, Elizabeth A., wife David; died Sept. 29, 1856-age 32 years, 3 months, 14 days.

" Albert, son David & Elizabeth; d. Jan. 17, 1853-age 1 day.

" Alice, dau. David & Elizabeth; d. Jan. 26, 1853-age 10 days

Gaudineer, Warren, son Elisha & Sarah J.; d. Feb. 22, 1853-age 3mos.

Smith, Capt. Henry Smith; May 8, 1819-Sept. 4, 1867.

Marian, Mary A. Marrian; Aug. 24, 1835-Mar. 11, 1864.

Bloomer, Phebe, wife Benjamin E. died Sep. 2, 1852-age 65yrs. 7mos.

Alexander, Mary, wife John Alexander, dau. Alex. & Mary Slater;

" Mary Slater, dau. John & Mary; Apr. 7, 1854-Sept. 12, 1854.

Stevenson, Agnes R. dau. John & Mary; died Mar. 4, 1863-age 5yrs. 2mo.

Hamilton, John, son Alex. & Sarah; died Jan. 22, 1841-age 14mos. 23d.

" Mary A. dau. Alex. & Sarah; died Jan. 24, 1841-age 3 years, 4 months, 17 days.

Parker, James C. Parker; Oct. 2, 1820-May 21, 1889.

" Jane Mulholland, wife James C. Parker; June 12, 1820-Sept. 7, 1885.

" James, son James & Jane; Mar. 6, 1856-July 28, 1881.

" Hugh, son James & Jane; Mar. 19, 1860-Sept. 27, 1880.

Davenport, Elizabeth, wife John Milton; died Aug. 12, 1856-age 25 years, 8 months, 7 days.

Emerson, Emma A., dau. Charles & Adeline; died Dec. 17, 1855-age 4 years, 9 months, 24 days.

Robinson, Jennett, wife David; died Oct. 25, 1864-age 43 years.

" Alexander, son David & Jennett; d. May 29, 1853-age 8mos.

Hamilton, Elizabeth, dau. Alex. & Elizabeth; d. Sep. 6, 1848-age 11mos.

" Margaret, dau. Alex. & Elizabeth; d. July 22, 1849-age 11da.

Cedar st.

White,   Sarah, wife James; died July 1,1871-age 55yrs. 6mos.

"   Mary Anne, dau.James & Sarah; died Apr.8,1853-age 1yr.3mo.

Rogers,   Hannah, wife Linzie; died Dec.7,1861-age 43yrs. 2mos. 16da

"   Corp.Samuel Rogers; "Co.B. 48th.N.Y.Inf."

"   John E., son Samuel & Mary E.; Aug.17,1864-

"   Ella F., dau.P.L.& Hannah; died Jan.9,1864-age 3yr. 5mo.

"   James F., son P.L.& Hannah; died May 18,1852-age 3yr. 3mo.

Hustis,   Sarah, dau.Caleb & Debriah A.; died Apr.9,1852-age 2yr.1mo.

"   Schuyler L. son Henry & Mary A.; d.Mar.27,1851-age 8mos.

Conklin, William Conklin; died Feb.24,1863-age 73yrs. 5mos. 6days.

"   Phebe, wife William; died Feb.21,1878-age 87yrs. 6mos. 9da.

Travis,   Cornelius N.Travis; died Apr.26,1856-age 31 years.

"   Benjamin Travis; died Apr.29,1855-age 69 years.

"   Phebe Travis; died April 1,1859-age 72 years.

Huestis, Howard H., son William H.& Adelia; died Dec.30,1855-
                        age 4 years, 25 days.

Ladue,   Augusta, dau.Abraham & Mary A.; died Dec.26,1851-age 6yrs.

Annin,   Melissa, dau.Samuel & Elizabeth; d.Nov.1,1867-age 7yr.2mo.

Monroe,   Lewis Monroe; died May 21,1857-age 68yrs. 5mos. 23days.

Mosier,   Amos Mosier; died Nov.23,1850-age 58yrs. 6mos. 7days.

"   Jane, wife Amos; May 3,1790-Sept.23,1872.

Secor,   Seth Secor; died May 28,1868-age 72 years, 10 months, 24da

Jaycox,   Elizabeth, wife Hamilton; died May 7,1854-age 40yrs. 1mon.

"   Eugene, son Hamilton & Elizabeth; died May 4,1851-age 6yr.

Miller,   Mary R., dau.William & Jane; died Nov.26,1852-age 2yr.4mo.

"   John, son William & Jane; died Dec.19,1852-age 4yrs. 6mos.

Bell,   John Bell; died Oct.6,1882-age 57 years, 4 months, 6 days

Bailey,   Elizabeth Bailey; died Jan.17,1871-age 47yrs. 4mos. 13days

Cedar st.

Davenport.	Phebe, wife Sylvenus W.; died Nov.21,1857- age 41 years, 5 months, 5 days.
Scholefield,	Seth Scholefield; died Jan.22,1857-age 85 years, 5 days
"	Dorcas, wife Seth; died Nov.16,1866-age 88 years.
McGovern,	John McGovern; "Co.I. 6th.N.Y. H.A."
Schedule,	William H., son William & Elizabeth; died Apr.19,1843- age 5 years, 8 months, 19 days.
LaForge,	George LaForge; died Feb.12,1892-age 75 years.
"	Mary Mekeel, wife George LaForge; died Aug.18,1894- age 76 years, 10 months, 4 days.
Lawrence,	Stephen Lawrence; died Apr.9,1855-age 53 years, 10 mos.
"	Martha Lawrence; Mar.24,1852-Sept.18,1873.
Disbrow,	Sophia Disbrow; died May 1,1894-age 83yrs. 1mon. 10day
Sheldon,	Emily J.Bailey, wife S.Sheldon; died Feb.3,1867- age 28 years, 3 months, 9 days.
Merritt,	Maria A.Davis, wife Vincent Merritt; June 7,1822-July 17,1871.
"	Josie, son Vincent & Maria; died May 13,1859-age 1yr.
"	Willie, son Vincent & Maria; Apr.18,1856-July 13,1856.
"	Mary, dau.Vincent & Maria; Apr.11,1854-Oct.2,1854.
"	Henry, son Vincent & Maria; died Feb.8,1861, age 9 years, 7 months, 6 days.
Parsons,	Peter S.Parsons; Dec.10,1819-June 15,1858.
"	Charles H.Parsons; Mar.18,1816-Dec.24,1853.
Mosher,	Harrison Mosher; died July 5,1855-age 33yrs. 11mos.
"	Elijah Mosher; died Apr.17,1870-age 56 years, 17 days
McCoy,	James McCoy; died Nov.25,1865-age 11yrs. 4mos. 21days.
Crawford,	Joseph Crawford; died Dec.14,1859-age 37 years.
Cronk,	Mary T., wife Charles E.; died May 6,1867-age 20yr. 2m.
Gibson,	Mrs Mary Gibson; 1826-1916.
Christian,	Isaac L. son Lewis & Phebe; died Sep.19,1865-age 5yr.2mo

Cedar st.

Hustis,   Elijah Hustis; Mar.5,1806-Mar.1,1879.

"   Delia Green, wife Elijah Hustis; Apr.13,1809-Apr.16,1877.

"   William, son Elijah & Delia; Mar.2,1845-Mar.29,1866.

"   Lydia, dau. Elijah & Delia; Aug.4,1841-Dec.23,1866.

Windberg, Charles C.Windberg; died Oct.30,1872-age 49yrs. 11mos.

Spalding, Jannett, dau. Andrew & Jane A.; died Jan.28,1860-age 4yrs.

Rose,   William Albert, son Samuel & Sarah; d.Sep.3,1860-age 2yrs.

Truman, James Truman; died Nov.1,1859-age 42 years.

Jaycox, William A.Jaycox; died Mar.12,1909-age 67 years.

"   Catherine Wiltsie, wife William Jaycox;
            Aug.28,1829-Feb.24,1880.

Briggs, Andrew Jackson Briggs; Jan.5,1821-Jan.20,1858.

Smith, Margaret, wid.A.J.Briggs, wife James Smith;
            March 11,1818-July 5,1906.

Briggs, Benjamin Briggs; died June 3,1861-age 69yrs. 11mos. 9days.

"   Phebe Briggs; died May 8,1875-age 75 years, 2 months.

Gray,   Freddie, son John & Mary F.; died Aug.24,1872-age 5mos.

Wood,   Luke Wood; died Apr.5,1869-age 82yrs. 2mos. 5days.

"   Mahala, wife Luke; died Feb.16,1872-age 65yrs. 5mos. 20da.

Post,   Carrie, wife William L.; died Sept.24,1867-age 28yrs. 5mos.

"   George R. son William & Carrie; died Sep.7,1867-age 5mos.

Lent,   John W.Lent; died Apr.21,1862-age 22yrs. 10mos. 13days.

Riggs, Susan Riggs; died Feb.11,1883-age 56 years, 9 months.

"   Hannah, wife Daniel; dau.Nicholas Nelson;
            died March 8,1878-age 66 years.

Higgins, Thomas, son Edward & Ann; died July 14,1854-age 3yr. 1mo.

Osborn, Warren E.Osborn; died May 24,1882-age 4yrs. 1mon. 7days.

"   Everett A.Osborn; died July 7,1881-age 3 months, 19 days.

Griffin, James Griffin; -----

Cedar St.

Taite, William, son Henry & Jane; died May 10,1856-age 2yrs. 8mos.

Warren, Esther, dau.John & Matilda; died June 30,1855-age 9yr. 16da

Taylor, James Taylor;   Mar.9,1827-Mar.18,1887.

" Elizabeth Ett, wife James Taylor; Dec.20,1825-Mar.9,1886.

" James, son James & Elizabeth;   Mar.9,1853-

" Vennisa, dau.James & Elizabeth;   Feb.9,1856-

" John W., son James & Elizabeth;   June 1,1856-

" Albert, son James & Elizabeth;   May 22,1861-

Miller, Mary H., wife A.; died Aug.30,1857-age 42 years, 4 months.

" Esebella L., dau.A.& Mary; died Nov.11,1839-age 15 months.

" Charles & Mary, children Arnaud & Mary; -----

Riggs, Lizzie, dau.Isaac & Maria; died Sept.7,1857-age 5 months.

Haight, Sylvanus C.Haight; died Mar.10,1884-age 54yrs. 9mos. 18da.

Turner, Rachel, wife Isaac; died Feb.19,1874-age 71yrs. 6mos. 14da.

Ladue, Charlie, son J.Q.& M.E.; died Aug.29,1861-age 3yrs. 7mos.

Hill, Sarah Grace, dau.James & Rachel E.; May 8,1857-Mar.17,1861.

" Annie Laurie, dau.James & Rachel; May 26,1860-Oct.26,1860.

Boyce, Eliza, wife James H.; died May 6,1855-age 23 years.

" Eugene Owen, son James H.& Frances H.; died Aug.1,1863-
age 5 years, 2 months, 18 days.

Wise, Benjamin Wise; died Dec.1,1871-age 78yrs. 1mon. 20days.

Nelson, James C.Nelson;   July 10,1794-Oct.6,1863.

" Sarah, wife James C.;   Aug.22,1803-Jan.29,1854.

" Jane Nelson; Feb.7,1824-Jan.19,1871.

Odell, Ferris D., son Charles R.& Mary P.; died Feb.20,1860-
age 8 years, 5 months.

Warren, Sylvester Warren; died Dec.19,1864-age 46yrs. 7mos. 22days

Nelson, Emma G., dau.Charles S.& Abby J.; d.Jan.12,1851-age 22mos.

Cedar st.

Reynolds,	Margaret Croft, wid. Sylvanus Haight,
			wid. Rev. John Reynolds;
			March 6, 1788 – June 14, 1873.

Marshall,	Samuel, son John & Hannah; died Nov. 17, 1862 –
			age 25 years, 9 months, 28 days.

Jefferds,	George E. Jefferds; died Nov. 7, 1854 – age 24yrs. 4mos.

"	Samuel Jefferds; died Apr. 16, 1862 – age 70yrs. 2mos. 24da

"	Mary A. dau. Samuel & Catherine; died Apr. 17, 1841 –
			age 21 years, 1 month, 4 days.

"	Emily, dau. Samuel & Catherine; died May 28, 1859 –
			age 19 years, 10 months, 11 days.

"	Perlina, dau. Jerome & Mary; died July 16, 1855 – age 2yr.

Eityengu,	Charles, son John L. & Dorathea; died Jan. 15, 1855 –
			age 1 year, 6 months, 28 days.

Lounsbury,	Philena, wife Allen A.; died Feb. 7, 1862 – age 18yrs. 4mo.

McCaffray,	Dorcas McCaffray; died Oct. 8, 1853 – age 77yrs. 10mos.

Stillwell,	Rachel, wife Burnett; died Dec. 19, 1871 – age 79yrs. 27da.

Truesdell,	John H. Truesdell; died Oct. 5, 1882 – age 53 years.

Yeomans,	Mary Emma, dau. Philemon & Hannah; died Feb. 12, 1854 –
			age 1 year, 5 months, 1 day.

Hamilton,	William Hamilton; died Mar. 29, 1872 – age 52 years.

Spellman,	Edward Spellman; "Co. G. 38th. N.Y. Inf."

"	Etta, dau. B. & P.; died Apr. 11, 1863 – age 6yrs. 3mos. 17da

Nagle,	Mary L. Nagle; died Oct. 9, 1867 – age 30 years.

Ferris,	William Ferris; died Apr. 10, 1855 – age 46yrs. 1mon. 5da.

"	Anna, wife Richard; died Aug. 7, 1857 – age 74yrs. 3mo. 19d

"	Jane, wife Isaac; died Sept. 29, 1868 – age 57yrs. 20days.

"	Milton Ferris; "Co. L. 6th. N.Y. H.A. Vol."
			died Mar. 10, 1894 – age 64 years.

Brunker,	William Marion, son William & Margaret; d. Oct. 28, 1852 –
			age 3 years, 8 months, 17 days.

"	Jane Creighton, dau. Wm. & Marg.; d. Jan. 8, 1861 – age 5y. 7m.

Cedar st.

Taylor,   Cinderella Taylor; ----

Dykeman,   Daniel Dykeman; died Jan.23,1870-age 44yrs. 1mon. 23days

"   Ellen J.Wood, wife Daniel Dykeman; died Jan.24,1876-
                    age 54 years, 7 months, 23 days.

"   Jennie, dau.Daniel & Ellen; died Sept.3,1876-
                    age 22 years, 2 months, 20 days.

"   William, son Daniel & Ellen; died Oct.20,1854-
                    age 2 years, 3 months, 7 days.

"   Wilber, son Daniel & Ellen; died Mar.27,1857-age 14mos.

"   Huestis W., son Daniel & Ellen; died Nov.16,1851-
                    age 2 years, 6 months, 14 days.

Barton,   Millard Filmore, son Andrew C.& Catherine; died Dec.14,1852-
                    age 2 years, 2 months, 25 days.

"   Estella Barton; died Sept.2,1861-age 1 year, 11 months.

"   Katy Amelia, dau.John L.& Katherine;
                    Aug.3,1856-Oct.8,1867.

"   Lavina, dau.John & Katherine;   May 12,1858-Nov.11,1859.

Butler,   Delia L., dau.R.P.& R.; died June 30,1867-age 9mos. 10days

"   Willet J., son R.P.& R.; died Aug.10,1872-age 2 months.

Skedgel,   Leonard, son Leonard & Margaret; d.Apr.14,1860-age 16yrs.

White,   Caleb Peck White; died Nov.25,1855-age 28yrs. 10mos. 14da.

"   Henry L.White; died Apr.1,1851-age 1yr. 4mo. 7da.

"   Charles P.White; died Jan.24,1856-age 1yr. 3mo. 22da.

Mekeel,   William Mekeel; died Aug.23,1859-age 66yrs. 11mos. 24da.

"   Lydia, wife William; died Aug.23,1853-age 52yrs. 18days.

"   Abigail, wife Thomas; died May 22,1865-age 90yrs. 11days.

Bunnell,   Lucy Bunnell;   1853-

Hines,   William Hines;   "Co.D. 128th.N.Y.Inf."

Sloan,   Robert, son James & Mary H.; died May 11,1853-
                    age 2 years, 7 months, 11 days.

Cedar st.

Odell,   George U. Odell; died July 19, 1862 - age 7yrs. 8mos. 3days.

"   George R., son Benjamin & Louisa; died Oct. 29, 1853 -
                        age 3 years, 1 month, 7 days.

Blakly,   Ellen, wife William; died Jan. 16, 1854 - age 57 years.

Ireland,   Amanda, wife Thomas; died Oct. 16, 1866 - age 64yrs. 7mos.

Fisher,   Ellen, wife David; Sept. 7, 1829 - Feb. 12, 1854.

Davis,   Marianita Davis; -----

Miller,   William J. Miller; died May 15, 1872 -
                        age 46 years, 7 months, 12 days.

A number of stones down.

Old Cemetery at

Cold Spring, Putnam Co.

New York.

On Mountain Avenue

Index

Ahern,	19.	Dale,	2.
Alden,	2.	Daniels,	13.
Andrews,	18.	Darrer,	17.
Armstrong,	5.	Davenport,	3, 5.
Atherstone,	5.	de St.Croix,	9.
Atkinson,	8.	Devine,	17.
		Dillon,	16.
Bailey,	17.	Dolan,	7,10.
Barhyte,	2.	Dougherty,	1, 3,15.
Barnes,	3,13,18.	Doyle,	18.
Barton,	16.	Drummond,	15.
Bauckham,	13.	Duffy,	7.
Baxter,	10.	Duncanson,	3.
Beatty,	12.	Dunn,	7,10.
Beers,	8.	Dutcher,	5.
Beesley,	13.	Dykeman,	3, 8.
Birdsall,	3, 4,13.		
Bliss,	20.	Eagan,	16.
Bloomer,	1, 6.	Evans,	19.
Bowne,	2, 3.		
Bourne,	8.	Feeley,	13.
Braidy,	7.	Ferris,	9,10.
Brandon,	14.	Finnin,	14,19.
Bride,	16.	Fisher,	17.
Bronson,	11.	Fitzgerald,	13.
Buchman,	11.	Flagler,	8.
Budd,	2.	Forster,	19.
Bull,	14.	Foster,	19.
Bunnell,	20.	Foshay,	2.
Burnes,	18.	Fowler,	16.
		Frase,	19.
Cahill,	14.	Frost,	19.
Calix,	20.		
Callahan,	7.	Gaghegan,	7.
Campbell,	6.	Gavin,	4.
Candee,	3.	G---ston,	21.
Carbory,	16.	Gillies,	1.
Cargill,	9.	Goodsell,	1.
Carrigan,	17.	Gorman,	18.
Chrilly,	12,17.	Greenleaf,	5.
Cleary,	15.	Grier,	8.
Colwell,	13.	Griffin,	12.
Creighton,	18.	Grogan,	7.
Corbin,	7.		
Costolo,	8.		
Couch,	17.		
Crosby,	4.		
Cronk,	9.		

B

Index

Haight,	4, 8, 17.	McAnally,	17.
Hald,	3.	McClelland,	1.
Hale,	19.	McCutcheon,	18, 20.
Hamilton,	15.	McDowell,	10.
Harris,	2, 4.	McErlean,	18.
Harron,	18.	McGowan,	18.
Harvey,	18.	McGurk,	17, 18.
Hasy,	15.	McIlrevy,	18.
Henyan,	2.	McIntire,	8.
Hoffman,	7.	McKendley,	3.
Holdane,	2.	McKeel,	9.
Howell,	8.	McPeach,	16.
Hunter,	14.	McPeck,	16.
Huestis,	6.	McRanells,	15.
Hustis,	1, 6, 8, 13, 19.	Maher,	14.
Hyatt,	10.	Mead,	4, 9, 11.
		Meeks,	19.
Ireland,	2, 17.	Mekeel,	2, 9, 10, 20.
		Merrick,	21.
Jacox,	4.	Moan,	13.
Jaycock,	2.	Molyneaux,	11.
Jaycox,	4, 9, 20.	Monks,	7.
Jewett,	1.	Monroe,	11.
Johnson,	3.	Moore,	21.
Jolley,	17.	Mosher,	11.
Jones,	14.	Moshier,	2.
		Murphy,	13, 15, 18.
Kelley,	15.	Murray,	7.
Kelly,	15.	Myers,	17.
Kenney,	14.		
Kidd,	11.	Nelson,	4, 5, 11, 12, 16.
Kiernan,	7.	Nevin,	18.
King,	6.	Newman,	7.
Kipp,	21.	Nichols,	11.
Kirwan,	17.		
Knapp,	13, 20.	O'Brien,	1, 14, 16.
Knowles,	20.	Odell,	17, 22.
		O'Niell,	15.
Lawrence,	1, 12.	Osborn,	1.
Lawson,	15.		
Lavy,	15.	Palmer,	19.
Lefong,	2.	Pelizalde,	18.
Lickley,	14.	Penman,	19.
Lloyd,	22.	Pickens,	19.
Lockwood,	3.	Purdy,	7.
Loveless,	11.		
Lynch,	15.	Quinn,	7.
Lyons,	19.	Quirk,	10.

Index

Reed,	13.
Reilley,	18.
Ridgway,	18.
Robbins,	1.
Robertson,	3.
Rodie,	19.
Roe,	16.
Rogers,	15.
Rowan,	15.
Russell,	19.
Sargent,	17.
Sarvise,	7,22.
Secor,	2.
Semonds,	19.
Sheehan,	22.
Shields,	6.
Short,	1.
Simonson,	11.
Sinclaire,	9.
Smith,	3,10.
Smyth,	20.
Snook,	6.
Snouck,	4.
Southard,	19.
Steen,	6.
Stockholm,	16.
Stotesbury,	9.
Stuart,	8.
Sutton,	4.
Sweeney,	14.
Sylvester,	20.
Tevlen,	12,15.
Thompson,	20.
Tows,	16.
Travice,	17.
Travis,	1,12.
Truesdell,	9.
Turner,	1,17.
Turhill,	14.
Walker,	4.
Wallace,	10.
Walsh,	16.
Ward,	15,21.
Warner,	12.
Warren,	1, 2, 9,12,16,18,21.
Weeks,	2.
Whellan,	17.
Wilson,	12.
Wixson,	2.
Wood,	2, 8.
Wooley,	2.
Wright,	2,12,19,21.
Zindle,	10.

Cold Spring
Mountain Avenue.

McClelland,	Susannah, wife Samuel; died Apr.28,1831-age 44 years.
"	William, son Samuel & Susannah; died July 13,1829- age 1 year, 10 months, 12 days.
Short,	Jane, wife John; died Dec.27,1824-age 40 years.
Gillies,	John Brown Gillies; born in Scotland; died May 7,1825-age 37 years.
Jewett,	Ashby Jewett; died Apr.15,1828-age 25yrs. 3mos. 2days.
Turner,	Hannah Turner; died June 14,1867-age 82 years.
Robbins,	John Robbins; died Dec.4,1847-age 62 years.
Lawrence,	Frances Lawrence; died Jan.28,1854-age 49yrs. 8mos. 24da
Warren,	Peter Warren; died Jan.10,1840-age 37 years, 2 months.
"	Benjamin Warren; died Nov.10,1825-age 42 years.
"	Juliaett, dau.Benjamin & Hannah; died Apr.13,1831-age 17y
Doherty,	Daniel Doherty; died Feb.27,1825-age 27 years.
"	Margaret, dau.John & Elizabeth; died June 6,1823-age 6mo
Hustis,	Gilbert Hustis; died July 27,1844-age 49yrs. 5mos. 15day
"	Phebe, wife Gilbert; died Jan.27,1845-age 46yrs. 9mos.
"	Phebe J., dau.Gilbert & Phebe; died Oct.3,1841- age 5 years, 11 months, 24 days.
"	John, son Gilbert & Phebe; died Dec.25,1827-age 3yr. 10mo.
Travis,	Phebe, dau.Benjamin & Phebe; Aug.14,1823-Oct.5,1824.
"	Gilbert Travis; died May 8,1819-age 26yrs. 5mos.
O'Brien,	Ann O'Brien; died March 14,1862-age 75 years.
Bloomer,	Frances Osborn, dau.Benjamin & Phebe; died Nov.29,1850- age 28 years, 4 months, 18 days.
Hustis,	William Hustis; died June 26,1819-age 55yrs. 3mos.
"	Phebe, wife William; died April 15,1844-age 70yr. 9mo.
Goodsell,	Elizabeth Goodsell; Jan.1,1812-Aug.24,1884.

Mountain Ave

Warren, Mary A., dau. Harry & Elizabeth; d. Nov. 1, 1832-age 3yrs. 1mon

Wright, Isaac Wright; died Apr. 4, 1881-age 91yrs. 2mos. 13days.

" Phebe, wife Isaac; died May 19, 1831-age 34yrs. 7mos. 17da.

Lefong, Margaret, wife Tepell; died July 31, 1828-age 42yrs. 3mos.

Secor, Sarah, wife Alexander; died Apr. 2, 1852-age 86yrs. 3mos. 25d

Bowne, Benjamin Bowne; died Feb. 12, 1835-age 64yrs. 8mos. 9days.

" Rachel, wife Benj.; died Feb. 21, 1802-age 22yrs. 6mos. 28da.

" Susannah B., wife Benj.; died Feb. 12, 1854-71yrs. 3mos.

Weeks, Chancy Weeks; died May 28, 1825-age 54 years.

Holdane, Robert, son Henry & Fanny; died Mar. 24, 1814-age 25 days.

Wood, Deborah Secor, wife Luke Wood; died Feb. 3, 1827-age 30 years

Mekeel, Nancy, wife Charles; died Jan. 20, 1850-age 51yrs. 8mos. 16da

Henyan, Mary A., dau. James & Susan; died May 18, 1852-age 1yr. 21da.

Harris, Thomas D., son Isaac & Hannah; died July 23, 1825-age 2yrs.

" Infant son Isaac & Hannah; died July 21, 1825-age 20 days.

Budd, Mary, dau. William & Elizabeth; died Jan. 20, 1820-age 14yrs.

" John, son William & Elizabeth; died Sept. 1, 1831-
age 21 years, 11 months, 22 days.

Moshier, Sarah, wife Elijah; died Sept. 15, 1826-age 62yrs. 6mos.

Ireland, Ephriam Ireland; died Feb. 6, 1862-age 86 years, 10 days.

" Tamer, wife Ephriam; died Sept. 4, 1851-age 73yrs. 4mos. 18da

Barhyte, William Barhyte; died Aug. 15, 1840-age 62yrs. 9mos. 25days

Jacocks, Mary A., dau. William & Jane; died Oct. 1, 1826-age 11mos. 3da.

Dale, John Dale; died Oct. 3, 1841-age 64 years.

Foshay, Daniel Foshay; died July 31, 1845-age 13 months, 9 days.

Alden, Ibena, dau. Manoah & Sarah; died Dec. 11, 1825-age 14mos. 18da.

Wixson, James, son Reuben T. & Caroline; died Sept. 16, 1835-
age 3 years, 2 months, 2 days.

Woolley, Edward, son Gideon & Maria; died Sept. 20, 1824-age 1yr. 6da.

Mountain Ave.

Duncanson,	Caroline Duncanson; died Jan.26,1811-age 1yr. 5mo. 23da.
Robertson,	Ann, dau.John B.& Matilda; died Dec.1,1826-age 13mo 12da.
Johnson,	Henry Johnson; died Oct.28,1825-age 42 years.
"	Sarah J. dau.Henry & Polly; died Sept.6,1824- age 2 years, 1 month, 6 days.
McKendley,	Ann, wife William; died Nov.27,1826-age 28yrs. 4mos. 2da.
Dougherty,	Elizabeth, wife John; died Nov.14,1855-age 62yrs. 10mos.
"	John Dougherty; died April 6,1830-age 40 years.
"	Eleanor, dau.John & Elizabeth; d.Feb.10,1841-age 11yr.10mo
"	Angela, dau.William & Miriam; died Sept.17,1855-age 1yr.
"	James H. son William & Miriam; died Sept.9,1848- age 1 year, 5 months, 6 days.
Davenport,	Morris Davenport; died Mar.19,183- age 44yrs. 6mos.
"	Esther Warren, wife Morris Davenport; died May 31,1876- age 80 years, 21 days.
Lockwood,	Robert Parroll, son Jared & Rebecca; died Aug.26,1847- age 1 year, 1 month, 7 days.
Dykeman,	Elisha, son Hezekiah & Esther; died Apr.23,1832-age 14mo
"	Mary J. dau.Hezekiah & Esther; d.Jan.4,1837-age 3yr. 6mo.
"	Davenport S., son Hezekiah & Esther; died Oct.14,1849- age 21 years, 11 months, 22 days.
Birdsall,	Seymour Birdsall; died Aug.31,1850-age 59yrs. 5mos. 14da.
"	Elizabeth, wife Seymour; died Dec.9,1864-age 72 years.
Candee,	Timothy Candee; died July 26,1833-age 50 years.
Barnes,	Lucy A.Candee, wife Thomas Barnes; died July 2,1861- age 78 years.
Candee,	Sheldon, son Timothy & Lucy; died Aug.25,1824- age 1 year, 7 months, 26 days.
Hald,	Elizabeth Hald; died May 26,1842-age 67 years.
Bowne,	Esther, wife William; died Oct.22,1825-age 24yrs. 3mos.
Smith,	Sarah, dau.Nathan & Huldah; died Nov.2,1825-age 15mos.

Mountain Ave.

Harris,	Isaac Harris; died June 4,1840-age 50 years, 4 months.
"	William W., son Isaac & Hannah; died Jan.8,1835- age 17 years, 7 months, 19 days.
Sutton,	William Sutton; died Dec.10,1836-age 50 years.
"	Thomas Sutton; died Mar.23,1828-age 89yrs. 7mos. 7days.
Haight,	Sylvanus W., son Henry W.& Jane; died Apr.12,1847- age 14 years, 8 months, 29 days.
"	John, son Henry & Jane; died Feb.2,1844-age 4yr. 3mo. 13da.
Snouck,	John Snouck; died Feb.20,1839-age 57 years, 4 months.
"	Eunice, wife John; died Apr.17,1839-age 50yrs. 4mos.
Crosby,	Jacob W.Crosby; died Aug.1,1847-age 53yrs. 5mos. 5days.
"	Jane, wife Jacob; died Jan.25,1839-age 34yrs. 11mos.
"	Catherine M., dau.Jacob & Jane; died Aug.26,1825- age 5 years, 3 months, 25 days.
Nelson,	Mary, dau.Elisha & Phebe J.; died Jan.18,1844- age 5 years, 11 months, 22 days.
"	Elizabeth, dau.Elisha & Phebe; died Oct.14,1838-age 10mo.
"	Phebe Jane Birdsall, wife Elisha Nelson; July 9,1817-July 24,1845.
Snouck,	Frances, wife Matthew Snouck, dau.Justis Nelson; Aug.7,1759-May 25,1820.
Mead,	Nancy, wife Benjamin; died July 20,1836-age 35 years.
Jaycox,	David Jaycox; died Feb.12,1849-age 44 years.
"	Thomas Jaycox; died Sept.15,1854-age 63 years, 17 days.
"	Sarah, wife Thomas; died Feb.16,1859-age 70 years.
Jacox,	Isaiah Jacox; died Aug.23,1840-age 88yrs. 3mos. 9days.
"	Esther, wife Isaiah; died Oct.19,1848-age 90 years.
Gavin,	Michael, son Thomas & Margaret; died May 1,1852- age 3 years, 6 months, 16 days.
Mead,	Isaac Mead; died Apr.13,1811-age 60yrs. 1mon. 27days.
Walker,	Charles S.Walker; died Sept.7,1865-age 25yrs. 1mon.

Mountain

Davenport,	George Davenport; died Feb.8,1819-age 38 years.
"	John Davenport; died July 27,1842-age 63yrs. 6mos.
"	Mary, wife John; died May 7,1817-age 37yrs. 8mos. 17da.
"	C.W.Davenport; died Mar.20,1849-age 37yr. 4mo. 14da.
"	Sarah Amelia, dau.Cornelius W.& Margaret B.; died Dec.15,1842-age 9yrs. 5mos.
"	Elijah Davenport; died Apr.25,1841-age 57 years, 28 days
"	William Davenport; died Mar.27.1852-age 76yrs. 3mo. 22da
"	Frances, wife William; died June 2,1824-age 47yrs. 3mos.
"	Josiah, son William & Frances; died June 16,1821- age 13 years, 8 months, 27 days.
"	Elizabeth, dau.William & Frances; died June 17,1818- age 16 years, 7 months, 9 days.
"	John, son William & Frances; died June 17,1818- age 12 years, 9 months, 18 days.
"	Samuel W., son Stephen & Mary; died Sept.23,1843- age 1 year, 1 month.
"	Philip, son Stephen & Mary; died Apr.25,1834-age 6 weeks
"	Rachel, dau.Stephen & Mary; died June 7,1835-age 2mo. 23da
"	Isaac Davenport; died Mar.18,1808-age 59yrs. 11mos. 20da
"	Elizabeth, wife Isaac; died Jan.13,1828-age 70yrs. 7mos.
"	Thomas Davenport; Apr.11,1750-July -- 1790.
"	Martha, wife Thomas; Jan.26,1755-Apr.16,1789.
"	Samuel, son Samuel & Caroline; May 18,1838------
Dutcher,	Elmore, son Julia & Henry; died Oct.21,1887-age 4 years.
"	Henry, son Julia & Henry; age 10 months.
Armstrong,	Alexander, son George & Mary; ------
Greenleaf,	John Greenleaf; died Nov.22,1824-age 28yrs. 9mos. 2days
Atherstone,	William Atherstone; died Dec.1,1835-age 39 years, 4 days

Mountain Ave.

Snooks, Edward, son Peter & Mary; died Jan.17,1831-age 9yr. 11mo.

" James, son Peter & Mary; died Jan.6,1834-age 16yrs. 1mon.

" John Snook; died June 17,1818-age 35 years, 6 months.

Nelson, Sarah, wife Warren; died Apr.27,1850-age 46yrs. 1mon. 14da

" Phebe J., dau.Warren & Sarah; died Aug.23,1858-age 28yrs.

" John M. son Warren & Sarah; died Oct.13,1850-
age 17 years, 11 months, 28 days.

" Isaac, son Elisha & Frances; died Sept.4,1821-age 4mos.

" Justus E., son Elisha & Frances; died Oct.15,1822-
age 2 months, 12 days.

Hustis, Ann Eliza, dau.Joseph R. & Elizabeth; died Mar.14,1853-
age 5 years, 7 months, 8 days.

" Infant Johnathan & Elizabeth; died Oct.30,1826-age 15da.

" Henry, son Thomas D.& Elizabeth; died Mar.24,1844-
age 4 years, 6 months, 16 days.

" Samuel D., son Thomas & Elizabeth; died Apr.4,1844-20mos.

Huestis, Johnathan Huestis; died Nov.24,1850-age 70yrs. 5mos. 10da.

" Elizabeth, wife Johnathan; died Dec.18,1858-
age 71 years, 28 days.

Bloomer, Beverly Bloomer; died May 28,1848-age 31yrs. 2mos. 28days.

" Frances, wife Beverly; died Aug.15,1840-age 20yrs. 6mos.

King, Catherine Ann, dau.Rev.L.W.& M.M.; died Apr.22,1844-6yrs.

" Lydia J. dau.Rev.L.W.& M.M.; died June 24,1843-age 6mo.

Shields, Nancy, wife Laurence; died Aug.28,1860-age 48 years.

" Jane, dau.Laurence & Nancy; age 12 years.

Steen, James Steen; died Mar.1,1858-age 77yrs. 3mos. 19days.

" Eliza, wife James; died Oct.10,1846-age 48 years.

" James, son James & Eliza; died Feb.11,1831-age 2yrs. 9mos.

Campbell, Arthur Campbell; died June 2,1833-age 49 years.

" Mary, wife Arthur; -------

Mountain Ave.

Callahan,	David Callahan; died June 5,1826-age 35 years.
"	Ellen, wife David;
"	Ellen Callahan; died June 26,1823-age 1 year, 1 month.
Duffy,	Bernard Duffy; died May 8,1860-age 66 years.
Quinn,	Ann, wife Patrick; died Jan.4,1864-age 77 years.
Sarvise,	Robert Sarvise; died Oct.5,1831-age 32yrs. 6mos. 18days
Grogan,	Maria, dau.Philip & Mary; died Apr.2,1851-age 14mos.
Murray,	John Murray; died Sept.9,1865-age 24yrs. 2mos.
Braidy,	Margaret, wife Thomas; died Sept.27,1871-age 27yrs. 5mos
"	Margaret, Infant dau.Thomas & Margaret; -----
Dolan,	Michael Dolan; died Jan.21,1864-age 40 years.
Gaghagan,	John Gaghagan; died Apr.26,1864-age 47 years.
Dunn,	Bridget Dunn; died Jan.14,1858-age 30 years.
Corbin,	Amey, dau.William & Mahaley; died Aug.27,1837-age 1 year
"	James H., son William & Mahaley; died Dec.26,1833- age 2 years, 8 months, 8 days.
Hoffman,	John Harrison, son William & Elizabeth; died Apr.20,1845 age 7 months, 25 days.
"	James William, son William & Elizabeth; died Sept.30,1842-age 26 days.
Kiernan,	Michael Kiernan; died April 11,1851-age 37 years.
"	Ellen, dau.Michael & Margaret; died Oct.9,1849-age 1mo.
"	Rose, wife Thomas; died June 14,1853-age 62 years.
Monks,	John Monks; died Jan.20,1851-age 35yrs. 2mos. 12days.
"	John, son John & Sarah; died July 10,1849-age 3mo. 19da.
Purdy,	Ezekiel Purdy; died Sept.23,1831-age 39 years, 7 months.
"	Margaret, wife Ezekiel; died Feb14,1866-age 64yrs. 8mos.
Newman,	Robert Newman; "Co.L.6th.N.Y. H.A."

Mountain Ave.

Atkinson,	Joseph, son Amos & Hannah; died Dec.14,1864-age 5 years.
McIntire,	William McIntire; died June 4,1863-age 30 years.
Stuart,	Charles C., son Abraham & Elizabeth; d.Sep.24,1846-15mos.
Costolo,	Thomas, son John & Johana; died Mar.14,1858-age 11yr. 6mo
Grier,	Rev.Thomas Grier; died May 19,1834-age 54 years.
Bourne,	Susan J., dau.Abram & Delilah; d.Jan.25,1835-age 15mos.
Dykeman,	B.Dykeman; died April 28,1864-age 69 years.
"	Sarah, dau.Benjamin & Asenath; Aug.11,1832-----
"	Isaac, son Benjamin & Asenath; died Sept.1,1829-age 1yr.
Flagler,	Harvey Flagler; died May 27,1842-age 29 years, 23 days.
"	William H. son Harvey & Sarah; died Mar.2,1840-age 18mos
Hustis,	Robert Hustis; died Feb.15,1833-age 73yrs. 8mos. 8days.
"	Tamer, wife Robert; died Mar,26,1850-age 81yrs. 3mos. 28d
Haight,	Joshua Haight; died Oct.3,1858-age 64yrs. 7mos. 17days.
"	Sarah, wife Joshua; died Feb.23,1857-age 59 years, 23 day
"	Sarah J. dau.Joshua & Sarah; died Oct.29,1853-age 24yrs.
"	David K., son Joshua & Sarah; died May 12,1850-age 25yrs
"	Mary E. dau.Joshua & Sarah; died Mar.9,1846-age 13yr. 6mo
"	John, son Joshua & Sarah; died June 21,1840-age 20yr.9mo.
"	James H. son Joshua & Sarah; died Nov.12,1839- age 21 years, 5 months, 27 days.
Beers,	Mary, dau.William & Abigail; died April 10,1847- age 18 years, 2 months, 24 days.
Wood,	Sarah H., dau.William & Jane; died Oct.19,1850- age 4 years, 11 months, 6 days.
"	William, son William & Jane; died July 17,1851- age 2 years, 2 months, 20 days.
"	Samuel, son Samuel & Sarah; died Aug.22,1847-age 6mos.
Howell,	Charles M.Howell; died Oct.5,1816-age 2 years, 6 months.

Mountain

Stotesbury,	Samuel, son Samuel;
"	John E. Stotesbury; died Nov.27,1850-age 19yrs. 4mos.
Sinclaire,	Charles William, son Thomas & Leah G.; died July 14,1834
de St.Croix,	Peter Lewis, son Peter L.& Philena; died Nov.9,1834- age 3 years, 8 months, 23 days.
Truesdell,	Ann Maria, wife Darius, dau. Joshua & Sarah Haight; died Oct.1,1851-age 25 years.
"	Asa, son Darius & Ann; died Feb.23,1851-age 11mo. 16da.
"	David, son Darius & Ann; Mar.13,1849-
Mekeel,	Mary A., dau. Thomas & Deborah; died July 25,1848- age 22 years, 2 months, 3 days.
Cronk,	Eliza J., wife John; died Apr.29,1845-age 29yrs. 6mos.
"	John, son John & Eliza; died Feb.21,1845-age 3 days.
"	George, son Joshua & Mary; died Oct.13,1842-age 9yr.8mo.
"	Mary E. dau. Joshua & Mary; died June 21,1842-age 3mos.
"	William, son John & Jane; died May 21,1845-age 14mos.
"	Nicholas Cronk; died Sept.28,1843-age 63 years.
"	Nancy, wife Capt. Nicholas; died Nov.29,1821-age 36yrs.
"	Mary, dau. Nicholas & Elizabeth; died May 6,1832-10mos.
Jaycox,	Silvenus J. son William H.& Elizabeth T. died July 30,1843-age 4mos. 20days.
"	Elizabeth J. wife William; died Jan.11,1850- age 28 years, 6 months, 12 days.
"	LeGrand, son Isaac & Frances; died Oct.13,1843- age 4 years, 1 month, 18 days.
Cargill,	Isaac M., son Henry & Susan; died Feb.21,1844- age 2 years, 3 months, 19 days.
"	William H., son Henry & Susan; d.Sep.11,1855-age 8mo.10d.
Mead,	Darius Mead; died Oct.27,1846-age 49yrs. 2mos. 12days.
Warren,	Peter I., son Samuel & Barbara; died Apr.30,1835-age 1y.
Ferris,	Sarah A. dau. Isaac & Jane; died June 30,1838-age 4yr.6m

Mountain Ave.

Ferris,   Mary A., dau. William & Phebe; died Feb.5,1841-age 8yr. 5mo.

"   Amy, dau. Philander & Mary; died Oct.13,1837-age 1 year.

"   Mary C., dau. Philander & Mary; died Aug.28,1842-
                                   age 4 years, 4 months, 17 days.

"   Kezia, son Philander & Mary; d. July 1,1842-age 7mos.

Smith,   Richard Smith; died May 16,1855-age 82 years.

"   Nancy, wife Richard; died May 31,1836-age 60yrs. 3mos. 24da

"   Jordan, son Richard & Nancy; died July 18,1832-age 31 years

"   Rivers Smith; died Apr.22,1838-age 38 years, 5 months.

Wallace,   Uriah, son John & Ann E.; Feb.15,1841----

Mekeel,   Sarah, wife Stephen; died Mar.29,1833-age 23yrs. 8mos. 22da.

"   Susan, wife Stephen; died Apr.1,1847-age 31yrs. 1mon. 27da.

"   James W., son Stephen & Susan; died Apr.1,1835-age 4mos.

McDowell, William, son John & Ann. died Sept.14,1833-age 1yr. 13da.

Zindle,   William H., son Jonas & Moraly; died May 20,1839-age 3yrs.

"   William, son Jonas & Moraly; died Mar.24,1834-age 6mos.

"   Charles, son Jonas & Moraly; died Jan.15,1831------

Hyatt,   Alvey Hyatt; died Aug.14,1849-age 41 years, 3 months.

"   William H., son Alvey & Prudence; died July 15,1837-age 7mo.

Quirk,   Michael Quirk; died Jan.19,1867-age 41 years.

Dunn,   Eleazer Dunn; died April 9,1835-age 21 years.

Baxter,   Thadeus Baxter; died Aug.14,1847-age 77yrs. 1mon. 7days.

"   Hannah, wife Thadeus; died Dec.4,1840-age 62yrs. 5mos. 26da

"   Jane, wife Elisha C.; died Oct.5,1851-age 42 years, 18 days

"   Betsey A. wife Elisha; died Mar.29,1854-age 26yrs. 3mos.

"   Frances, wife Elisha; died Nov.27,1858-age 56yrs. 5mos. 8da

"   Charles, son Elisha & Jane; died Aug.29,1843-age 21 days.

Dolan,   Bridget, wife John; died Dec.16,1863-age 35 years

Mountain Ave.

Buchanan, Henrietta, dau. John & Lydia; died July 22, 1848-
              age 3 years, 10 months, 25 days.

"   Joseph, son John & Lydia; died June 28, 1848-age 4mos.

"   Mary A., dau. Jesse & Clara; died July 2, 1845-age 23yr. 3mo

"   Harriet, dau. Jesse & Clara; died Jan. 5, 1838-
              age 7 years, 5 months, 29 days.

Mosher,   Elizabeth, wife Henry, dau. Justus & Phebe Secor;
              died Sept. 2, 1850-age 21yrs. 8mos.

"   Frances, dau. Henry & Elizabeth; died May 22, 1850-age 4mos.

Monroe,   Julia, dau. Gilbert & Fanny J.; Mar. 20, 1840-----

"   Almira, dau. Gilbert & Fanny; died Mar. 15, 1844-age 2yr. 1mo

"   Phebe, dau. Lewis & Martha; died Sept. 3, 1838-
              age 17 years, 4 months, 27 days.

Simonson, Mary Cornelia Simonson; died Feb. 28, 1850-
              age 17 years, 9 months, 26 days.

Mead,   Gilbert Mead; died June 10, 1844-age 62yrs. 6mos. 21days.

"   Sarah Mead; died Sept. 6, 1855-age 51yrs. 1mon. 4days.

Kidd,   Anna, wife Capt. Alexander Kidd; died Dec. 4, 1838-age 75yrs.

Nelson,   Elisha Nelson; died Apr. 15, 1852-age 74 years.

Molyneaux, Daniel Molyneaux; died Jan. 27, 1849-age 74 years.

"   Susan, wife Daniel; died July 15, 1840-age 58 years.

"   Susan, dau. Daniel & Susan; died Mar. 12, 1838-
              age 18 years, 10 months, 10 days.

Nichols, Marvin R. Nichols; died June 20, 1852-age 42yrs. 1mon. 4da.

"   Catherine, wife Marvin; died May 27, 1846-age 26yrs. 10mos.

"   James Nichols; died Dec. 12, 1844-age 63 years.

"   Rollins, wife James; died June 10, 1845-age 62yrs. 3mos.

"   Annis, dau. James & Rollins; died June 1, 1838-age 13yr. 10m.

Bronson, Elizabeth, dau. Solomon; died Nov. 12, 1844-age 38 years.

Loveless, James K., son Harvey & Abigail; died Oct. 6, 1849-
              age 3 years, 11 months, 26 days.

Mountain Ave.

Griffin,	Lewis, son Daniel & Sarah; died Jan.31,1838-age 2yr. 11mo.
"	John E. son Daniel & Sarah; died Jan.19,1845- age 3 years, 3 months, 4 days.
Travis,	William Augustus, son Lewis & Nancy; died Sept.22,1844- age 4 years, 5 months, 10 days.
Warner,	Sarah Warner; died Jan.6,1835-age 55 years.
Beatty,	Sarah Beatty; died Dec.3,1834-age 28 years.
Lawrence,	Gilbert Lawrence; died June 11,1861-age 66 years.
"	Mary A., wife Gilbert; died Apr.1,1837-age 34 years.
"	Sarah, dau.Enoch & Martha; died Aug.16,1840-age 20mos.
"	Ariah Lucy, dau.Enoch & Martha; died June 21,1841- age 1 year, 6 months, 16 days.
Warren,	Harry Warren; died Mar.3,1851-age 46yrs. 7mos. 6days.
"	Elizabeth J., wife Harry; died Dec.23,1838- age 28 years, 10 months, 28 years.
"	Davenport, son Harry & Cornelia E.; died Apr.1,1853- age 3 years, 3 months, 23 days.
Wright,	Susan, wife George; died Apr.26,1843-age 28yrs. 1mon. 29da
Nelson,	Emmalinda, dau.H.J.& H.L.; died Jan.15,1850- age 4 years, 6 months, 25 days.
"	Infant dau.H.J.& H.L.; May 25,1841----
Wilson,	John H., son Martin & Lydia; Mar.4,1840----
Tevlen,	Hugh Tevlen; died May 19,1857-age 46yrs. 9mos. 4days.
Chrilly,	John Chrilly; died June 3,1865-age 38 years.
Nelson,	Deborah A., wife George; died Mar.20,1847-age 26yr. 2mo.
Warren,	Samuel Warren; died Dec.13,1834-age 66 years.
"	Anna Warren; died Feb.14,1843-age 77 years.
"	John S.Warren; died June 11,1837-age 47 years, 5 months.
Lawrence,	Jesse Lawrence; died May 24,1858-age 87yrs. 1mon. 5days.
"	Rachel, wife Jesse; died May 21,1841-age 72yrs. 5mos. 15da

Mountain Ave.

Fitzgerald,	Johana, wife Maurice; died June 25,1849- age 49 years, 8 months, 14 days.
Bauckham,	Mary, wife Henry; died July 11,1838-age 27 years.
"	Mary, dau. Henry & Mary; age 3 months.
Colwell,	Jane, dau. Charles & Elizabeth; died Feb.8,1840-age 5yrs.
Knapp,	Catherine, wife William; died Apr.6,1852-age 27yrs. 8da.
Hustis,	Isaac Hustis; died Apr.11,1873-age 72yrs. 6mos. 26days.
"	Eliza, wife Isaac; died Apr.26,1839-age 37yrs. 2mos. 8da
"	Phebe, dau. Isaac & Eliza; died Apr.7,1859-age 25yr. 1mo.
"	William, son Isaac & Eliza; died Nov.13,1842- age 19 years, 2 months, 15 days.
Fitzgerald,	John Fitzgerald; died Sept.3,1857-age 34 years, 14 days.
Birdsall,	David Birdsall; died June 7,1838-age 81yrs. 1mon. 19days
"	Hannah, wife David; died Mar.8,1851-age 78yrs. 8mos. 11da
"	Aaron Birdsall; died Oct.5,1846-age 48 years.
"	Esther, wife Aaron; died Apr.4,1874-age 74yrs. 2mos. 9da.
"	William H. Birdsall; died Feb.8,1847-age 2yrs. 8mos. 8day
Daniels,	William H., son John & Selina; died Sept.3,1847- age 1 year, 1 month, 7 days.
Barnes,	William Leonard, son Charles & Mary; died Dec.10,1835- age 1 year, 7 months, 14 days.
Reed,	George Reed; died March 10,1835-age 63 years.
Moan,	John Moan; died December 4,1873-age 80 years.
"	Catherine, wife John; died Mar.14,1873-age 70 years.
Beesley,	Charlotte, wife C. Beesley; died May 16,1851-age 36 years.
Feeley,	James, son Anthony & Mary; died Aug.28,1860-age 22 years.
"	Ann, dau. Anthony & Mary; died Aug.4,1842-age 1yr. 8mo.
Murphy,	Mary Teresa, wife John A. Murphy, dau. Anthony & Mary Feeley died Dec.3,1870-age 22yr. 8mo. 22da.

Mountain Ave.

Sweeney,	Edward Sweeney; died Apr.7,1859-age 61yrs. 5mos. 23days.
"	Catherine, wife Edward; died Aug.4,1859-age 52 years.
O'Brien,	Catherine, wife James; died Aug.10,1865-age 20yrs. 11mos.
"	James, son James & Catherine; died July 28,1865-age 21days
Kenney,	Dorcas Kenney; May 14,1881-----
"	Elizabeth Kenney; died Apr.23,1839-age 29 years.
"	Rosana Kenney; died July --,1838-age 1 year, 2 months.
Brandon,	John Brandon; died Mar.11,1865-age 48 years, 11 months.
Maher,	Roger Maher; "Co.D. 10th.N.Y.Infantry."
Cahill,	Mary, dau.Edward & Eliza; died Dec.31,1851-age 1yr.4mo.16da.
"	Ann, wife Edward; died Mar.24,1848-age 27 years.
"	John, son Edward & Ann; died Apr.5,1848-age 15 days.
Finnin,	Mary, dau.Thomas & Mary; died Jan.25,1850-age 1yr. 2mo.
"	William Finnin; died Jan.2,1874-age 58 years.
"	Margaret Finnin; -------
"	Bridget, wife William; died Feb.26,1870-age 55 years.
"	Mary, wiffe, William; died Mar.27,1848-age 27 years.
"	William, son William & Mary; died Mar.28,1848-age 1 day.
Lickley,	Abraham Lickley; died Jan.22,1836-age 33yrs. 9mos. 21days.
Tuthill,	Malissa J., dau.John H.& Catherine; d.Sep.21,1836-age 13mo
"	Charles W., son John H.& Catherine; d.Jan.30,1840-age 11mo
"	Cornelia, dau.John H.& Catherine; d.May 10,1834-age 1mo.
Jones,	William Jones; died Sept.16,1847-age 3 years, 14 days.
"	George E.Jones; died Aug.28,1842-age 10 months.
"	Susannah, dau.John & Dorothy; died May 18,1841-age 3yr.8mo
Bull,	Robert Bull; died Jan.8,1857-age 54 years.
Hunter,	John Hunter; died April 24,1837-age 25 years.

Mountain Ave.

Rowan,	Michael Rowan; died Oct.28,1848-age 40 years.
"	Thomas, son Michael & Mary; died Dec.27,1841-age 4yr. 9mo.
"	James H.Rowan; died Dec.23,1840-age 1year, 8mos. 25days
O'Neill,	Rosanna, wife Henry; died May 5,1872-age 58 years.
McRanells,	Sarah McRanells; died Aug.14,1840-age 27 years.
"	James McRanells; died Aug.27,1841-age 5yrs. 4mos. 10days
"	Mary A.Mcranells; died Sept.17,1839-age 1 year, 5 months.
"	Jane McRanells; died Sept.2,1840-age 1 year, 4 months.
Lawson,	Milly A., wife Robert; died Sept.28,1845-age 39yr. 7mo.
Drummond,	Mary J., wife William H.; died Sept.30,1845-age 21 years.
Kelley,	John Kelley; died April 7,1866-age 36 years.
"	Sarah Kelley; died Dec.25,1860-age 11 months, 3 days.
Hamilton,	John W., son Alexander & Elizabeth; died May 11,1847-age 1 year, 9 months, 7 days.
Ward,	Bridget, wife Edward; died April 6,1868-age 54 years.
Dougherty,	James Dougherty; May 27,1838-age 39 years.
Hasy,	John Hasy; died Sept.3,1838-age 36 years.
Lynch,	Patrick Lynch; died Oct.1,1839-age 45 years.
Rogers,	Thomas Rogers; died June 15,1848-age 48 years.
Cleary,	Judith Cleary; died Mar.17,1858-age 66 years.
Tevlin,	Bridget Tevlin; died Aug.21,1840-age 57 years.
"	Mary, dau.James & Catherine; died Jan.29,1838-age 5mos.
"	Mary, dau.James & Catherine; died Sept.23,1847-age 18mos.
Murphy,	Julia Anna, dau.Nicholas & Julia; Apr.12,1852-Sep.2,1853.
Kelly,	James Kelly; died July 7,1846-age 36 years.
"	James Kelly; died Dec.30,1846-age 6 months.
Lavy,	Mary, James, Daniel; children James & Ann; -----

Mountain Ave.

Stockholm,	Charles, son Aaron & Sarah; died May 22,1852-age 3mos.
Dillon,	Patrick Dillon; died May 16,1849-age 37 years.
McPeck,	James McPeck; died May 19,1872-age 60 years.
McPeach,	William, son James & Sarah; died Mar.28,1853-age 1yr. 8mo
Warren,	Sarah F., dau.Isaac & Mary A.; died Nov.5,1841-age 21mos.
"	John N.Warren; died Oct.8,1840-age 48yrs. 3mos. 9days.
Tows,	Emma, dau.James & Ann; died July 28,1851-age 3yr. 2mo. 19d
"	George, son James & Ann; d.July 5,1850-age 3mos. 13days.
Bride,	Mary Bride; died Feb.2,1855-age 30 years.
"	Mary Ellenor, dau.John & Joanna; died Feb.8,1855- age 2 years, 6 months, 28 days.
Roe,	Mary Barton, wife Admiral R.Roe; died July 28,1855- age 48 years, 8 months, 2 days.
Fowler,	Daniel Fowler; died Mar.30,1844-age 40yrs. 7mos. 5days.
"	Margaret, wife Daniel; died Feb.17,1840-age 24 years.
"	Robert W., son Daniel & Margaret; d.Apr.16,1841-age 14mo.
"	Jane, wife Daniel; died Oct.22,1835-age 22yrs. 8mos. 6da.
Nelson,	Mary J., wife George W.; died July 30,1854-age 20yrs. 4mo
"	Frederick, son George & Mary; died Sept.17,1854-age 6mos.
Warren,	Mary Agnes, dau.Henry R.& Ann E., died Mar.16,1850-age 5y.
"	Henrietta, dau.Henry & Ann; died Nov.5,1837-age 1yr. 3mo
"	John P.Warren; died May 14,1838-age 66yrs. 4mos. 14days.
"	Mary, wife John P.; died Sept.23,1840-age 54 years.
"	Ann Eliza, wife Harry R.; died Dec.12,1857-age 40yrs.2mo.
Eagan,	Ellen Walsh, wife John Eagan; died June 30,1875-age 48yr.
Walsh,	Thomas Walsh; -----
O'Brien,	Charles O'Brien; died Nov.6,1863-age 55 years.
Carbory,	John Carbory; died Sept.16,1857-age 41 years.

Mountain Ave.

Chrilley,	Ann, wife James; died April 24,1854-age 57 years.
McGurk,	Ellen McGurk; died April 3,1857-age 63 years.
"	Peter McGurk; died February 15,1858-age 38 years.
Kirwan,	Agnes, wife Michael; died June 27,1848-age 32 years.
Darrer,	James Darrer; died Mar.6,1841-age 76yrs. 6days.
Devine,	Patrick Devine; Feb.22,1822-Dec.10,1864.
"	Mary Ann Devine; died Feb.2,1882-age 64 years.
Carrigan,	Patrick Carrigan; died Mar.17,1848-age 39 years.
"	Mary Carrigan; died Mar.4,1854-age 14 years, 2 days.
Haight,	Laura, wife Charles; died Oct.1,1841-age 26 years, 7 mos.
"	Mary, dau.Charles & Laura; died Oct.14,1839-age 6mos. 22da.
"	John, son Charles & Laura; died Feb.6,1841-age 10mos.
Fisher,	Amy Maria, wife David; died Sept.23,1849-age 19yrs. 8mos.
"	Alida, dau.David & Mary; died Dec.19,1847-age 6mos. 6days
"	Mary A., dau.David & Mary; died Jan.26,1854-age 5yr.4mo.
Sargent,	Mary Sargent; died Jan.11,1841-----
Turner,	Gilbert Turner; died Oct.14,1854-age 32yrs. 4mos. 27days
Odell,	Abijah, son Abijah & Harriet; died Nov.5,1841-age 4yrs.
Myers,	Johnathan, son John & Elizabeth; died Mar.8,1843-age 2 months, 17 days.
Bailey,	Emery J., son James & Margaret; died Aug.13,1844-age 8mos.
Whellan,	Thomas Whellan; died Aug.12,1849-age 31 years.
Ireland,	Abraham E.Ireland; died July 3,1847-age 41yrs. 8mos. 28da.
Couch,	Samuel Couch; "Native of Cornwell,Eng.;" died Oct.27,1846-age 58yrs. 4mos.
McAnally,	Ann McAnally; died Feb.11,1861-age 44 years.
Travice,	Nancy, wife Reuben; died Sept.17,1843-age 54yrs. 3mos.
Jolley,	Mary Eliza, dau.David & Maria; died Mar.6,1844-age 17 years, 4 months, 17 days.

Mountain Ave.

McCutcheon, Robert McCutcheon; died Dec.4,1856-
              age 67 years, 9 months, 3 days.

"   Margaret, wife Robert; died Jan.22,1860-age 68 years.

Gorman,   Daniel Gorman; died Feb.6,1854-age 24 years.

Burnes,   James Burnes; died April 22,1846-age 33 years.

"   John Burnes; died May 23,1850-age 31 years.

Doyle,   Mary Burnes, wife James Doyle; d.Sept.12,1851-age 29yrs

Reilley,   Michael Reilley; died Aug.22,1849-age 27yrs. 3mos.

Murphy,   Patrick Murphy; died Aug.8,1846-age 27 years.

McIlrevy,   Daniel McIlrevy; died July 17,1848-age 25 years.

McGowen,   James McGowen; died Apr.14,1851-age 32 years.

McErlean,   Matilda, dau.Edward & Martha; died Mar.20,1844-age 1yr.

McGurk,   Isabella, dau.James & Isabella; died Dec.14,1840-
              age 1 year, 4 months, 1 day.

Nevin,   Ann, dau.Michael & Mary; died Jan.31,1846-
              age 10 years, 11 months, 25 days.

"   Elizabeth, dau.Michael & Mary; ----

Murphy,   James, son James & Mary; d.Aug.5,1846-age 4mos. 4days.

Ridgway,   Jeanette, dau.Alanson & Phinna; died June 7,1842-
              age 5 years, 3 months, 11 days.

Pelizalde, Louis M.Pelizalde; July 4,1821-July 28,1840.

Harron,   Jane, wife Johnathan; died Apr.29,1840-age 35 years.

Warren,   Daniel Warren; died Apr.9,1835-age 61yrs. 3mos. 8days.

"   Susannah, wife Daniel; died July 30,1854-age 76yrs. 7mo.

"   Margaret, dau.John & Jemima; d.Mar.8,1839-age 1mo. 16da.

Andrews,   John P.Andrews; Jan.1,1844-

Harvey,   George H. son Aaron & Maria; d.June 10,1842-age 14mos.

"   Maria A. dau.Aaron & Maria; d.Mar.3,1841-age 1yr. 5mo.

Creighton, John Creighton; died Sept.14,1861-age 71 years.

Mountain Ave.

Hustis,   David, son Elijah & Deliverance; died Feb.6,1841-age 7yrs.

Hale,   Stewart Hale; died Feb.4,1863-age 60 years.

"   Susan, wife Stewart; died May 20,1849-age 38 years.

"   Mary, wife Stewart; died Apr.27,1842-age 39 years.

"   Mary J., dau.Stewart & Mary; died Sept.19,1851-
           age 17 years, 5 months, 8 days.

Meeks,   Ann Elizabeth, wife John L.; died Nov.4,1827-age 27yrs.3mo.

Semonds,   Richard Semonds; died Nov.30,1843-age 28 years.

Fraser,   Ann, wife James; died Nov.18,1842-age 42 years.

Palmer,   John Palmer; died Dec.-- 1840-age 20 years.

Wright,   John P.Wright; died Jan.7,1840-age 4 years.

Penman,   William Penman; died Aug.1,1839-age 49 years, 6 months.

Russell,   Charles B.Russell; died Oct.23,1842-age 39yrs. 2mos.

Rodie,   William Rodie; died Aug.2,1863-age 62yrs. 11mos. 27days.

"   Isabella, wife William; died Feb.28,1852-age 48yrs. 8mos.

"   Isabella, dau.William & Isabella; died Aug.27,1848-
           age 5 years, 6 months.

Foster,   Polly, wife John; died May 4,1835-age 26 years, 1 month.

"   Margaret, wife John; died Feb.25,1841-age 29yrs. 11mos.

Frost,   John, son Joseph & Alzada; died Mar.1841-age 1yr. 8mo.

Southard, Almira, dau.Richard & Charity; died Mar.18,1853-age 7yrs.

Evans,   George H., son Isaac M.& Hannah; d.Oct.28,1841-age 1yr. 6da

Pickens,   Mary Pickens; died Mar.13,1864-age 80 years.

Lyons,   Susan, wife John; died Jan.19,1850-age 28 years.

"   Alexander, son John & Susan; died May 31,1841-age 2mo. 18da

Forster,   John Forster; died Apr.9,1837-age 73 years.

Finnin,   James Finnin; died Dec.5,1863-age 58 years.

Ahern,   Johnathan Ahren; died Aug.13,1839-age 30 years.

Mountain Ave.

Thompson,   Robert Thompson; died Jan.5,1850-age 50 years.

Sylvester, Mary, wife William; died Dec.18,1841-age 41 years.

"   William, son William & Mary; died May 20,1841-age 19yrs.

"   Mary J., dau.John F.& Sarah; died Oct.10,1844-age 3yrs.

Mekeel,   Almiry, dau.Sylvenus & Sarah; died Jan.6,1848-age 2yrs.

"   Harry Mekeel; died Aug.17,1872-age 61 years. 11 months.

"   Mary, wife Harry; died Aug.9,1869-age 55yrs. 8mos. 26da.

"   Sarah E., dau.Harry & Mary; died Mar.3,1848-age 4yr.10mo.

"   Mary J., dau.Harry & Mary; died Apr.3,1844-age 2yr. 1mo.

"   Joshua, son Harry & Mary; died Mar.27,1839-age 4 years.

"   Martha A.Mekeel; died Apr.1,1873-age 32yrs. 5mos. 9days.

"   Stephen H., son John & Hannah; died Dec.30,1841-age 28da.

"   Alexander, son Harry & Mary; died March 8,1853-
                         age 16 years, 1 month, 25 days.

"   Emily, dau.Harry & Mary; died Apr.7,1868-age 8yrs. 6mos.

Knowles,   John Wesley, son John & Charity; died Aug.7,1845-
                         age 1 year, 7 months, 15 days.

Knapp,   George, son Reuben & Susan; died Aug.-- 1848- -----

Bliss,   Infant dau.Joshua & Emeline; died May 25,1840-----

"   Harry E., son Joshua & Emeline; died Apr.23,1842-----

Bunnell,   Emelinda, dau.Miles & Bula; died Aug.12,1837-
                         age 8 years, 8 months, 10 days.

"   Juliett, dau.Miles & Bula; d.Apr.10,1838-age 5yr. 6mo.

Mekeel,   Harry Mekeel; died Aug.17,1872-age 61yrs. 11mos. 10days.

Jaycox,   Drake F.Jaycox; died Oct.25,1851-age 31 years, 7 months.

"   S.E.Jaycox; died Oct.14,1857-age 7yrs. 2mos.

Calix,   Ann M., dau.Alexander & Mary; died Aug.10,1845-age 10mos.

Smyth,   Nancy McCutcheon, wife William Smyth; died Jan.7,1862-
                         age 40 years, 6 months, 5 days.

Mountain Ave.

Merrick,	William E. Merrick; died Aug. 14, 1846-age 28yrs. 11mo. 17da.
"	George, son William & Sarah; June 3, 1839----
"	Mary E., dau. William & Sarah; died May 12, 1841-age 10mos.
"	Margaret, dau. William & Sarah; May 12, 1840-----
"	Maria, dau. William & Sarah; May 12, 1840-----
G----ston,	William, son Dean L. & Caroline A.; d. Mar. 25, 1853-age 10mo.
Ward,	Rosana Ward; died Feb. 10, 1870-age 70 years.
Warren,	Sylvanus Warren; Nov. 15, 1799-Feb. 19, 1859.
"	Phebe, wife Sylvanus; Aug. 13, 1804-Dec. 15, 1870.
"	Sarah, dau. Sylvanus & Phebe; d. Oct. 16, 1841-age 7yrs. 6mos.
"	Alexander, son Sylvanus & Phebe; died Feb. 14, 1841-age 1yr.
"	Cornelius, son Sylvanus & Phebe; died May 7, 1837- age 1 year, 2 months, 1 day.
"	Sarah E., dau. Sylvanus & Phebe; d. Jan. 3, 1829-age 1yr. 17d.
"	William J. son Sylvanus & Phebe; died June 25, 1828- age 3 years, 6 months, 22 days.
"	Alexander, son Sylvanus & Phebe; died Nov. 9, 1830-age 4 years, 6 months, 4 days.
"	Martha J., dau. Cornelius & Hannah; died May 10, 1834- age 18 years, 2 months, 4 days.
"	Cornelius Warren; died July 28, 1849-age 59yrs. 4mos. 13da.
"	Hannah Haight, wife Cornelius Warren;] Nov. 20, 1793-Nov. 7, 1886.
Kipp,	Susan F. Kipp; Jan. 16, 1856----
"	Mary J., dau. Samuel & Susan; died Nov. 19, 1827-age 2 years.
"	William M., son Samuel & Susan; Aug. 28, 1832-----
"	Samuel Warren, son Samuel M. & Susan; died Feb. 12, 1842- age 11 years, 5 months, 3 days.
Wright,	Charlotte, dau. Abram & Mary; died Apr. 8, 1842-age 1yr. 11mo.
Moore,	Nancy Moore; died Aug. 14, 1840-age 35 years, 4 months.

Mountain Ave.

Lloyd, Charles E., son John D. & Mary; died Sept.2,1847-age 13mos.

Sarvise, Elizabeth, dau. Robert & Catherine; died Jan.1,1829-
                                      age 2 years, 5 months, 7 days.

Sheehan, Roger, son John & Ellen; died Feb.12,1824-age 1 month.

"   John, son John & Ellen; died Oct.28,1826-age 1yr. 7mo. 7da.

Odell, John Odell; died July 5,1858-age 74 years.

"   Mary Odell; died Oct.14,1847-age 50 years.

"   Cas, son John & Mary; died March 5,1837-age 23 years.

    Many stones down. Some markers illegible.

Some old markers
in the Sears burying ground
Doansburg, Putnam Co.
New York

Doansburg

Bangs,   John Bangs; died Mar.30,1784-age 65 years.
"   Hannah, wife John; died Oct.29,1758-age 33 years.
"   Sarah Bangs; died Mar.1,1787-age 64 years.

Barnum, Capt.Joshua Barnum; died Oct.23,1822-age 85 years.
"   Adah, wife Capt.Joshua; died Apr.17,1810-age 73 years.
"   Johnathan Barnum; died Oct.7,1843-age 83 years.
"   Judge Stephen Barnum; died July 12,1825-age 64 years.
"   Major Joshua Barnum; died June 4,1818-age 53 years.
"   Thankful, wife Major Joshua; died Nov.30,1841-age 73yrs.
"   Dr.Stephen C.Barnum; died Aug.11,1849-age 60 years.
"   Clarissa, wife Dr.Stephen; died May 14,1834-age 40yrs.
"   Hannah, wife Dr.Stephen; died Apr.14,1861-age 66 years.
"   Capt.Azor Barnum; died Sept.9,1807-age 61 years.
"   Azor Barnum,Jr.; died Apr.28,1846-age 71 years.
"   Sally, wife Azor,jr.; died Oct.13,1807-age -7 years.

Burgess, Ezekiel Burgess; died Feb.16,1784-age 79 years.
"   Sarah, wife Ezekiel; died Dec.18,1774-
"   Naomi, dau.Capt.Jeremiah; died Mar.1,1784-age 22 years.

Chapman, Thomas Chapman; died June 6,1827-age 68 years.
"   Peter Chapman; died Oct.8,1776-age 33 years.

Crane,   Zebulon Crane; died Aug.17,1848-age 60 years.
"   Weltha, wife Zebulon; died Sept.6,1860-age 71 years.
"   Zebulon Crane; died Dec.31,1814- age 68 years.

Crosby, Joshua Crosby;
"   Lydia, wife Joshua; died Sept.10,1781-age 67 years.
"   Hannah, dau.Joshua & Lydia; died March 1757-age 13 years
"   Mercy, wife Theodorus; died Aug.20,1811-age 70 years.

Doansburg

Crosby, David Crosby; died Oct. 20, 1793 – age 85 years.
" Reliance, wife David; died Feb. 25, 1788 – age 75 years.
" Desire Crosby-Penney;
" Moses Crosby; died July 2, 1821 – age 66 years.
" Abner Crosby; died May 5, 1813 – age 67 years.
" Ruth, wife Abner; died Oct. 1, 1816 – age 67 years.
" David Crosby; died Nov. 16, 1816 – age 79 years.
" Bethia, wife David; died July 2, 1776 – age 41 years.
" Peter Crosby; died Nov. 9, 1841 – age 68 years.
" Ruth, wife Peter; died July 31, 1830 – age 67 years.
" Charles C. Crosby; died Nov. 15, 1848 – age 51 years.
" Jane, wife Charles C.; died Dec. 9, 1857 – age 64 years.
" Eli Crosby; died Nov. 22, 1827 – age 78 years.

Doane, Ruth Doane; died Sept. 30, 1801 – age 69 years.
" Elnathan Doane; died Aug. 13, 1806 – age 59 years.
" Phebe, wife Elnathan; died June 10, 1788 – age 32 years.
" Elnathan Doane; died Nov. 11, 1845 – age 53 years.
" Edmond Doane; died July 6, 1825 – age 49 years.
" Demas Doane; died July 23, 1830 – age 44 years.
" Roxana, wife Demas; died June 7, 1838 – age 45 years.

Foster, Edmond Foster, Esq.; died May 5, 1845 – age 77 years.
" Sarah, wife Edmond; died Mar. 1, 1847 – age 77 years.
" James Foster; died Aug. 18, 1814 – age 81 years.
" Thankful, wife James; died July 27, 1772 – age 31 years.
" Bethsheba, wife James; died Sept. 12, 1820 – age 72 years.

Gage, Elihu Gage; died Aug. 14, 1802 – age 76 years.
" Grace Gage; died Feb. 28, 1814 – age 78 years.

Doansburg

Gage,	Thomas Gage;
"	Rebecca, wife Thomas; died Dec.5,1759-age 53 years.
Gray,	Hannah, wife Nathan; died 1789-age 78 years.
Hall,	Peter Hall; died July 2,1795-age 75 years.
"	Abigail Hall; age 86 years.
Hoyt,	Oliver, son Henry; died Apr.29,1792-age 2 years.
Jones,	Nehemiah Jones; died Dec.18,1805-age 71 years.
Kent,	Rev.Elisha Kent;
"	------ wife Rev.Elisha Kent;
Lawrence,	Samuel Lawrence; died Nov.10,1831-age 84 years.
"	Thankful, wife Samuel; died Aug.30,1811-age 52 years.
Paddock,	Thomas Paddock; died June 11,1799-age 77 years.
"	Mary, wife Thomas; died July 8,1778-age 55 years.
"	Peter Paddock; died Apr.10,1760-age 63 years.
"	Sarah, wife Peter; died Oct.22,1776-age 80 years.
"	Stephen Paddock; died May 2,1832-age 82 years.
"	James Paddock; died Aug.9,1761-age 67 years.
Penney,	William Penney; died Feb.21,1786-age 70 years.
"	Archibald Penney; died Oct.1,1840-age 67 years.
"	Henrietta, wife Archibald; died Dec.15,1854-age 69 years
"	Robert Penney; died Apr.28,1836-age 60 years.
"	William Penney,Jr.; died Aug.8,1807-age 65 years.
"	Sarah, wife William,Jr.; died Mar.23,1814-age 74 years
"	Capt.John Penney; died Sept.27,1826-age 69 years.
"	Desire Crosby, wife Capt.John Penney; died June 5,1849-age 90 years.

Doansburg

Perry,	Simeon Perry; died Sept.8,1853-age 94 years.
"	Ebenezer Perry; died May 6,1862-age 63 years.
Raymond,	John Raymond; died Feb.15,1829-age 85 years.
"	Mary, wife John; died July 27,1787-age 40 years.
Reed,	Rev.Daniel Reed; died Feb.6,1854-age 83 years.
"	Sarah, wife Rev.Daniel; died Oct.22,1856-age 79 years.
Sears,	Thomas Sears; died Apr.26,1804-age 59 years.
"	Deborah, wife Thomas; died Sept.13,1828-age 79 years.
Waring,	John Waring; died Feb.17,1809-age 73 years.
"	John Waring,Jr.; died Apr.15,1812-age 43 years.
"	Mary Waring; died Dec.13,1839-age 89 years.
"	Stephen Waring; died Jan.22,1815-age 43 years.
"	Joanna Waring; died Apr.28,1779-age 48 years.
"	Susannah Waring; died Aug.10,1837-age 76 years.
Williams,	Joanna Williams; died Apr.5,1867-age 87 years.
"	Susan E.Williams; died Oct.25,1872-age 60 years.
Young,	Deacon Elkanah Young; died May 20,1809-age 59 years.
"	Huldah, wife Deacon Elkanah; died Feb.14,1830-age 73yrs

Baptist Ground

Farmers Mills, N.Y.

Farmers Mills-Bapt.

Bell,	Mary, wife Andrew; died Feb.8,1862-age 28yrs, 2mos. 5days
Drew,	Sarles Drew; Apr.30,1824-Dec.3,1909.
"	Bethia Patrick, wife Sarles Drew; Feb.13,1827-Oct.28,1853.
Dyckman,	Rev.Judson Dyckman; died Oct.11,1875-age 70 years, 3 months
"	Corinda, wife Rev.Judson; died Oct.19,1872- age 73 years, 2 months, 29 days.
"	Charles R., son Rev.J. & Corinda; died Dec.14,1856- age 25 years, 9 months, 3 days.
"	Louisa, dau.Rev.Judson & Corinda; died Mar.6,1852- age 14 years, 9 months, 16 days.
Griffin,	Euphemia L., wife Charles C.; died Apr.17,1895- age 30 years, 2 months, 11 days.
Hopkins,	Charles R. Hopkins; died June 19,1887-age 32 years, 4 mos.
"	Leonard K. Hopkins; died May 1887-age 59 years.
Horton,	Freeman Horton; died Mar.20,1860-age 22 years, 16 days.
Kelley,	Seth Kelley; died June 11,1848-age 80yrs. 3mos. 18days.
"	Esther, wife Seth; died Mar.14,1852-age 86yrs. 4mos. 26da
Knapp,	William X. Knapp; died May 15,1852-age 46yrs. 4mos. 7days.
"	-------- ------ died Oct.1,1865-age 61yrs. 3mos. 8days.
Ladue,	Emeline Wright, wife William H. Ladue; June 8,1853-April 13,1898.
Lee,	Joseph Lee; died May 3,1846-age 72 years, 6 months, 3 days
"	Abigail, wife Joseph; died Dec.10,1855-age 80yrs. 5mos.
"	Obediah C. Lee; Feb.24,1821-June 23,1876.
"	Hester R., wife Obediah C.; died Oct.14,1870-age 42yrs.11mo
"	Sarah, dau.Obediah & Hester; died July 2,1863- age 1 year, 6 months, 10 days.
"	Joseph Lee; died Dec.16,1883-age 46 years, 7 months, 19da
"	Dena A. Lee; died Apr.23,1907-age 62yrs. 4mos. 28days.

Farmers Mills-Bapt.

Lee,   Thomas H. Lee; Aug.31,1857-Apr.2,1886.

"   Joseph W. Lee; died May 25,1864-age 45yrs. 9mos. 8days.

"   Rachel, wife Joseph W.; died Apr.5,1863-age 38yrs. 6mos.

"   Sarah M., dau.J.W. & R: died June 20,1853-age 4yr. 4mo.

"   Thomas Lee; Sept.10,1802-Mar.30,1888.

"   Esther, wife Thomas; died Nov.4,1870-age 63yrs. 8mos.

"   Infant dau.Thomas & Esther; died Feb.1,1882-age 14 days.

"   Gracie Lee; died Dec.21,1878-age 1 month, 17 days.

"   John Lee; Oct.24,1825-Apr.2,1908.

"   Chloe, wife John; died Nov.21,1891-age 62 years.

"   Mary H., dau.John & Chloe; died May 30,1855-age 1yr. 11mo.

"   George C., son John & Chloe; died Apr.12,1888-age 30yrs.

"   Bell, dau.George & Emma; died Oct.27,1883-age 3yrs. 10mos.

"   Annie B., dau.George & Emma; died Dec.1,1878-age 3 months.

"   Absolom Lee; died Mar.21,1851-age 53yrs. 11mos. 4days.

"   Matilda, wife Absolom; died Apr.15,1869-age 72yrs. 1mon.

"   Anson, son Absolom & Matilda; died Apr.7,1858-
            age 19 years, 9 months, 19 days.

"   Milden, son Absolom & Matilda; died Mar.20,1837-age 1mon.

"   Eunice, dau.Absolom & Matilda; died Dec.19,1834- -----

"   Isaac C. Lee; died Feb.14,1852-age 26 years, 1 month, 28da

"   James J., son James A. & Clorinda; died Mar.31,1886-
            age 17 years, 2 months.

"   Sarah Amanda, dau.James A.& Clorinda; died Sept.10,1860-
            age 3 months, 17 days.

Lockwood,Sylvia, wife Stephen Lockwood, dau.Samuel & Sarah Terry;
            died Dec.17,1844-age 62yrs. 1mon.

Kent,   Thadeus S. Kent; Apr.8,1842-Dec.25,1907.

"   Emeline, wife Thadeus; June 3,1844-Nov.30,1899.

Farmers Mills-Bapt.

Kent,	Infant son Thadeus & Emeline; Nov.10,1869--------
"	Jane, dau.Thadeus & Emeline; died Aug.16,1878-age 3mos.
Mead,	Squire W. Mead; Mar.4,1840- -------
"	Phebe M. wife Squire; Dec.4,1839-Apr.26,1899.
"	Tunis Mead; died Jan.29,1886-age 74 years.
"	Elizabeth, wife Tunis; died May 2,1878-age 50 yrs. 1 mon.
Meade,	Gilbert Meade; Aug.1,1810-Dec.25,1880.
"	Sarah Wright, wife Gilbert Meade; March 10,1814-May 27,1879.
Patrick,	Charles Patrick; died April 15,1880- age 82 years, 10 months, 17 days.
"	Mary, wife Charles; died Mar.24,1849-age 47yrs. 1mon. 6da.
Robinson,	Rev.Nathaniel Robinson; died Aug.20,1869- age 81 years, 1 month, 14 days.
"	Adah Kelley, wife Rev.Nathaniel Robinson; died Oct.9,1883- age 93 years, 4 months, 28 days.
"	Olive, dau.Nathaniel & Adah; died Sept.10,1823- age 1 year, 8 months, 10 days.
"	Coleman Robinson; May 2,1816-Jan.30,1892.
"	Chloe Jane Henion, wife Coleman Robinson; July 26,1819-January 28,1890.
"	Peter Robinson; died May 21,1849-age 88yrs. 2mos. 13days
"	Phebe, wife Peter; died May 25,1834-age 70 years, 28 days
"	Charlotte, wife Peter; died Dec.10,1853-age 81 years.
"	Samuel Robinson; Feb.9,1799-Oct.14,1884.
"	Betsey Wixon, wife Samuel Robinson; Aug.14,1803-Mar.9,1865
"	Elisha Robinson; May 17,1797-Feb.22,1860.
"	Adah Ladue, wife Elisha Robinson; Feb.15,1800-Feb.21,1898
"	Ruth Ann Robinson; Jan.15,1832-June 13,1910.
"	Sarah Robinson; died Feb.25,1844-age 78yrs. 10mos. 22day

Farmers Mills-Bapt.

Robinson, Andrew Robinson; died Mar.31,1843-age 76 years.

"   Jemima, wife Andrew; died June 3,1803-age 35 years.

"   Betsey, wife Andrew; died May 24,1812-age 33 years.

Russell, Joseph P. Russell; died July 7,1881-age 62yrs. 9mos. 5day

"   Letty Wright, wife Joseph Russell;
                 July 29,1823-Apr.6,1896.

"   Silas Russell; July 12,1818-Apr.21,1896.

"   Rebecca, wife Silas; died Apr.2,1851-age 31yrs. 9mos.

"   Rachel Lee, wife Silas Russell; Oct.18,1827-Mar.25,1893.

"   Silas P. Russell; died Feb.14,1860-age 1yr. 2mo. 5da.

Smalley, Nathan C. Smalley; Oct.17,1809-May 17,1891.

"   Adelia Wright, wife Nathan Smalley;
                 Sept.29,1814-Feb.11,1890.

"   Emily J. dau.Nathan & Adelia; died Apr.12,1866-
                 age 16 years, 10 months, 14 days.

"   Zacharia Smalley; died Jan.14,1871-age 85 years.

"   Priscilla, wife Zacharia; died Jan.14,1876-age 92 years.

"   Isaac Smalley; died Jan.22,1885-age 84yrs. 3mos. 13days.

"   Elizabeth, wife Isaac; died June 15,1837-age 44 years.

"   Amy, wife Isaac; died Mar.10,1847-age 37 years.

"   Esther, wife Isaac; died Dec.8,1879-age 79 years, 2 months

"   Clarissa, dau.Isaac & Elizabeth; died Mar.27,1887-
                 age 63 years, 7 months, 17 days.

"   Erastus Smalley; died July 9,1883-age 51yrs. 8mos. 16days

"   Charles S., son Erastus & Kenturah; died Mar.24,1867-
                 age 10 months, 24 days.

"   Augustus B. Smalley; May 12,1848-Jan.1,1916.

"   Mary Manurvia, wife A.B.Smalley; died Sept.7,1877-
                 age 24 years, 10 months, 11 days.

"   Charles W., son Augustus & Mary; died July 11,1882-
                 age 7 years, 9 months, 7 days.

Farmers Mills-Bapt.

Smalley, Minnie, dau. Augustus & Mary; died Dec.24,1877-age 4 years
" Warren Smalley; died Oct.25,1888-age 70 years.
" Herman R. Smalley; Mar.28,1879-Mar.18,1904.
" Maud Smalley; Feb.17,1893-Mar.29,1904.
" Elizabeth Smalley; died June 3,1906-age 66yrs. 6mos. 28da
" Frank, son Robert D. & Marietta; died Dec.4,1883-
age 5 years, 11 months, 24 days.

Smith, Joseph L. Smith; Sept.21,1825-Feb.15,1895.
" Joanna Lee, wife Joseph Smith; died Jan.13,1890-age 62yrs.
" Emma J. dau. Joseph & Joanna; died Apr.13,1911-age 60 years
" Naomi, dau. Joseph & Joanna; died May 23,1848-age 23 mos.
" Ray Smith; died June 30,1828-age 42 years.
" Isaac, son Ray & Clorinda; died Aug.6,1853-age 25 years.
" Jacob, son Ray & Clorinda; died June 18,1834-age 2yrs.11mo.

Spencer, John H. Spencer; died May 9,1877-age 40yrs. 3mos. 2days.
" Ruth Ann Dyckman, wife John H. Spencer; died Feb.6,1917-
age 76 years, 2 months, 27 days.

Sprague, Eli Sprague; Dec.11,1835-Aug.16,1912.
" Phebe J., wife Eli; died July 14,1873-age 34yrs. 1mon. 9da
" Luman, son Eli & Phebe; -------
" Infant dau. Eli & Phebe; -------
" Martha Jane, dau. Eli & Phebe; died May 15,1858-age 12days
" Mary A., dau. Eli & Phebe; died Nov.13,1860-age 16 days.
" Luman Sprague; died June 17,1862-age 50yrs. 11mos. 18day
" Louisa, wife Luman; died Aug.23,1863-age 51yrs. 4mos. 12da
" Pamelia, wife John; died Mar.24,1804-age 37 years.
" Pamelia Sprague; died Dec.24,1848-age 22yrs. 6mos. 15days.
" Orry Sprague; died July 3,1848-age 50yrs. 10mos. 24days.

Farmers Mills-Bapt.

Sprague,   Elizabeth, wife Orry; died June 19,1841-age 45yrs. 10mos.

"   Persis, wife Samuel; died Jan.21,1864-age 40yrs. 2mos.

Tompkins,   Nelson Tompkins; died Dec.6,1887-age 74yrs. 6mos. 13days

"   Fanny, wife Nelson; died May 11,1885-age 64yrs. 2mos.

Travis,   Susan Jane, wife Norman L.; died July 2,1853-
            age 30 years, 9 months, 26 days.

Warren,   Sarah Patrick, wife Hiram Warren; died Dec.16,1852-
            age 23 years, 9 months, 13 days.

"   Mary P., dau.Hiram & Mary; died Nov.16,1852-age 5mos.

Wixon,   Robert N. Wixon; died Jan.27,1906-age 65 years.

"   Virgil Wixon; died Aug.16,1910-age 38 years.

"   Eben Wixon; died Jan.15,1889-age 73yrs. 9mos. 17days.

"   Laura Robinson, wife Eben Wixon; died Feb.7,1900-
            age 81 years, 6 months, 2 days.

"   Elijah Eugene, son Charles & Mariann; died Apr.28,1848-
            age 1 year, 1 month, 27 days.

Wixom,   Betsey, wife Elijah; died Sept.1,1845-age 69 years.

Wixson.   Wright Wixson; May 19,1823-Dec.20,1900.

"   Sarah Brownell, wife Wright Wixson;
            April 21,1832-April 17,1902.

"   Charles E., son Wright & Sarah; died June 1,1860-
            age 9 years, 9 months, 11 days.

"   Isaac Wixson; died Mar.26,1853-age 66 years, 15 days.

"   Lucinda, wife Isaac; died Feb.25,1857-age 65yrs. 6mos.

"   Harriet, dau.Isaac & Lucinda; died May 18,1856-
            age 37 years, 24 days.

"   Charles E., son Isaac & Lucinda; died June 7,1855-
            age 29 years, 9 months, 25 days.

"   Warren, son Isaac & Lucinda; died Feb.21,1852-
            age 24 years, 2 months, 4 days.

"   Isaac Wixson,Jr.; died Dec.13,1851-age 22yrs. 2mos. 25da.

Farmers Mills-Bapt.

Wixson, Harvey Wixson; died Dec.21,1875-age 64yrs. 7mos. 12days.

" Eliza Ann Wixson; died Nov.12,1887-age 79yrs. 2mos. 22days

" Isaac J., son John & Cornelia Ann; died Mar.25,1849-
age 4 months, 28 days.

Wright, Johnathan Wright; died Sept.24,1870-age 64yrs. 9mos. 7days.

" Mary R., wife Johnathan; died May 24,1891-
age 79 years, 7 months, 7 days.

" Isaac L. Wright; died Feb.18,1883-age 67yrs. 1mon. 18days

" Abigail Lee, wife Isaac Wright; July 23,1820--July 23,1876.

" Absalom I., son Isaac & Abigail; died Oct.22,1853-
age 8 years, 2 months, 23 days.

" David S. Wright; died May 23,1897-age 77 years.

" Matilda, wife David; died Sept.13,1894-age 70 years.

" James S. son David & Matilda; died Feb.22,1860-
age 3 years, 2 months, 26 days.

" Mary Jane Knapp, wife Robert Wright; died Oct.28,1854-
age 28 years, 9 months, 26 days.

3 Cemeteries at

Farmers Mills, Putnam Co. N.Y.

   Private yard.
   New grounds.
   Old grounds.

Each alphabetical order

Private yard, Farmers Mills

Barrett,	Sarles Barrett; died July 8,1870-age 27 years, 29 days.
"	Mary Ann, wife Sarles; died Sept.26,1867- age 23 years, 8 months, 24 days.
"	Abner, son Warren & Mary; died Sept.9,1868- age 4 years, 4 months, 20 days.
Bennett,	Joseph E. Bennett; Mar.12,1815-Jan.13,1892.
"	Mary Dingee, wife Joseph Bennett; May 10,1815-Sept.19,1892.
Dean,	Benjamin N. Dean; Aug.28,1824-May 7,1887.
"	Emily Smalley, wife Benjamin N. Dean; Oct.5,1829-Sept.9,1900.
"	Theron Dean; Nov.12,1852- --------
"	Lettie C. Purdy, wife Theron Dean; Mar.28,1859-July 22,1898.
Hopkins,	Julia Ann Hopkins, dau.Abigail Russell; died Apr.9,1835-age 17 years.
Morley,	John Morley; Apr.3,1799-Mar.25,1886.
"	Susan, wife John; died Apr.16,1871-age 75 years, 4 mons
Parker,	Isaac W. Parker; "Co.G. 6th.N.Y. H.A.- G.A.R." Feb.11,1842-Feb.4,1913.
"	Isabel Smalley, wife Isaac W. Parker; Nov.17,1857-----
Robinson,	Coleman D., son Adonijah & Sophia; died Aug.7,1847- age 2 years, 3 months, 26 days.
Russell,	Abigail Russell; died Mar.19,1863-age 68yrs. 10mos. 15da.
Schreder,	William C. Schreder; Mar.6,1812-Mar.26,1890.
"	Mary Shaw, wife William C. Schreder; Jan.7,1812-Sept.12,1858.
Smalley,	Isaac Smalley; died in 1812-age 33 years.
"	Elizabeth, wife Isaac; died in 1818-age 35 years.
"	Freeman Smalley; died Apr.17,1891-age 83 years.
"	Clarissa, wife Freeman; died Nov.1,1843-age 33yrs. 4mos

Private Yard

Smalley,	Betsey, wife Freeman; died Sept.30,1874- age 62 years, 10 months, 10 days.
"	Mary, wife Freeman; died Jan.16,1878- age 53 years, 9 months, 27 days.
"	Elizabeth, dau.Freeman & Clarissa; died Oct.5,1846- age 17 years, 2 months, 11 days.
"	John J. son Freeman & Clarissa; d.May 22,1851-age 16yr
"	Elizabeth G. dau.Freeman & Betsey; died Nov.25,1874- age 28 years, 8 months, 16 days.
"	Esther, dau.Freeman & Betsey; d.Mar.27,1871-age 23yrs.
"	Susan L., dau.Freeman & Betsey; died Feb.25,1874- age 22 years, 4 months, 25 days.
"	Chloe, dau.Freeman & Betsey; d.May 9,1860-age 5yr.10mo
"	Caleb H. Smalley; Dec.16,1833-Jan.15,1912.
"	Marie L. wife Caleb; May 10,1836-Nov.18,1905.
"	Levi C. Smalley; May 31,1832-Dec.12,1881.
"	Harriet Morley, wife Levi Smalley; Apr.12,1836-Nov.8,1915.
"	Levi C. Smalley,Jr.; died Oct.4,1874-age 10mos. 25day
Sturdevant,	David Sturdevant; died Jan.9,1839-age 59 years.
"	Anna, wife David; died Feb.19,1837-age 59yrs. 11mos.
Sturdivant,	John Sturdivant; Aug.17,1813-May 22,1877.
Turner,	Martha Wright, wife Richard S Turner; Sept.7,1863-Sept.16,1893.
Wright,	William M. Wright; died Apr.22,1870-age 39yrs. 4mos.
"	Clarissa J., wife William M.; died Aug.20,1870- age 27 years, 1 month, 10 days.
"	Freeman S., son William M. & Clarissa J.; died Sept.25,1887-age 22yrs. 4mos.

New grounds
Farmers Mills

New Grounds

Bailey, Mary E., dau. John O. & Frances S.; died July 31, 1853-
age 2 years, 2 months, 24 days.

Barrett, Minnie E., dau. John & Juliaett; died Feb. 3, 1895-
age 15 years, 3 months, 20 days.

" Harvie, son John & Juliaett; died Sept. 12, 1886-age 16 days.

" Thompson, son Dingiay & Nancy; died Nov. 16, 1837-
age 20 years, 6 months, 11 days.

" Dingiay Barrett; died Apr. 20, 1833-age 39 years, 1 month.

" Jacob Barrett; died May 15, 1881-age 74 years.

" Nancy Davis, wife Jacob Barrett; died July 22, 1877-72yrs.

" Mary Jane, wife Warren; died Dec. 12, 1883-age 44yrs. 9mos.

" George F. Barrett; 1855-1920.

" Louisa O. Sprague, wife George F. Barrett; 1860- ------

" George W. Barrett; Aug. 5, 1844-Mar. 24, 1903.

" Emma Jane Merritt, wife George W. Barrett; Mar. 18, 1871----

" Sarah A. wife James; July 27, 1849-June 8, 1898.

Bond, Jane Ann, wife George; died Dec. 27, 1858-age 55 years.

Brewer, Mary Ann, dau. James & Laura; died Sept. 12, 1855-age 7mos.

" Estella, dau. James & Laura A.; died Feb. 10, 1860-age 10mos.

" William B., son James & Laura; d. June 18, 1868-age 2mo. 24da

" Albert E., son John & Lucretia J.; died Dec. 10, 1864-
age 14 years, 8 months.

" Adrian, son John & Lucretia; died Jan. 29, 1841-age 3yrs. 2mo.

" Jeremiah D. Brewer; Jan. 4, 1877-July 13, 1905.

" Fernando J. Brewer; Mar. 11, 1842-Apr. 2, 1912.

" Margaret M., wife Fernando J.; Mar. 22, 1852-Oct. 26, 1911.

Clauson, Anson Clauson; died Sept. 18, 1832-age 28 years.

" Alexander C. Clauson; died Keokuk, Ia. Sep. 15, 1861-age 32yr.

" Matilda, wife Alexander; died May 8, 1863-age 30yrs. 7mos.

New grounds

Copp,	Infant son Joseph & Laura; June 1,1858--------
"	Belden, son Joseph & Laura; died Feb.14,1861-age 5yrs.
Cunningham,	Sarah Ann, wife Isaac H.; died Apr.14,1840-age 24yrs.
"	John, son Isaac & Sarah; died June 26,1838-age 14mos.
Dakin,	Nathaniel Dakin; died May 4,1874-age 71 years.
"	Louisa, dau.Benjamin & Betsey A.; died Nov.16,1847-age 1 year, 4 months, 15 days.
Daniels,	Margaret B. Daniels; 1830-1915.
"	William Daniels; Oct.28,1850-Apr.15,1903.
"	Margaret Ann, wife William; died June 23,1872-age 48 years, 1 month, 6 days.
Davis,	George Davis; died Apr.7,1843-age 22yrs. 10mos. 23days.
"	Sophia, wife Joseph; died Apr.16,1846-age 50 years.
Doughty,	Hannah Ann, wife George W.; died May 13,1850-age 24yrs.
"	Caroline, dau.George & Hannah; died June 14,1855-age 18 years, 3 months, 3 days.
"	Justinia, dau.George & Hannah; d.Feb.12,1860-age 7mos.
"	George M., son George W. & Hannah A.; died Jan.28,1848-age 1 year, 8 months, 24 days.
"	Julia Ann, wid.David;B. Hazelton,wife George Doughty; died Jan.23,1862-age 37 years.
Flagler,	Huldah, wife Shadrack R.; died Oct.31,1844-age 20 years, 7 months, 28 days.
Hanyan,	Margaret, wife Zackariah; died May 29,1842-age 31 years, 2 months, 10 days.
"	John, son Zackariah & Margaret; died Aug.4,1834-16mos.
"	John Wesley, son Zackariah & Margaret; died Aug.4,1833-age 4 years, 6 months, 19 days.
Hazelton,	Austin W. Hazelton; died Feb.25,1839-age 50yrs. 5mos.
"	Polly, wife Austin; died June 16,1874-age 83 years.
"	David B. Hazelton; died Oct.2,1854-age 36yrs. 1mon. 9da.

New yard

Kirk,	George Kirk; died Oct.20,1882-age 68yrs. 3mos. 7days.
"	Elizabeth, wife George; died Aug.31,1880- age 66 years, 8 months, 13 days.
"	Demmon Kirk; died April 2,1911-age 82 years.
"	Mahala Hults, wife Demmon Kirk; died Feb.5,1903- age 65 years, 1 month, 5 days.
"	William Kirk; died June 12,1850-age 44yrs. 9mos. 16days.
"	Mary, wife William; died Nov.8,1880-age 77yrs. 6mos. 19da
"	James Kirk; died Feb.10,1901-age 75 years.
"	Delilah Wixon, wife James Kirk; died Oct.19,1876-age 47yr
"	Carrie, dau.James & Delilah; died Sept.10,1866- age 2 years, 4 months, 6 days.
"	John, son John & Mary; died Feb.19,1847-age 18yrs. 11mos.
"	Phebe Jane, dau.Warren & Mary; died Jan.13,1858- age 1 year, 8 months, 21 days.
"	Walter A., son Warren & Mary; Oct.31,1860-Mar.17,1861.
"	Byron, son Warren & Mary; Apr.29,1862-Sept.7,1862.
"	Frank C., son Warren & Mary; Aug.13,1865-Dec.30,1865.
Lee,	Robert T. Lee; died Sept.19,1858-age 64yrs. 10mos. 22days
"	Dena, wife Robert; died July 8,1886-age 97 years.
"	Andrew J. Lee; Dec.5,1834-June 17,1917.
"	Phebe E. Wright, wife Andrew J. Lee; Oct.26,1837---------
"	William H. Lee; Dec.8,1863-Oct.4,1919.
"	Robert J. Lee; July 16,1847-July 27,1915.
Lockwood,	John Peter Lockwood; died Dec.4,1908-age 70 years.
"	Esther Mead, wife John P. Lockwood; ---------
Mead,	Robert Mead; died Jan.24,1857-age 44 years.
"	Abby N.Smith, wife Robert Mead; died Jan.12,1893-age 74yrs
"	Harvey Mead; died Nov.12,1877-age 66yrs. 9mos. 19days.

New yard

Mead, Alvin Mead; Sept.16,1819-Dec.26,1891.

" Deborah, wife Alvin; died Oct.25,1889-age 67yrs. 11mos. 3days

" Squire S. Mead; died Feb.23,1895-age 71 years.

" Phebe, wife Squire S.; died Feb.21,1895-age 63 years.

" Estella, dau.Squire & Phebe; died Jan.31,1880-age 8yrs. 9mos.

" Charles, son Squire & Mary, brother Nathaniel, Ira, Eli;
April 2,1826-December 12,1890.

" Nathaniel Mead; Mar.6,1808-Nov.20,1893.

" Mary J., wife Nathaniel; Jan.17,1818-Dec.31,1899.

" Laura Ett, wife Squire Mead, relict Anson Clauson;
died July 12,1878-age 70yrs. 4mos.

" Eli Mead; March 23,1829-May 3,1900.

" Laura P., wife Eli; June 16,1846-July 8,1916.

" William D. Mead; June 10,1852-Sept.22,1915.

" Carrie L. Smalley, wife William D. Mead;
Apr.18,1863-Oct.31,1909.

" Alice B. Mead; June 8,1884-Feb.24,1891.

" William S. Mead; 1869-1915.

" Hattie L. Smalley, wife William S. Mead;--------

" Squire Mead; died April 2,1860-age 81 years, 21 days.

" Polly, wife Squire; died Oct.30,1837-age 51yrs. 7mos. 7days.

" Anson, son Ira & Julia; died Dec.30,1852-age 3yrs. 10mos. 12da

" Squire, son Ira & Julia; died Jan.4,1853-age 5 months, 14 days

" Burton, son Thomas L.& Williametta H.; died Sept.22,1886-
age 8 months, 21 days.

" Amos Mead; died Dec.26,1854-age 36 years.

" William, son Amos & Mary; died Sept.21,1847-age 1yr. 8mo. 21da

" Emily, dau.Gilbert & Sarah; died Nov.28,1847-age 4yrs. 9mos.

" William Mead; died Dec.17,1840-age 66 years, 4 months, 3 days

New yard

Mead,	Sarah, wife William; died Sept.12,1849-age 74yrs. 5mos.
Merritt,	Amos Merritt; Jan.27,1821-Nov.14,1903.
"	Emerett Patrick, wife Amos Merritt; Aug.5,1828-Apr.1,1891.
"	Abner A., son Amos & Emerett; June 2,1862-Nov.1,1865.
"	Emory A, son Amos & Emerett; Sept.26,1873-Mar.12,1880.
"	Jane Dakin, wife John Merritt; Aug.4,1883- age 49 years, 10 months, 25 days.
Miller,	Isaac B. Miller; May 6,1829-Oct.6,1894.
"	Aletta Lee, wife Isaac B. Miller; Mar.10,1832-Mar.31,1919.
Nickerson,	Daniel C. Nickerson; died Nov.4,1918-age 73yrs. 11mos.
"	Henrietta, wife Daniel; died Mar.8,1905-age 64yrs. 5mos.
"	George Nickerson; Apr.20,1869-Feb.20,1914.
"	Walter C., son George & Addie; died Aug.3,1899-age 6yrs.
Ogden,	Charles Ogden; died Dec.23,1844-age 19 years.
Patrick,	Jehial Patrick; died Oct.15,1861-age 76 years.
"	Lucinda, wife Jrhial; died Aug.1847-age 60 years.
"	Jemima, dau.Jehial & Lucinda; died Nov.4,1856-age 30yrs.
Phillips,	James F. Phillips; died Feb.25,1864-age 59yrs. 10mos.
"	Anna, wife James; died Feb.17,1880-age 72yrs. 8mos. 10da.
"	Seymour B. Phillips; died at Harpers,Ferry,Va.May 29,1863 age 20 years, 8 months.
"	John Phillips; died Oct.13,1820, or 26-age 38yrs. 6mos.
"	Joseph Phillips; died Apr.10,1812-age 50 years, 23 days.
Pierce,	Pauline Worden Pierce; Oct.5,1815-Mar.10,1889.
Resseque,	Sarah, wife Stephen; died Sept.6,1834-age 52 years.
Ressequie,	William D. Ressequie; son Peter & Julietta; Feb.28,1885-Apr.13,1913.
Robinson,	Martin E. Robinson; son Albert & Elizabeth; Sept.15,1897-Feb.22,1917.

Farmers Mills

Russell, Robert Russell; died Feb.3,1858-age 69yrs. 5mos. 18days.

" Mary, wife Robert; died Aug.10,1848-age 49yrs. 9mos. 22da.

" John Russell; died Aug.11,1889-age 81yrs. 3mos. 21days.

" Adah Mead, wife John Russell; died Apr.30,1876-
age 66 years, 3 months, 7 days.

" Benjamin, son John & Adah; died Oct.10,1853-age 17yrs. 6mos

" Lewis W., son Joseph P. & Letty Ann; d.June 7,1854-age 5yrs

" James Russell; Nov.12,1799-Apr.3,1884.

" Dena, wife James; died Dec.28,1831-age 32yrs. 8mos. 12days.

" James E., son James E. & Deny; died July 11,1852-age 21yrs.

" Anna Mariah, dau.James & Dena; d.Nov.15,1856-age 31yr. 1mo.

" Daniel Russell; died June 16,1871-age 48yrs. 1mon. 20days.

" Mary Jane Phillips, wife Daniel Russell; died Mar.7,1884-
age 52 years, 9 months, 21 days.

" Amanda M. dau.Daniel & Mary; died Feb.7,1886-age 17yr. 5mo.

" Annie M. dau.Daniel & Mary; died Oct.1,1866-age 9mo. 11da.

" Margaret, wife Austin; died Dec.16,1847-age 40yrs. 2mos.

" Lebben, son Austin & Margaret; died Mar.9,1837-age 8mos.

" Ophelia, dau.Austin & Margaret; died Nov.21,1859-age 9yrs.

" George H., son Austin & Margaret; died Sept.13,1865-
age 25 years, 3 months, 26 days.

Russel, William Russel; died Feb.7,1846-age 67 years.

" Theodotha, wife William; died Aug.31,1832-age 52yrs. 8mos.

" Amy, wife William; died June 27,1844-age 44yrs. 5mos. 22da.

" Eliza, wife William; died July 18,1863-age 80 years.

Smalley, William Smalley; "Co.G. 6th.N.Y. H.A." died July 11,1911-
age 83 years, 2 months, 19 days.

" Lucinda, wife William; died Mar.7,1888-age 40yrs. 9mos. 16da

" Jane, wife William; died May 28,1887-age 50yrs. 1mon. 18days

Farmers Mills-New

Smalley,	Judson J., son William & Thankful; d.July 16,1858-1mo.
"	Wright Smalley; died July 2,1898-age 84 years.
"	Elizabeth, wife Wright; died Aug.27,1887- age 69years, 6 months, 12 days.
"	Joseph Smalley; died June 18,1887-age 48yrs. 6mos.
"	Howard E. son William & Hattie; Apr.18,1905-Apr.22,1905
"	Joseph Smalley; died Mar.30,1845-age 53 years.
"	Elizabeth, wife Joseph; died Feb.6,1885-age 88yrs. 1mon
"	Harriet, wife James J.; died Apr.6,1850-age 35yrs. 4mos
"	Ann E. dau.James & Harriet; died Sept.16,1849- age 2 years, 6 months, 18 days.
"	Samuel P. son James & Harriet; d.Apr.26,1844-age 6mos.
Terwilliger,	Sarah E., dau.James & Sarah; died Nov.19,1837-age 3yrs.
Thompson,	Robert Thompson; died Sept.17,1840-age 67 years.
"	Nancy Russueque, dau.Robert & Sarah; died Dec.28,1844- age 48 years, 6 months.
Tompkins,	William Emit, son Nelson & Margaret; died Mar.1,1860-age 1 year, 7 months
Townsend,	Alonzo Townsend; Sept.25,1813-Aug.9,1877.
"	Ada Townsend; died Aug.18,1872-age 80 years, 19 days.
"	Harvey Townsend; died Mar.28,1855-age 26yrs. 11mos.
"	Adeline, dau.Alonzo & Ada; died Sept.27,1861- age 2 years, 2 months, 4 days.
"	Samantha, dau.Alonzo & Ada; died Dec.7,1858- age 2 years, 9 months, 19 days.
"	Egbert, son Alonzo & Ada; died Mar.22,1859- age 11 years, 6 months, 22 days
"	Ludia Jane, dau.Alonzo & Ada; died Mar.15,1872- age 21 years, 6 months, 14 days.
Tompkins,	Walter H. Tompkins; Oct.5,1848-Dec.18,1906.

Farmers Mills-New

Whitney,	Russell Whitney; died Nov.11,1848-age 23yrs. 11mos. 17days
"	Sarah J., wife Jeremiah; died Nov.23,1846-age 77 years.
Williams,	Jane, wife Thomas; died July 9,1868-age 79 years.
"	Harrison Williams; died Aug.26,1884-age 70 years.
"	Sarah, wife Harrison; died July 10,1889-age 70 years.
Wixon,	David Wixon; died Apr.4,1863-age 22 years, 11 months.
"	Eliza, wife Joseph; died Oct.22,1857-age 53 years.
Wixson,	Jasinthe, wife Egbert; died Sept.20,1864-age 60yrs. 3mos.
"	William, son Egbert & Jasinthe; died Aug.1,1865- age 23 years, 7 months, 26 days.
Worden,	Smith Worden; died Feb.25,1821-age 34 years, 10 months.
"	Martha, wife Smith; died Mar.20,1881-age 91yrs. 4mos. 9da.
"	Smith Worden; Nov.20,1817-Aug.29,1906.
Wright,	Robert D. Wright; died Dec.11,1863-age 30yrs. 3mos. 7days
"	Elizabeth, wife Robert; died Nov.28,1859-age 31yrs. 11days

Burial Plot,

near Fredericksburg

Putnam County, N.Y.

North of Towners Corners.

Near Fredericksburg

Fisher,	Mary, dau. Nathaniel & Lydia; died June 11, 1828-age 10yr
"	Eliza, dau. Moses & Betsey; died Apr. 14, 1828-age 16yrs.
Griffiths,	Joshua Griffiths; died Aug. 22, 1818-age 56 years.
Lewis,	Sarah, wife Enoch; died Nov. 22, 1787-age 40 years.
Newberry,	Edeley Newberry; died May 12, 1818-age 75 years.
"	Ruth, wife Edeley; died Apr. 18, 1818-age 72 years.
Pell,	Mary, wife Philip; died Aug. 15, 1781-age 27 years.
"	Margaret C., dau. Philip & Gloriana; died Nov. 22, 1779-age 21 years.
Squires,	Esther, wife Johnathan; died Mar. 22, 1814-age 51 years.
Sturges,	Nathan Sturges; died May 18, 1784-age 38 years.
Warden,	Susannah Warden; died Oct. 27, 1820-age 4 years.
Watkins,	Polly M., dau. Joseph & Abigail; died Mar. 15, 1821-age 15 years.
Wilcox,	Jemima, wife Roswell; Aug. 21, 1773-

Horton Farm Plot

Putnam County, New York

7 miles N.E. of Peekskill

W.P.Horton.
1920

Horton Farm

Adams, Mary Steele, wife Mildan Adams; died Aug.30,1888 -
    age 90 years, 2 months.

Horton, Joshua Horton; (R.S.) died Nov.11,1811 -
    age 60 years, 1 month, 20 days.

"   Phoebe Swartout, wife Joshua Horton; died Sep.8,1807-
    age 47 years, 7 months, 23 days.

"   Sarah Colegrove, wife Joshua Horton; died Apr.5,1847-
    age 81 years, 9 months, 6 days.

"   Isaac Horton; died April 4,1861 -
    age 81 years, 3 months, 17 days.

"   Margaret Odell, wife Isaac Horton; died May 1,1831 -
    age 48 years, 4 months, 6 days.

"   John Horton; died May 15,1837 -
    age 54 years, 2 months, 13 days.

"   Anne Steele, wife John Horton; died June 26,1858 -
    age 66 years, 10 months, 6 days.

"   Cyrus Horton; died February 13,1832 -
    age 47 years, 8 months, 12 days.

"   Sarah Mead, wife Cyrus Horton; died May 27,1842 -
    age 51 years, 4 days.

"   James Horton; died Sept.26,1825 -
    age 34 years, 6 months, 22 days.

"   Ann Nelson, wife James Horton; died Sept.27,1839-
    age 44 years, 10 months, 24 days.

"   Jasper Horton; died May 22,1828 -age 42 years, 20 days.

"   Samuel Horton; Nov.1775 - Jan.1776.

"   Elias Horton; Jan.15,1792 - Aug.10,1795.

"   Cyrus Benjamin Horton; died April 25,1885 -
    age 68 years, 1 month, 8 days.

"   Phebe Horton; died May 15,1871 -
    age 65 years, 5 months, 14 days.

"   Catherine Steele Horton; died Feb.25,1825 -
    age 10 years, 10 months, 13 days.

Horton Farm

Horton,   Sarah Ann Horton; died January 27, 1811 -
             age 4 months, 23 days.

"   Ezra James Horton; died February 7, 1825 -
             age 2 months, 17 days.

"   William Nelson Horton; born & died Feb. 4, 1844.

"   Cyrus James Horton; died Mar. 16, 1844 - age 1 mon. 12 days.

"   James S. Horton; died December 4, 1825 -
             age 1 year, 2 months, 8 days.

"   Phebe Jane Horton; died January 3, 1822 -
             age 1 year, 1 month, 22 days.

Mead,   Anna Mead; died January 30, 1835 -
             age 70 years, 3 months, 18 days.

Nelson,   Jane Horton, wife Morris Warren Nelson;
             died January 12, 1844 -
             age 47 years, 2 months, 13 days.

Steele,   Catherine Steele; died December 4, 1848 -
             age 82 years, 7 months, 10 days.

Baptist Church

Hortentown, Putnam Co. N.Y.
1924

25 markers back of church &
48 "   up On the hill.

copied by W.P.Horton.

Hortontown church

Denny,	Marcus C. Denny; died July 10, 1881 -age 36 years.
Grosier,	Sophia Grosier; died 1852 - age 73 years.
Horton,	Henry Horton; "Corp. Co. L. 6th. N.Y. Vol. Artillery." died May 2, 1903 -age 60 years.
"	Henrietta Horton; Feb. 4, 1852 - Sept. 20, 1852.
"	Samuel Horton; May 6, 1849 - Nov. 21, 1852.
"	Orry D. Horton; July 27, 1853 - Oct. 27, 1864.
"	Alvah Horton; Dec. 8, 1816 - Feb. 11, 1896.
"	Sarah, wife Alvah; died June 16, 1866 - age 42 years, 1 month, 2 days.
"	Warren, son John G. & Melissa; Sept. 30, 1870 - Feb. 5, 1883.
Knapp,	Mary J. Denna, wife Jm. H. Knapp; died Feb. 21, 1883 - age 52 years, 7 months, 20 days.
Lawrence,	Alsada Lawrence; died Nov. 4, 1914 - age 87 years, 25 days.
Light,	Alonzo Light; "Co. L. 5th. N.Y. H.A." died Apr. 24, 1916 -age 73 years.
Miller,	Charles H. Miller; died Mar. 20, 1904 -age 76 years.
"	Julia A. Miller; died Sep. 14, 1902 -age 54yrs. 5mos.
Reynolds,	Robert E. Reynolds; "Co. E. 15th. Regt. N.Y. Engrs. died 1913. -----
"	Sarah Reynolds; 1849 - 1912.
"	Clara M. Reynolds; 1893 - 1912.
Russell,	Fanny Russell; died 1841 - age 41 years.
Shaw,	Jackson Shaw; died Oct. 26, 1891 -age 68yrs. 3mo. 29da.
Stevens,	Abram B. Stevens; Sept. 10, 1848 - Dec. 5, 1901.
"	Lottie S. Stevens; died November 19, 1897 - age 3 years, 2 months, 20 days.
"	Sadie E., dau. Abraham E. & Sarah E.; died Feb. 13, 1880- age 6 years, 3 months, 5 days.

Hortontown

Wixson, Elijah Wixson; died Aug. 5, 1867 -
          age 72 years, 2 months, 26 days

"   Elizabeth Knapp, wife Elijah Wixson;
          died July 28, 1878 - age 76 years

Wright, John Wright; died May 9, 1860 - age 58yrs. 9mos. 8days.

(These first 25 are back of church)

Barrett, George Lyman Barrett; died Sept. 14, 1848 -
          age 1 year, 6 months, 18 days.

"   Alitha Jane, dau. H. & S. A.; died Feb. 4, 1855 -
          age 5 years, 6 months, 7 days.

"   Eivielly, dau. H. & S. A.; d. July 21, 1845 - age 5mo. 22da.

Brett, William H. Brett; died Aug. 29, 1852 - age 21 years.

Brown, Samantha, wife Daniel E.; died Mar. 31, 1863 -
          age 22 years, 1 month, 16 days.

"   Georgiana, dau. Hiram & Keziah; died Aug. 3, 1864 -
          age 8 years, 3 months, 11 days.

Disbrow, Solomon Disbrow; 1812 - 1898.

    Anna M. Conklin, wife Solomon Disbrow; 1820 - 1891.

    William H., son Solomon & Anna; 1852 - 1860.

"   Olive E., dau. Solomon & Anna; 1857 - 1860.

Horton, Daniel Horton; died Dec. 31, 1852 - age 53yrs. 4mos. 27da.

    Jefferson Horton; died Apr. 26, 1888 - age 84 years.

"   Margaret Ann, wife Jefferson; died Aug. 31, 1860 -
          age 55 years, 8 months, 11 days.

"   Emily, dau. Benjamin R. & Margaret; died Dec. 22, 1855 -
          age 21 years, 5 months, 26 days.

"   Samuel Horton; died Feb. 23, 1864 -
          age 78 years, 5 months, 8 days.

"   Alithea, wife Samuel; died July 18, 1874 -
          age 87 years, 3 months.

"   John I. Horton; died Feb. 22, 1817 - age 50yr. 4mo. 17da.

Hortontown

Horton, John Horton; Jan. 31, 1791 - May 24, 1863.

" Susan, wife John; Sep. 23, 1800 - Apr. 5, 1865.

" Joseph S. Horton; died May 10, 1866 -
age 59 years, 8 months, 11 days.

" George, son Joseph & Elizabeth; died Dec. 30, 1840 -
age 4 years, 11 months.

" Gilbert A. Horton; died Apr. 20, 1865 -
age 37 years, 1 month, 3 days.

" Elijah Horton; died Sep. 27, 1854 - age 75yrs. 5mos.

" Hannah, wife Elijah; d. June 4, 1850 - age 72yrs. 6mos.

" Ann, sister Hannah; born 1762 - died Oct. 19, 1847.

" James Horton; died Mar. 1, 1884 - age 80 years.

" Elizabeth, wife James; died Oct. 14, 1874 -
age 62 years, 6 months, 8 days.

" William R., son Richard R. & Adelaide E.;
died Feb. 27, 1864 - age 3y. 11m. 6d.

" Evelena, dau. Walter & Jane E.; died Aug. 15, 1876 -
age 1 year, 4 months, 11 days.

Ladue, Daniel Ladue; died July 4, 1855 - age 56yrs. 2mos. 13da.

" Ithamar Ladue; died Apr. 22, 1849 - age 46yrs. 2mos. 23day

" William J. Ladue; May 6, 1865 - --------

" Charles E. Ladue; died July 10, 1854 -
age 24 years, 7 months, 7 days.

" Jane E., wife Cornelius S.; died Feb. 7, 1876 -
age 27 years, 5 months, 20 days.

Miller, Henry E. Miller; died Dec. 3, 1866 -
age 66 years, 9 months, 19 days.

" Charlotte, wife Henry E.; died Dec. 27, 1880 -
age 80 years, 3 months, 18 days.

" Charlton W., son Henry & Charlotte; died Feb. 19, 1838 -
age 5 years, 10 days.

Hortontown

Perry,   Edward Perry; died April 24, 1831 -
                    age 60 years, 4 months, 18 days.

          Mary, wife Edward; died Oct. 10, 1863 -
                    age 88 years, 5 months, 1 day.

Purdy,   Caleb Purdy; Aug. 26, 1782 - Mar. 15, 1861.

*   "   Hester, [MILLER] wife Caleb; Jan. 25, 1788 - Dec. 10, 1866.

    "   ~~John~~ [JOB] Purdy; died Aug. 13, 1819 - age 58yrs. 1mon. 25days

    "   Phebe Purdy; died Nov. 13, 1834 - age 70yrs. 4mos. 17days

Reed,   George Reed; died Nov. 8, 1852 - age 29yrs. 7mos. 19days.

    "   Frances I. Miller; wife George Reed, William J. Ladue,
                & Alvah Horton; Aug. 21, 1826 - May 7, 1880.

Ridgway, William H. Ridgway; died October 30, 1852 -
                    age 20 years, 8 months, 21 days.

Smith,   Surlina B., dau. Philemon & Hetty; died Aug. 29, 1838 -
                    age 1 year, 7 months, 4 days.

Surrine, Orinda, wife William H.; died Sept. 21, 1868 -
                    age 38 years, 9 months, 11 days.

          (These last 48 markers are on a plateau up)
          (back of the church.   )

* HESTER (MILLER) PURDY, WAS THE 10TH AND LAST CHILD OF JOHN (TRUXON) MILLER [JR.], REVOLUTIONARY PATRIOT, OF PINES BRIDGE, WESTCHESTER CO., 1731-1808. HE IS BURIED HERE BESIDE HIS WIFE HESTER. GRAVES ARE MARKED WITH ROUGH FIELD STONES. "MILLER HILL" WAS NAMED AFTER HIM.

Two burial plots

known as Odell & Pulling Plots

near Hortontown, Putnam Co. N.Y.

Odell Plot
On Shaw Hill, and one mile West of Hortontown, Putnam Co.

Ketcham, Joseph Ketcham; died Oct.12,1820-age 61 years.

" Anna Ketcham; died May 1,1812-age 24 years.

Travice, Neomi, relict John Travice; died Apr.25,1829-age 68 years.

Travis, John Travis; died Apr.18,1818-age 13 years, 8 months.

Odell, It is claimed there are quite a few Odells buried in this yard--but there were no markers.

A small burial plot
about 200 yards from the highway, at bottom of the hill
Hortontown, Putnam County, N.Y.

Knapp, Abraham Knapp; Mar.16,1816-Feb.8,1887.

" Esther, wife Abraham; died July 17,1845; age 45 years, 4 months, 5 days.

" Enos, son Abraham & Esther; died July 16,1860-age 17yrs.

Pilling, Garison, son Abraham & Hannah; died June 22,1826- age 2 or 12 years, 9 months.

" Betsey, dau.Abraham & Hannah; died June 8,1836- age 9 years, 4 months, 10 days.

" Nancy, dau.Abraham; & Hannah; died Mar.23,1831- age 1 year, 2 months, 20 days.

Two Burial Plots

Jefferson Valley &
Tompkins Corners

Putnam County, N.Y.

The Post Plot
At Tompkins Corners, Putnam County N.Y.

Nichols, William Nichols; died July 8, 1875 - age 88 years.

Post,   James Post; died Apr. 21, 1854 - age 56 years.

"   Joel Post; died Mar. 11, 1885 - age 65 years.

"   Amanda, dau. James & Rachel; died Nov. 9, 1835 - age 16 years

- - - - - -

The Kirkum Plot
On Wood street, Jefferson Val.
Putnam County, N. Y.

Anderson, Peter Anderson; died Dec. 8, 1797 - age 80 years.

"   Mary, wife Peter; died Mar. 1, 1812 - age 73 years.

Angevine, Sarah, wife Peter; died July 30, 1823 - age 42 years.

Carpenter, Phebe, wife Thomas; died Aug. 24, 1815 - age 40 years.

Kirkum,   Zebedee Kirkum; died Oct. 1788 - age 50 years.

"   Lydia, wife Zebedee; died Sept. 1793 - age 53 years.

Roe,   William Roe; died Oct. 16, 1795 - age 34yrs. 10mos. 11days.

"   Caleb L. Roe; son William & Mary; died Mar. 4, 1809 -
                    age 21 years, 11 months, 12 days.

Near Secords Corners
On New York City reservation land
of its water supply at
Kent, Putnam Co. N.Y.

Near Secords Corners.
On land of New York City Water Shed,
These bodies were removed from Carver Plot,
at Coles Mills, when Making the basin for
storage reservoir at Kent, Putnam County, N.Y.

Abbott,   Thankful Cole, wife Elijah T. Abbott;
                    died Apr.21,1837-age 73 years, 5 months

Cole,   Horace B. Cole; died Jan.17,1843-age 32 years.

"   Zilla, dau. Horace B. & Elizabeth; died Apr.3,1836-
                    age 4 years, 4 months.

Pierce,   Timothy Pierce; died April 30,1839-
                    age 63 years, 2 months, 22 days.

"   Mahitable, wife Daniel; died April 16,1837-
                    age 85 years, 4 months, 3 days.

Pinckney, Lewis Pinckney; died July 9,1831-age 70 years.

"   Orpha, wife Lewis; died June 29,1836-
                    age 67 years, 8 months, 16 days.

Yeamans,   Chloe, wife William; died Apr.11,1851-age 80 years.

"   Rachel, daut. William & Chloe; died Nov.20,1830-
                    age 20 years, 10 months, 3 days.

           Several common field stones.

Baptist Church

Kent Cliffs

Putnam County, New York

Bap. Kent

Adams,	Jemima J. Adams;	Apr. 28, 1855-May 23, 1913.
"	Enos B. Adams;	July 18, 1846-Apr. 24, 1917.
"	Susan C., wife Enos B.;	Mar. 30, 1846-May 2, 1900.
"	Kempton E. Adams;	Feb. 14, 1881-Sept. 13, 1914.
"	Milden Adams;	died Sept. 13, 1869-age 65 years.
"	Moses Adams;	died May 20, 1851-age 82 years, 9 months.
"	Phebe, wife Moses;	died Aug. 19, 1849-age 71yrs. 7mos.
"	Ada Adams-Rundle;	Rundall
"	Harriet Adams-Rundle;	"
"	Arthur A. Adams;	Nov. 13, 1875-Mar. 17, 1880.
"	Lena B. Adams;	Oct. 26, 1894-Dec. 15, 1894.
"	Andrew J. Adams;	Jan. 31, 1831-Oct. 14, 1911.
"	Julia A., wife Andrew J.;	Jan. 1, 1832-Mar. 7, 1910.
"	James M., son Andrew J. & Julia;	died Oct. 7, 1865- age 14 years, 7 months, 27 days
"	Chester, son Andrew & Sadie E.;	Feb. 27, 1907-Apr. 27, 1908
"	Marion, dau. Andrew & Sadie;	Nov. 8, 1904-Aug. 27, 1909.
Barrett,	Elijah Barrett;	died Oct. 28, 1890-age 58 years.
"	Hannah Barrett;	died Dec. 21, 1854-age 56 years, 3 months
"	Jackson, son William Jr. & Hannah;	died Aug. 11, 1853- age 18 years, 10 months, 14 days
"	Dennis Barrett;	died Mar. 11, 1890-age 71 years, 9 mos.
Brown,	Stephen Brown Jr.;	died Apr. 23, 1854-age 32 years.
"	Stephen Brown;	died Apr. 20, 1852-age 73 years.
"	Jane, wife Stephen;	died Apr. 2, 1856-age 70 years, 3 mos.
Caragan,	Elizabeth, wife John;	died Mar. 28, 1856-age 66 years.
Cargin,	Gilbert Cargin;	1831-1904.
"	Emeline, wife Gilbert.	1837-1913.
Barrett,	Marvin P. Barrett;	died Feb. 25, 1875-age 30yrs. 10mos.

Bap. Kent

Chadwick,	Cyrus H. Chadwick; died Dec. 11, 1860-age 18yrs. 4mos.
"	James Chadwick; died Nov. 17, 1864-age 25 years, 3 mos.
Conklin,	Asenath L., dau. Joseph G. & Martha; died Apr. 29, 1864-age 1 year, 4 months, 14 days.
"	Susan C., dau. Joseph & Martha; died May 27, 1865-age 4mo.
"	Henrietta, dau. Joseph & Martha; died June 7, 1877-age 8 years, 11 months, 22 days.
Chadwick,	Grace, dau. Morris & Iva; died Aug. 12, 1887-age 20mos.
Curry,	Rachel Curry-Townsend;
Ferris,	Darius Ferris; Aug. 24, 1812-Mar. 19, 1891.
"	Malinda Light, wife Darius Ferris; Apr. 22, 1820-Jan. 30, 1901.
"	Peter M. Ferris; Nov. 20, 1828-July 14, 1860-
"	Phebe, wife John; died Mar. 8, 1862-age 71 years, 9 months
"	Sarah Mariah, wife Orville C.; died June 24, 1847-age 35 years, 2 months.
Foshay,	Charles A., son George & Juliaett; died Mar. 24, 1856-age 9 months.
Hunt,	Ichabod Hunt; Apr. 12, 1831-Apr. 21, 1910.
Hyatt,	Phebe M., dau. Absolam & Sarah C.; died Mar. 7, 1860-age 8 years, 9 months, 28 days.
Light,	J. J. Light; "Co. I. 59th. N.Y. Inf."
"	Rev. Allen E. Light; "Pastor 1st. Baptist Church 1876-1895" died April 10, 1895-age 63 years.
"	Margaret Light-Tompkins;
"	Abigail, wife Elijah; died Aug. 9, 1861-age 59yrs. 4mos.
"	Moseman B. Light; May 1, 1815-Dec. 8, 1888.
"	Sally M., wife Moseman; Nov. 30, 1826-Mar. 19, 1903.
"	George F., son Moseman & Sally; died Nov. 12, 1860-age 3 years, 8 months, 10 days.
"	Malinda Light-Rundall;

Bap. Kent

Light,	Malinda Light-Ferris;
Knapp,	Sarah, wid. Jacob; died Jan.22,1878-age 73 years.
Mabie,	Albert, son Daniel K. & Ann E.; d.Nov.4,1847-age 2mos.
Mead,	John Mead; died Mar.4,1826-age 77 years.
"	John S. Mead; died Aug.22,1840-age 66 years, 6 months.
"	Hannah, wife John S.; died Sept.6,1830-age 50 years.
Nichols,	Cornelius B. Nicholas; Sept.25,1822-Jan.27,1895.
"	Chlorinda Nichols; Nov.7,1821-July 18,1891.
"	Hannah G., dau. Cornelius & Chlorinda; died Sept.22,1853 age 3 years, 2 months, 10 days.
"	Nathaniel Nichols; died Apr.8,1861-age 60 years, 1 mon.
"	Elizabeth, wife Nathaniel; died Oct.3,1855- age 53 years, 3 months, 22 days.
Rundall,	Gilbert P. Rundall; born 1802-died Feb.5,1888.
"	Ada Adams, wife Gilbert Rundall; born 1799-died Jan.1889
"	Clarissa E. Rundall; 1829-1911.
"	Charles Rundall; Jan.7,1826-Dec.29,1905.
"	Harriet Adams, wife Charles Rundall; March 22,1828-April 14,1865.
"	Malinda Light, wife Charles Rundall; July 4,1829-July 5,1903.
Rundell,	Mary M., wife Wesley H.; died March 16,1883- age 23 years, 1 month, 3 days.
Smalley,	Mary, wife Samuel; died Aug.10,1877-age 75 years.
"	William R. Smalley; "Co.G. 150th. N.Y.Inf."
"	Rucy Letty, wife Nathaniel; died Mar.16,1864- age 41 years, 2 months, 12 days.
"	Susan, wife James; Oct.11,1769-Feb.6,1845.
"	Mary Smalley-Townsend;
Russell,	Stephen, son Thomas; died Sept.4,1827-age 61yrs. 4mos.

Bap. Kent

Smawley,   Isaiah Smawley; died July 7,1856-age 100 years, 3 mos.

"   Hannah, wife Isaiah; died Dec.15,1848-
         age 87 years.

Tompkins, Ernest H., son George H.& Margaret E.;
         Sept.2,1890-Apr.6,1902.

"   Clayton E., son George H.& Margaret E.;
         Jan.7,1898-Dec.13,1899.

"   Howard Tompkins; Nov.2,1817-Mar.2,1890.

"   Margaret Light, wife Howard Tompkins;
         born 1834-died March 10,1874.

Townsend, Stephen Townsend; died Apr.26,1893-age 82yrs. 2mos.

"   Mary Smalley, wife Stephen Townsend; died Dec.30,1878-
         age 68 years, 4 months, 17 days.

"   Coleman S.Townsend;   Dec.7,1851-Feb.23,1915.

"   Rachel Curry, wife Coleman Townsend;
         Apr.9,1835-Apr.24,1915.

"   Coleman Townsend;   Jan.24,1827-Jan.28,1895.

"   Joshua Townsend; died Nov.9,1858-age 70 years, 11 months

Williams, Solomon Williams; died Jan.1,1873-age 76yrs. 11mos. 23da

"   Rachel, wife Solomon; died Apr.11,1872-age 79 years.

"   Major Williams;   June 15,1830-Dec.10,1896.

"   Mary E., wife Major; died Mar.25,1860-age 17yrs. 7mos.

Wilson,   John H.Wilson; "Private Co.F. 133rd.N.Y.Vol.Inf."
         died Oct.8,1904-age 67 years.

Wixon,   Ada M., wife Bently; died Nov.7,1895-age 64 years.

Bailey Plot
near Kent Cliffs,
Putnam Co. N.Y.

Bailey Plot

Bailey,	Joseph H. Bailey; "Surgeon U.S. Army." Oct.20,1803-Apr.1,1883.
"	Mary A., wife Joseph H.; Mar.8,1812-Oct.26,1880.
"	Joseph H., son Joseph & Mary; Sep.15,1831-Aug.21,1834.
"	Thomas H. Bailey; May 15,1849-March 16,1900.
"	John Oppie Bailey; died June 16,1905-age 91 years.
"	Frances S. Worden, wife John O. Bailey; Sept.30,1820-Aug.1,1882.
"	Mary Read, dau. Rev. M.A. & Agnes B.; Dec.19,1883-Sept.22,1884.
"	Helen Sinclair, dau. Rev. M.A. & Agnes B.; died Mar.6,1877-age 1 year, 25 days
"	Matthew Sinclair Bailey; Dec.2,1864-July 2,1865.
"	Doct. Rowland Bailey; died July 9,1835-age 72 years.
"	Abigail Bailey; died June 10,1851-age 72 years.
Dusenbury,	Charles Dusenbury; died Sept.13,1877-age 74 years.
Hunt,	Nancy A. Hunt; died Dec.1,1872-age 87 years.
Knox,	Lewis A., son Lewis & Patia; died Apr.17,1832-age 7mos
Mabie,	Mary Marion, daut. Moses T. & Mary R.; died July 30,1849-age 10mos. 8days

Barrett Ground

2½ miles from Kent Cliffs

on the Mahopac Mines
highway

Putnam County, N.Y.

Barrett Ground

Barrett, John Barrett; died April 2, 1817-age 76 years.

" Marcus Barrett; died Apr. 21, 1825-age 76 years.

" Anna, wife Marcus; died May 25, 1811-age 65 years, 5 months

" Gideon Barrett; died Jan. 14, 1820-age 48 years.

" Hannah, wid Gideon, wife Benona Barrett;
died Nov. 3, 1861-age 84 years.

" Benona Barrett; died Dec. 19, 1865-age 70 years.

" Isaac C. Barrett; died Nov. 10, 1853-age 80 years.

" Rachel, wife Isaac C.; died July 24, 1858-age 86 years.

" Isaac Barrett; died Mar. 7, 1824-age 69 years.

" John Barrett; died Dec. 26, 1861-age 79 years, 1 month.

" Sarah Barrett; died May 22, 1890-age 102 years, 7 months.

" Allen Barrett; Jan. 20, 1811-Aug. 7, 1878.

" Isaac Barrett; "Co. D. 6th. N.Y. H.A."

" Vincent Barrett; died July 16, 1862-age 49yrs. 2mos. 26days

" Sarah A., wife Vincent; 1829-1909.

" Olive E., dau. Vincent & Sarah; 1857-1880.

" Dora K., dau. Vincent & Sarah; 1853-1916.

" Emeline, wife Stephen; died Sept. 27, 1887-age 56yrs. 7mos.

" Jessie L., dau. Stephen & Emeline; died Feb. 26, 1886-
age 24 years, 1 month, 3 days.

" Hattie C., dau. Stephen & Emeline; died Feb. 18, 1885-
age 18 years, 10 months, 29 days.

" Addie B., dau. Stephen & Emeline; died Oct. 18, 1887-a
age 21 years, 7 months, 1 day.

" Jane, wife John; died Apr. 19, 1868-age 46 years.

" Obed Barrett; died May 29, 1896-age 93 years, 10 months.

" Elizabeth A., wife Obed; died Oct. 22, 1872-age 71yrs. 3mos.

" Edward Barrett; died May 22, 1885-age 70 years.

Barrett ground

Barrett, Peter Barrett; Sept.15,1830-Apr.16,1900.

" Sarah Townsend, wife Peter Barrett; Sept.14,1848-July 15,1890.

" Gideon Barrett;

" Eunice, wife Gideon; died Nov.19,1861-age 70 years, 19da.

" Ebenezer, son John & Eunice; died Nov.20,1848-age 23yrs.

" Sena, dau.Laban & Delila; died Jan.21,1863- age 27 years, 9 months, 10 days.

" Ann Eliza, dau.Obed & Elizabeth; died Jan.28,1844-age 14da

" Gideon, son Alfred & Mary; died Mar.13,1853-age 14 mos.

" Alfred Barrett; died Oct.3,1855-age 41yrs. 1mon, 7days.

" John Barrett; died Apr.7,1861-age 77 years.

" Eunice, wife John; died Apr.21,1868-age 89 years.

" Sarah A., dau.Solomon & Lydia; died Feb.23,1860-age 12yrs

" Phebe E. dau.Solomon & Lydia; died Aug.8,1852-age 13mos.

" Peter H. son Solomon & Lydia; died Sept.7,1846-age 7mos.

" Ebenezer Barrett; died May 31,1864-age 80 years.

" Reuben Barrett; died Sept.4,1851-age 14 years, 1 month.

" Gideon Barrett; died Mar.28,1877-age 73 years.

" Vincent Barrett; died at Harpers Ferry,Va. Apr.6,1863- age 33 years, 10 months, 25 days.

" Allen Barrett; died Aug.7,1878-age 67 years, 7 months.

" Sarah D.Barrett; died Dec.1,1890-age 77yrs. 10mos. 21da.

" George D., son Allen & Sarah; died Apr.8,1843- age 1 year, 2 months, 27 days.

" George W., son John & Margaret; died Sept.27,1853- age 2 years, 2 months, 10 days.

" John Peter, son John & Margaret; died Jan.5,1850-age 5mos

" Laretta, dau.Albeon & Sarah; died Apr.5,1838-age 3yr. 5mo.

" Emma L.Barrett; died Dec.9,1840-age 13 months

Barrett

Barrett,	Amanda, dau. John & Sarah; d. Dec. 19, 1832 - age 2yrs. 9mos.
"	Annis Barrett-Mead;
"	Lucinda Barrett-McDonal;
"	Esther E. Brewer, wife Henry Barrett; Aug. 7, 1842 - Mar. 16, 1914.
Brewer	Fowler Brewer; died Sept. 5, 1886 - age 67yrs. 3mos. 27days.
"	Betsey A. Brewer; died Feb. 13, 1899 - age 74 years, 2 months
"	Daniel Brewer; died May 7, 1889 - age 72 years.
"	Martha, wife Daniel; died Mar. 2, 1861 - age 42 years.
"	Elizabeth, wife Daniel; died Apr. 20, 1870 - age 84yrs. 20da
"	Daniel Brewer; died Mar. 6, 1865 - age 75 years.
"	Susan Brewer; died April 22, 1864 - age 53 years.
"	Mima Jane Brewer-Pinckney;
"	Esther E. Brewer-Barrett;
Hitchcock,	Col. David Hitchcock; died Dec. 25, 1862 - age 67 years, 28 da
Hunt,	Daniel Hunt; died June 17, 1849 - age 84 years.
Lockwood,	Peter Lockwood; died July 28, 1863 - age 59 years, 22 days.
"	Hannah, wife Peter; died Feb. 8, 1868 - age 60yrs. 4mos.
"	Gideon, son Peter & Hannah; died Mar. 5, 1868 - age 22 years, 1 month, 11 days.
"	Eunice, dau. Peter & Hannah; died Feb. 24, 1868 - age 16 years, 10 months, 2 days.
"	Cordelia Lockwood; died May 4, 1870 - age 24 years.
"	Hannah Lockwood; died Sept. 4, 1892 - age 53 years, 5 months
"	Eunice, dau. Peter & Hannah; died Dec. 20, 1851 - age 17 years, 29 days.
McDonal,	Warren McDonal; Nov. 10, 1828 - Apr. 22, 1854 -
"	Lucinda Barrett, wife Warren McDonal; Aug. 3, 1827 - Feb. 23, 1890.
"	Annetta McDonal; July 21, 1851 - Mar. 2, 1855.

Barrett

McDonal,	Mary McDonal; Dec.14,1853-Apr.3,1903.
Mead,	Annis Barrett, wife Moses F.Mead; died Mar.20,1843- age 28 years, 9 months, 11 days.
Pinckney,	Ezra Pinckney; Sept.29,1852-Nov.6,1910.
"	Mima Jane Brewer, wife Ezra Pinckney; Apr.4,1856-Mar.9,1902.
Satterlee,	Cornelius Satterlee; died Mar.4,1879-age 20yrs. 6mos.
Sutton,	Delia, wife Reuben R.; died Oct.24,1857-age 24 years.
Townsend,	Sarah Townsend-Barrett;
"	John H.Townsend; died May 6,1881-age 48 years, 4 months.
"	Robert D., son John & Emeline; died July 18,1861-11mos.
"	Charles R., son John & Emeline; died February 22,1856- age 7 months.
Wildey,	Ida M., wife Jacob T.; died Nov.20,1888- age 31 years, 1 month, 26 days.
"	Hattie L., dau.Jacob T.& Ida M.; died June 5,1886-age 3 months.
"	Steven W., son Jacob T. & Ida M.; died Mar.8,1888-age 7 months, 3 days.

Many markers illegible.

Williams Plot

near Kent Cliffs

Putnam County, New York

Williams

Booth,   Samuel Booth; "Co.K. 2nd.Regt.N.Y.Cav.Vol."
                    Mar.3,1844-Dec.7,1876.

"   Davison, son William & Maggie;
                    June 22,1892-December 16,1892.

"   Alonzo D.Booth; Oct.25,1869-Feb.21,1880.

"   Cora J.Booth; July 20,1866-Feb.21,1869.

Everett,   Mary P.Everett-Hanion;

Hanion,   Louisa, dau.Elias & Betsey; died Jan.26,1851-
                    age 2 years, 6 months, 21 days.

"   Mary P.Everett, dau.Betsey & Elias; died Mar.5,1847-
                    age 7 years, 1 month, 17 days.

McDowell,   Hannah J.Williams, wife John H.McDowell;
                    died Sept.7,1864-age 45 years.

Williams,   Alonzo Williams; died Sept.23,1887-age 66yrs. 5mos.

"   Julia, wife Alonzo; died Oct.19,1886-age 64 years.

"   Dennis Williams; July 23,1821-Feb.12,1899.

"   Almira, wife Dennis; Dec.24,1826-Jan.17,1907.

"   Hannah J.Williams-McDowell;

Wixon,   Peleg Wixon; died Sept.14,1857-age 62 years.

Methodist Church
Ground at Lake Mahopac
Putnam Co. N.Y.

Index   Lake Mahopac

Agor,	10.	McDonnall,	5.
Albin,	3.	Martin,	4.
Alfort,	4.	Miller,	1, 8, 11.
Arnold,	2.	Morgan,	3.
Aubry,	3.	Moore,	3.
Austin,	3, 9.	More,	11.
Bailey,	2.	Morrow,	3.
Baldwin,	5, 7, 8.	Nichols,	2.
Barnum,	6.	Nickerson,	10.
Berry,	10.	O'Brien,	1.
Biven,	8.	Pinckney,	7.
Blattman,	3.	Powers,	6.
Blydenburgh,	3.	Price,	9.
Boyd,	10.	Richards,	8.
Cargan,	3.	Saxtan,	10.
Carr,	3.	Seabury,	4.
Clark,	3.	Seaman,	7.
Cole,	10, 11.	Selvage,	9.
Coleman,	3.	Shear,	3, 5.
Conklin,	3.	Sillwood,	3.
Craft,	2, 4.	Sloat,	2, 6.
Dean,	9.	Smith,	3, 4, 6, 8, 10.
Dibble,	6.	Sprague,	3.
Dingee,	1.	Strang,	5, 9.
Drawyer,	10.	Tilford,	2.
Erickson,	1.	Townsend,	2.
Ferguson,	2.	Travis,	2.
Ferris,	9.	Turrell,	6.
Findley,	3.	Ulmer,	6.
Foshay,	6.	Vail,	1, 6.
Frost,	1.	VanWagener,	2.
Ganong,	6, 8.	Vredenburgh,	3.
Ganun,	7.	Warren,	5.
Ganung,	7.	Webber,	4.
Hart,	5.	Westcott,	7.
Heroy,	11.	Williams,	7.
Hitchcock,	7.	Wixson,	4, 5.
Hyatt,	2, 3.	Wright,	1, 5, 7.
Islieb,	4.	Zickler,	4.
Lent,	2, 3, 4.		
Lockwood,	3.		

Lake Mahopac

Wright,	Robert Wright; died April 5, 1883- age 87 years, 4 months, 25 days.
"	Zillah, wife Robert; died Jan. 1, 1858- age 58 years, 2 months, 17 days.
"	William Wright; died Nov. 10, 1858- age 77 years, 10 months.
"	Margarey, wife William; died Jan. 19, 1844-age 62yrs.
"	Sarah J., dau. William & Margery; died June 8, 1855- age 31 years, 9 months, 5 days.
"	Delila, dau. William & Margery; died Nov. 22, 1844- age 17 years, 5 months, 20 days.
"	Elias Wright; son Daniel C. & Mary; died Sept. 7, 1853- age 34 years, 6 months, 14 days.
"	Margaret A. Frost, wid. Elias; died Mar. 29, 1901- age 73 years, 7 months, 11 days.
"	Abner S., son Elias & Margaret; died Nov. 13, 1905- age 55 years, 5 months, 5 days.
"	Ann, dau. Stephen & Dorinda; died Nov. 2, 1848- age 1 year, 6 months, 26 days.
"	George Wright; died Apr. 19, 1852-age 78 years.
"	Mary, wife George; died Feb. 16, 1830-age 57 years.
Vail,	John Vail; died Jan. 15, 1871-age 73 years, 6 months.
Erickson,	Erick J. Erickson; 1823-1891.
Miller,	Absalom Miller; June 10, 1819-Feb. 17, 1892.
O'Brien,	Daniel O'Brien; died July 20, 1850-age 36 years.
"	Leonard, son Daniel & Eliza Jane; died Apr. 1, 1846-age 5 weeks.
"	Ray, son Daniel & Eliza Jane; died June 5, 1849- age 2 years, 1 month, 15 days.
"	Martha R., dau. Daniel & Eliza J.; died July 9, 1852- age 3 years, 2 months.
Dingee,	Stephen, son Allen M. & Elizabeth; died Sept. 14, 1835- age 1 year, 6 months, 10 days.

Lake Mahopac

VanWagener, Rachel, wife Richard; died July 15, 1842-
age 31 years, 11 months, 2 days.

Travis, Mary, wife Hiram; died Apr.30,1852-
age 34 years, 10 months, 12 days.

Hyatt, Margaret A., wife Moseman B.;
died May 9,1860-age 25 years, 16 days.

Nickols, Sarah, wife Josiah; died Aug.2,1852-age 86 years.

Ferguson, Eleazer Ferguson; died Nov.24,1845-
age 48 years, 6 months, 20 days.

" Betsey Ferguson; died Jan.26,1882-
age 82 years, 5 months, 9 days.

" Rosanna, wife John; died May 17,1852-age 31 years.

Sloat, Elizabeth, dau.Bud F. & Mary; died Sept.3,1850-
age 19 years, 22 days.

Bailey, Hester Ann, dau.Harvey N. & Eunice A.;
died Mar.29,1858-age 11 months, 20day

Lent, David A. Lent; died Jan.15,1895-age 75 years.

" Ann Retta, wife David A.; died Sept.22,1881-age 65yrs

Craft, Dewitt Clinton, son Elijah B. & Joanna;
died Sept.8,1851-age 6 years, 9 months

Tilford, James A. Tilford; "Corp.Co.D. 59th.Regt. N.Y.Vol."
born July 15,1836-
died Georgetown,D.C. May 7,1862.

" Charles Tilford; "Sergt.Co.D. 59th.Regt; N.Y.Vol."
July 8,1836-July 18,1913.

Arnold, James Arnold; died Mar.31,1861-age 77 years.

" Mary, wife James; died Dec.28,1873-age 92 years.

Townsend, Job, son Stephen A. & Emily;
died Feb.23,1880-age 8 months.

" Alzora, dau.Stephen & Emily; died Apr.3,1888-
age 10 years, 7 months, 10 days.

" James Townsend; died Nov.26,1876-age 51 years.

" Mary A. Arnold, wife James Townsend;
died Apr.1909-age 82 years, 11 months.

Lake Mahopac

Blydenburgh,	Charles S., son J.S. & Harriet; died July 14, 1870-age 1 year.
Cargan,	Perry O.; "Co.D. 6th.N.Y. H.A." died Nov.14, 1896-age 74 years.
"	Hannah Matilda, dau. Noah & Juliaette; died Oct.21, 1859-age 13mos. 19days.
Morgan,	Emeline, wife Daniel; Apr.10, 1848-Dec.12, 1905.
Moore,	William Moore; died Dec.4, 1855-age 73yrs. 3mos.
Sprague,	Hester Smith, wife James Sprague; Mar.17, 1837-Feb.3, 1889.
Lockwood,	Infant son George & Delia; died Mar.28, 1870-19 days.
Blattman,	Harry J., son Frank J. & Betsey A.; died July 23, 1879-age 1men. 12days.
Coleman,	John G. Coleman; died July 13, 1888-age 34 years.
Albin,	George E. Albin; died May 16, 1889-age 19 years.
Findley,	Julia M., wife William; Sept.23, 1845-Jan.13, 1888.
Hyatt,	George Hyatt; died Dec.14, 1864-age 22yrs. 3mos.
Austin,	John W. Austin; Aug.21, 1837-Sept.26, 1880.
Shears,	Israel B. Shears; Aug.17, 1820-Mar.5, 1871.
Conklin,	Franklin H., son Ira J. & Sarah E.; died Feb.26, 1860-age 1 year, 9 months
Vredenburgh,	Ann Eliza, wife Daniel Vredenburgh, dau. James & Rhoda Lent; died July 26, 1865-age 31yrs. 10mos.
Sillwood,	Richard Sillwood; Dec.11, 1835-Dec.11, 1915.
"	Jennie Merrow, wife Richard Sillwood; Oct.24, 1842-Oct.23, 1912.
Carr,	Charles T. Carr; Jan.2, 1853-Jan.8, 1884.
"	Mary Carr; died Sept.1, 1897-age 67 years.
"	Jane Carr; died Apr.5, 1861-age 1 year, 2 months.
Clark,	Emerson Clark; --------
"	Nellie Carr, wife Emerson Clark; 1858-1909.

Lake Mahopac

Smith, Johnathan Smith; Mar.10,1835- -------

" Mary A., wife Johnathan; Nov.15,1834- -------

" George C., son Johnathan & Mary; died Mar.19,1872-
    age 9 years, 11 months, 10 days.

Wabber, Caroline, dau.Joseph & Elizabeth; died Nov.21,1869-
    age 3 years, 6 months, 3 days.

Zickler, Fintz Zickler; July 29,1802-Feb.21,1878.

" Elizabeth Islieb, wife Fintz Zickler;
    Nov.3,1804-Nov.22,1885.

Aubry, Ambrose Aubry; Dec.5,1804-Dec.11,1865.

Alfort, Augustus Alfort; died Oct.20,1862-age 57yrs. 9mos.

" Caroline, wife Augustus; died April 19,1879-
    age 59 years, 29 days.

Martin, Silas W. Martin; died Feb.15,1881-age 32 years.

Lent, William A. Lent; died Dec.9,1863-age 36yrs. 8mos.

" James Lent; Feb.26,1804-Mar.8,1890.

" Rhoda, wife James; died June 4,1861-age 59yrs. 11mos.

" Martha J., wife George; Oct.5,1829-Jan.22,1901.

" Charlie, son Isaac & Lavina; died Dec.19,1863-
    age 10 years, 5 months.

Wixson, Abram B.Wixson; Nov.18,1819-Jan.11,1887.

Craft, Maria Craft; died Jan.7,1847-age 47 years.

" Maria Ann, dau.Ira & Lucy; died Aug.11,1851-
    age 24 years. 9 months, 22 days.

" Ann Maria, dau.Ira & Lucy; died 1825-age 5 years.

" John Craft; died Feb.11,1879-age 71 years, 20 days.

" Hannah, wife John; died Sept.30,1868-age 63yrs. 10mos.

" Emily G., dau.John & Hannah; died Sept.27,1853-
    age 21 years, 1 month, 9 days.

Seabury, Charley, son George B. & Hester A.; d.Apr.24,1861-4days

Lake Mahopac

Hart,	William Hart; died Nov.22,1866-age 77 years.
"	Harlan, wife William; died June 5,1838- age 49 years, 4 months, 24 days.
"	Nancy, wife William; died Mar.9,1866-age 69 years.
Baldwin,	Henry S. Baldwin; Nov.11,1801- -----
"	Eliza, wife Henry; Feb.7,1808-Dec.23,1884.
"	Daniel, Baldwin; died Jan.24,1842-age 65 years, 2 days.
"	Hannah Strang, wife Daniel Baldwin; March 13,1779-March 13,1865.
"	Henry, son Henry S. & Eliza; died Mar.25,1838- age 3 years, 6 months.
Wixson,	John Wixson; died Sept.19,1870-age 75yrs. 6mos. 17da.
"	Betsey, wife John; died Jan.7,1880-age 80yrs. 5mos.
"	Ann Eliza, dau. John & Betsey; died Nov.14,1861- age 35 years.
"	John W., son John & Betsey; d.Apr.2,1840-age 6 months.
"	Caroline, dau. John & Betsey; d.Nov.18,1831-age 2mos.
McDonall,	John McDonall; died Oct.3,1865-age 21 years. 2 months.
"	----- " died Sept.29,1833-age 2yrs. 8mos. 21da.
Wright,	Zilpha, wife John; died Apr.30,1836-age 37yrs. 7days.
"	Theodore, son Gilbert & Eliza; d.Jan.12,1839-age 7mos.
"	Caleb Wright; died Aug.19,1853-age 81yrs. 1mon. 18da.
"	Mary Ann, wife Caleb; died Sept.20,1858- age 86 years, 4 months, 22 days.
Shear,	Martin Shear; died Nov.12,1863-age 82 years.
"	Letitia, wife Martin; died Apr.3,1854-age 63 years.
"	Elisha H., son Israel & Charlista; died Apr.5,1856-age 1 month, 20 days.
Warren,	Esther G. wife Clark; died Nov.5,1857-age 22yrs. 11mos.
"	Emma Jane, dau. Clark & Esther; died July 11,1859- age 3 years, 6 months, 29 days.

Lake Mahopac

Smith,   Abel Smith; died Oct.12,1829-age 61 years

"   Barsheba, wife Abel; died Feb.17,1850--------

"   Mary Smith; died May 31,1856-age 40yrs. 5mos. 12days.

"   Warren Smith; died Apr.1,1841-age 2 years.

"   Theresa E., dau. James & Emma; died Sept.23,1853-
          age 3 months, 8 days.

Foshay, G.H. Foshay; died May 29,1848-age 40yrs. 8mos. 11days.

"   James Foshay; died Aug.7,1881-age 83yrs. 3mos. 11days.

"   Zipporah, wife James Foshay & relict Robert Powers;
          died Aug.11,1887-age 95yrs. 6mos.

"   Euphemia A. Foshay; died July 14,1876-age 42yrs. 2mos.

Powers, Robert Powers; died Sept.20,1827-age 39yrs. 1mon. 21da.

"   R.A. Powers; died Aug.6,1872-age 49 years.

Ulmer, Julian Foshay Ulmer; "U.S. Navy"
          Nov.17,1895-July 11,1917.

Vail.   Samuel Vail; died Mar.23,1832-age 42yrs. 5mos. 11days.

"   Betsey, wife Samuel; died May 20,1844-
          age 52 years, 9 months, 20 days.

Sloat,   Lyman Sloat; died Jan.13,1861-age 34 years.

"   Isaac Sloat; died April 26,1861-age 62 years.

"   Philena, wife Isaac; died April 22,1859-age 66 years.

"   Elizabeth H. Sloat; --------

Ganong, Daniel Ganong; died Dec.17,1868-age 86yrs. 10mos. 29days

"   Adah, wife Daniel; died Dec.4,1875-age 87yrs. 11mos.

Barnum, Noble S. Barnum; died Nov.9,1881-age 55yrs. 11mos.

Turrell, Ephriam Turrell; Sept.22,1811-Feb.23,1867.

"   Easter, wife Ephriam; died Sept.5,1850-age 38 years.

Dibble, George E., son Elbert & Phebe; died Apr.27,1849-
          age 7 years, 1 month, 6 days

Lake Mahopac

Williams, Sarah, wife Samuel; died Mar.25,1850-age 35 years.

Hitchcock, Daniel Hitchcock; died May 22,1870-age 77yrs. 10mos.

"   Patience, wife Daniel; died Mar.23,1825-age 33 years.

"   Sarah Ann, wife Daniel; Dec.5,1823-Aug.12,1876.

"   James, son Daniel; died Feb.6,1841-age 2yrs. 4mos.

"   Hiram Hitchcock; "Co.G. 6th.N.Y. H.A." -------

Pinckney, Aaron Pinckney; died June 23,1825-age 39 years.

"   Nancy, wife Aaron; died April 5,1818-
                 age 55 years, 4 months, 10 days.

Wright,   John Wright; died May 10,1889-age 87yrs. 7mos.

"   Sarah A., wife John; died Sept.30,1880-age 70yrs. 6mos

"   Ebenezer, son John & Sarah; died April 12,1848-
                 age 20 years, 2 months, 23 days.

"   Edward Wright; May 15,1826-July 2,1911.

"   Phebe E. Austin, wife Edward Wright;
                 April 13,1825-December 13,1903.

"   Charles E., son Edward & Phebe; died Dec.9,1858-
                 age 4 months, 18 days.

"   Willie Clayton, son Edward & Phebe;
                 died Mar.10,1862-age 10 days.

Baldwin, Reuben D. Baldwin; died Dec.27,1882-age 76 years.

"   Eleazor H. Baldwin; died Aug.27,1868-age 84 years.

"   Hannah, wife Eleazor; died Jan.7,1874-age 85 years.

"   James, son Henry & Rachel; died March 7,1826-
                 age 44 years, 6 months.

Westcott, Ira Westcott; died Apr.4,1841-age 28yrs. 1mon. 18da.

Seaman,   Huldah, wife Stephen; died May 17,1868-age 66yrs. 5mos.

Ganun,   Julia A., wife Edwin C.; Dec.10,1840-May 16,1864.

Ganung,   Naomi, wife Gilbert; died May 12,1847-age 96 years.

Lake Mahopac

Biven, William G., son F.C. & Laura A.; died Nov.29,1873-
age 1 year, 5 months, 14 days.

" Felix C. Biven; Dec.1,1836-Nov.30,1915.

" Laura Augusta Baldwin, wife Felix C. Biven;
Apr.24,1850-Feb.28,1916.

" Augusta Hannah, dau.Reuben D. & Calista;
died Oct.17,1856-age 16yrs. 10mos.

Richards, Phebe Miller, wife John W. Richards; died June 24,1853-
age 29 years, 3 months, 1 day.

Miller, Hannah C., dau.Benjamin H. & Deberah; died Jan.9,1846-
(27yrs.) age 21 years, 4 months, 20 days.

" Henrietta, dau.Benjamin & Deborah; died Jan.12,1838-
age 23 years, 6 months, 18 days.

" Salome, dau.Benjamin & Deberah; died Mar.18,1856-
age 24 years, 4 months, 6 days.

Ganong, John Ganong; died Mar.10,1840-age 81 years, 9 months.

" Anna, wife John; died Sept.12,1827-age 70 years.

" Mary Elizabeth, dau.Abel W. & Eliza; d.May 16,1827-
age 1 year, 6 months, 23 days.

" John Arthur, son Abel & Eliza; died Sept.30,1827-
age 3 years, 11 months.

" Elizabeth, wife Reuben; died Oct.26,1841-age 80 years.

" Joseph Ganong; died July 5,1865-age 75 years.

" Chloe, wife Joseph; died Apr.30,1881-age 85 years.

Smith, Jonah Smith; died Oct.16,1827-age 44yrs. 1mon. 19days.

" Mary, wife Jonah; died Apr.27,1868-age 84yrs. 7mos.

" Elias Smith; Oct.24,1807-May 10,1890.

" Maria, wife Elias; died Oct.9,1860-age 56yrs. 9days.

" George W., son Jonah & Mary; died July 14,1850-age 28yrs

" Margaret, dau.Jonah & Mary; died Nov.2,1827-
age 9 years, 9 months, 6 days.

Lake Mahopac

Austin,	George W. Austin; Oct.8,1818-Sept.14,1889.
"	Elmira Dean, wife George Austin; Oct.2,1829-June 2,1914.
"	Henry P., son George & Elmira; died Aug.30,1864- age 6 years, 3 months, 20 days.
"	Infant George & Elmira; Aug.30,1856--------
"	" " " " " Aug.26,1859--------
"	" " " " " Aug.19,1861.--------
Dean,	Johnathan Dean; died Apr.15,1889-age 93yrs. 3mos.
"	Pamelia Price, wife Johnathan Dean; died Oct.14,1874- age 72 years, 11 months.
"	James H., son Johnathan & Pamelia; died May 27,1832-age 9 years.
"	Joseph Dean; died Nov.1833-age 84 years.
"	Anna Dean; died Feb.1844-age 87 years.
Ferris,	David A. Ferris; died Dec.8,1846-age 23yrs. 10mos.
"	Julia Ann, wife David; died Sept.4,1847-age 19yrs. 10mos
"	Elizabeth, wife Samuel; died May 18,1838-age 36 years.
"	Clarissa, dau.Samuel & Elizabeth; died June 6,1843- age 17 years, 10 months, 6 days.
"	Sarah A., dau.Samuel & Elizabeth; died April 29,1834-age 2 years.
"	Ezra H., son Samuel & Esther; died Jan.15,1842- age 2 years, 1 month, 15 days.
"	William C., son Samuel & Esther; died Mar.12,1854- age 1 year, 9 months.
"	Betsey, wife David; died July 1,1848-age 72 years.
Strang,	Robert Strang; died Mar.30,1893-age 78yrs. 3mos.
"	Susan Ferris, wife Robert Strang; died Feb.20,1884- age 63 years, 3 months, 20 days.
Selvage,	Catherine, wife Samuel B.; died Aug.13,1853- age 28 years, 12 days.

Lake Mahopac

Drawyer, Calista, dau. John & Rachel; died Dec. 8, 1844-
age 6 years, 7 months, 8 days.

" Adella, wife Hiram H.; died May 29, 1844-
age 31 years, 2 months, 20 days.

Agor, James W., son John & Anna; died Dec. 22, 1827-
age 2 years, 5 months, 17 days.

Berry, Samuel A. Berry; died Dec. 18, 1850-age 45 years.

Nickerson, James Leonard, son Nathaniel & Jemima;
died Dec. 20, 1829-age 1 year, 2 mos.

" James L. Nickerson; died Oct. 2, 1853-age 22yrs. 5mos.

Saxtan, Emily, wife Charles; died Aug. 27, 1858-age 23yrs. 5mos.

Boyd, Rufus M. Boyd; died July 10, 1853-age 43 years.

Smith, Able Smith; died Sept. 28, 1896-age 85yrs. 10mos. 13days.

" Belinda, wife Able; died July 28, 1873-age 58yrs. 11mos.

" Ann M., wife Able; died Aug. 6, 1917-age 96yrs. 7mos.

" James Smith; died Aug. 24, 1871-age 69yrs. 8mos. 12days.

" Nancy, wife James; died May 11, 1885-age 83 years.

" Kezia Smith; died Dec. 6, 1855-age 21yrs. 1mon. 7days.

" Julia Smith; died Nov. 19, 1829-age 2 years, 5 months.

" Kezia Smith; Mar. 3, 1807-Dec. 4, 1848.

" Sarah Ophelia, dau. Joseph & Betsey; died Feb. 18, 1847-
age 1 year, 11 months, 13 days.

" Hester, wid. Johnathan; died Dec. 1, 1861-age 78 years.

" Samuel Smith; died May 13, 1850-age 42 years, 7 months.

" Jemima, wife Samuel; died Nov. 12, 1894-age 86yrs. 5mos.

" Johnathan, son Samuel & Jemima; died Nov. 24, 1833-
age 2 years, 9 months, 19 days.

" Susan Jane, dau. Samuel & Jemima;
died Jan. 25, 1868-age 29 years.

Cole, ------- died July 24, 1882-age 63 years.

Lake Mahopac

Heroy,	Mortimer M. Heroy; died Mar.21,1873-age 55yrs. 8mos.
"	2 infants Mortimer & Susan; --------
Miller,	Samuel Miller; died Dec.1845-age 25 years.
"	Henrietta, dau.Samuel & Calista; died Sept.22,1845- age 1 year, 3 months.
Cole,	Calista, wife Alanson Cole; wid.Samuel Miller; died July 24,1882-age 63 years.
More,	Jannett, wife Clark; died Nov.4,1851-age 35yrs. 2mos.
"	Eugene Alonzo, son Clark & Jannett; died Mar.8,1842- age 8 months.
"	Samuel M., son Clark & Jannett; died April 16,1846- age 8 months, 18 days.

    Legrand T.; died Oct.2,1851-age 7yrs. 3mos. 22days.

    John; died June 21,1852-age 11 years, 2 months, 4 days.

    Phebe Ann; died Oct.7,1851-age 1 year, 18 days.

        (These 3 children are probably More)

These burial plots

known as Entrott & Hadden plots

are near Lake Oscawana

Putnam Co. N.Y.

Entrott Plot
near Christians Corners,
N-E. Lake Oscawana, Putnam Co. N.Y.

Entrott,   Henry Entrott; died May 15,1837-age 82 years, 9 months.

Austin,   George W., son Philip & Sarah; died July 27,1848-age 11da

Conklin,   Martin W., son Jesse & Mary; died Oct.6,1849-age 10mo.13d

"   Infant Jesse & Mary; died Mar.10,1846-age 21 days.

McDonald,   Jerome McDonald; died about 1865------

- - - - - - -

Hadden Plot
At Christians Corners -
East of Lake Oscawana,
Putnam Co. N.Y.

Curry,   Jackson Curry; died May 10,1919-age 85yrs. 4mos. 10days.

Hadden,   William Hadden; died Nov.24,1876-age 80 years, 10 months.

"   Mary Elizabeth, dau. William & Sarah; died Dec.7,1873-
             age 34 years, 8 months.

"   Albert, son William & Sarah; died Jan.4,1834-
             age 5 years, 6 months, 15 days.

"   Albert M. Hadden; died July 8,1872-age 36yrs. 5mos. 11days.

"   Sarah, dau. Albert & Amy; died Feb.1,1876-age 4yrs. 9mos.

"   Mary Elizabeth, dau. Albert & Amy; died Feb.9,1876-
             age 7 years, 7 months, 22 days.

"   Willie J., son Albert & Amy; died Oct.12,1863-
             age 6 years, 4 months.

Baptist Church ground
at Ludington,
Putnam County, N.Y.

Ludington, Bap.

Ballard,	Isaac Ballard; died Sept.5,1882-age 81 years.
"	Jane, wife Isaac; died June 9,1871-age 63 years.
Bennett,	Peter Bennett; died Nov.20,1867-age 65 years.
Bowen,	John A. Bowen; died Dec.18,1883-age 80 years.
Brownell,	Morgan W. Brownell; died Mar.4,1884-age 82 years.
Cornwell,	Prince Cornwell; died Dec.29,1855-age 105 years.
Dakins,	Zephania Dakins; died Aug.11,1878-age 78 years.
Disbrow,	Solomon Disbrow; died Aug.30,1851-age 70 years.
Kirk,	Calvin Kirk; died Apr.23,1880-age 75 years.
Lewis,	Henry Lewis; died June 1,1864-age 81 years.
"	Abigail, wife Henry; died Apr.12,1852-age 61 years.
Light,	Henry Light; died Apr.20,1852-----
Ludington,	Frederick Ludington; died July 23,1852-age 78 years.
"	Susan, wife Frederick; died Aug.29,1855-age 60 years.
Mead,	William Mead; died Sept.10,1870-age 67 years.
"	Lewis Mead; died Jan.15,1842-age 77 years.
"	Sarah, wife Lewis; died Aug.3,1845-age 81 years.
Merritt,	Anderson Merritt; died Feb.6,1887-age 85 years.
Smith,	Greeche Smith; died Mar.17,1866-age 90 years.
Sprague,	Joseph Sprague; died Mar.16,1879-age 89 years.
"	Fanny, wife Joseph; died Dec.25,1874-age 79 years.
White,	Joshua White; died Jan.24,1851-age 61 years.
"	Samuel White; died Apr.20,1859-age 75 years.

Private burial ground

West of Ludingtonville, Putnam Co.

New York

Private Ground
West of Ludingtonville

Disbrow, Anon Disbrow; died Feb.27,1865-age 61 years.

" Locky, wife Anon; died Mar.3,1877-age 72 years.

Ketcham, Thaddeus Ketcham; died Apr.24,1831-age 31 years.

" Ezekiel Ketcham; died Oct.26,1853-age 82 years.

" Mary, wife Ezekiel; died Aug.3,1849-age 67 years.

Merritt, Phebe, wife Stephen; Sept.22,1772-May 7,1842.

Baptist Church Yard

Mahopac Falls

Putnam County, N.Y.

Index A.B.C.D.E.F.G.H.

Abberley,	19.
Agor,	1, 3, 6,11,13,14,16,17,18,19.
Ames,	14.
Arnold,	18,20.
Austin,	6,14,17.
Ballard,	10.
Banker,	5.
Barker,	4.
Barrett,	1, 2, 3, 4, 8, 9,10,12,14,15,16,17,18,20,21.
Benjamin,	1, 2,20.
Beyea,	4.
Bishop,	1.
Boyd,	18.
Bray,	21.
Briggs,	6.
Brush,	17.
Buckley,	7.
Butterfield,	6.
Carhart,	7.
Carpenter,	4.
Carver,	9,15.
Cary,	15.
Cavanaugh,	6.
Clauson,	16.
Cole,	1, 9,11,12,14,15,17,21.
Colwell,	7.
Conklin,	7.
Crawford,	2,19.
Cronk,	8,10.
Curry,	1, 2,11,14,16,18,19.
Dean,	17.
DeForest,	19.
Denike,	19.
Depew,	5.
Dingee,	1.
Early,	6.
Frost,	17.
Gay,	9.
Griffin,	17.
Guy,	15.
Hadden,	4,14,15,17,19,20.
Hall,	8.
Hallock,	19.
Hamilton,	7.
Hart,	11.
Hawke,	1.
Hawkins,	10.
Hazen,	18.
Hazleton,	1,13.
Herrick,	8.
Heroy,	5,19.
Hill,	3, 5, 6, 7,16,17.
Hinds,	11.
Hitchcock,	6.
Horton,	7,11,17,18,21.

Hughes,	11.
Hulse,	15.
Hunt,	21.
Hunter,	13.
Hyatt,	10,11,14.

Index J.K.L.M.O.P.Q.R.S.T.V.W.Y.Z.

Jenkins, 6.
Jennings, 14.
Johns, 1.
Kemp, 8.
Kinsman, 21.
Kirkum, 4.
Lent, 2.
Lockwood, 13,16,18.
Lounsbury, 18.
Ludington, 9.
McBride, 20.
Maynard, 6.
Mead, 19,20.
Miller, 2.
Moore, 16,17.
Munger, 8.
Oakley, 20.
Odell, 9,18.
Pearce, 10.
Pierce, 17,19.
Pinckney, 2, 3, 4, 6, 7, 8, 9,18,20,21.
Post, 15,17,20.
Potter, 21.
Power, 3.
Pratt, 16.
Purcell, 5.
Quillin, 19.
Retan, 14.
Riedl, 18.
Sackrider, 7,13,15,19.
Sampson, 2.
Secor, 8.
Simpkins, 6.
Sloat, 1.
Smith, 5, 7, 9,11,16,20.
Sprague, 11.
Stokum, 6.
Sutton, 14.
Tompkins, 15,17,20.
Travis, 3, 7, 8, 9.
Vivian, 1.
Waite, 19.
Wardell, 7.
Warren, 7.
Williams, 2,14,17.
Wilson, 19.
Willson, 4.
Wixon, 20.
Wixsom, 9,10.
Wixson, 3,10.
Wright, 3,14.
Young, 14.
Zemnen, 4.

Bap. Mahopac Falls

Hazleton, David Hazleton; died Mar.24,1848-age 57 years. 2months.
" Amy, wife David; died Feb.6,1876-age 84 years.
" Joseph H., son David & Amy; died Feb.9,1854-
        age 22 years, 1 month, 25 days.
" Eliza M., dau. William B. & Mary A.; died Sept.1,1853-
        age 1 year, 3 months, 27 days.

Agor, Orren Agor; died May 12,1867-age 64yrs. 9mos. 23days.
" Adah, wife Orren; died Aug.13,1834-age 27 years, 8 month
" Ezra, son Orren & Adah; died May 29,1846-
        age 13 years, 7 months, 20 days.
" Sarah Ann Agor; died Oct.29,1857-age 46 years, 6 months

Sloat, Sara A. Sloat; died Oct.1,1868-age 37 years.
" Arvilla, wife William H.; died May 29,1868-age 68 years

Agor, William Agor; died Mar.16,1848-age 75 years, 18 days.
" Elizabeth Cole, wife William Agor;
        died Feb.15,1841-age 66 years.
" Charles Agor; died Oct.13,1858-age 62 years, 11 months.
" Elizabeth, wife Charles; died Sept.18,1850-
        age 54 years, 8 months, 3 days.
" Eliza, dau. Charles & Elizabeth; died June 28,1846-
        age 20 years, 1 month, 7 days.

Vivian, James Vivian; died May 30,1887-age 23 years, 21 days.

Hawke, John, son John & Louisa; died Aug.9,1882-age 19 days.
" Annita, dau. John & Louisa; died Oct.19,1886-age 2yr. 6mo.

Dingee, Julia, dau. Caroline; died Oct.21,1872-age 16yrs. 11mos.

Johns, John Johns; died Apr.20,1888-age 39 years, 2 months.

Bishop, Jacob Bishop; died Sept.11,1862-age 60 years, 9 months.

Benjamin, Daniel H. Benjamin; Oct.9,1851-Nov.3,1881.

Curry, James W. Curry; May 17,1807-July 10,1864.
" Sarah Barrett, wife James Curry; Jan.10,1813-Jan.19,1884

Bap. Mahopac Falls

Barrett,   Marcus Barrett; died May 5,1853-age 78 years, 6 days.

"   Mary, wife Marcus; died Dec.24,1864-age 82yrs. 8mos.

"   Seth Barrett; died June 3,1872-age 59yrs. 3mos. 14days

Curry,   Phebe J., wife James; died May 1,1864-age 17yrs. 10mos.

"   Moseman, son James & Phebe; died Sept.13,1864-age 8mos.

"   Jerome, son James H.& Sarah; died Mar.4,1855-
            age 3 years, 9 months, 8 days.

Benjamin, Mary J., wife William; died Feb.18,1865-age 20 years.

"   David Benjamin; June 13,1816-June 2,1892.

"   Rachel Barrett, wife David Benjamin;
            Nov.3,1810-Dec.15,1892.

Lent,   William M.Lent; died Feb.3,1865-age 30 years, 6 months.

"   Erastus, son William & Rachel; died June 5,1860-age 17mo.

Barrett,   Eveline, wife Henry; died May 14,1871-age 36yrs. 8mos.

"   Levi G., son Henry & Eveline; died July 16,1847-
            age 8 years, 11 months, 11 days.

Sampson,   Rev.David Sampson; died Aug.8,1859-age 60yrs. 2mos.

Pinckney,   Alvah Pinckney; Jan.13,1828-Feb.22,1907.

"   Eliza Crawford, wife Alvah Pinckney;
            May 28,1838-Jan.9,1902.

Williams,   Cornelius F.Williams; died Aug.27,1854-age 63 years.

"   Letta, wife Cornelius; died Apr.12,1857-age 75yrs. 3mos

Crawford,   Wayne C.Crawford; May 9,1830-Feb.12,1898.

"   Ward H.Crawford; died Jan.16,1894-age 67 years, 11 mos.

"   Warren W.Crawford; died Sept.12,1868-age 40yrs. 5mos.

"   Mary E. wife Cyrus A.; died May 28,1867-
            age 23 years, 9 months, 24 days.

Miller,   Mary E.Miller; died May 14,1877-age 50yrs. 9mos. 14da.

"   Elizabeth, wife Smith; died Apr.5,1881-age 81yrs. 10mos

Bap. M.P.

Power,	Mary, wife James B.; died May 21,1862-age 23yrs. 3mos.
Wixson,	James Wixson; died Feb.18,1849-age 76yrs. 8mos. 19days
"	Elizabeth, wife James; died July 31,1839-age 72 years.
Wright,	Daniel Wright; died Feb.23,1865-age 70 years.
"	Stone down.
"	Phebe, dau.Daniel & Chloe; Sept.30,1848------
"	Alfred H.Wright; died Mar.4,1882-age 60yrs. 3mos. 25days
Hill,	Sarah, wife Noah; died May 13,1846-age 76 years, 15 days
Barrett,	Ella Hill, wife Ferris Barrett; died Dec.2,1879-age 41yrs
Hill,	Anthony Hill; died Feb.22,1867-age 74 years.
"	Dorothy, wife Anthony; died July 2,1878-age 80 years.
"	William W.Hill; died July 24,1863-age 33 years.
Pinckney,	Stephen Pinckney; 1790-1873.
"	Sarah, wife Stephen; died Feb.9,1848-age 56yrs. 3mos.
"	Levi, son Stephen & Sarah; died Oct.28,1833-age 10yrs.
"	Antha J. dau.Stephen & Sarah; d.Nov.12,1832-age 10mos.
"	Perry Pinckney; died Nov.26,1879-age 60yrs. 2mos. 29days
"	Stone down;
"	Nathan, son Perry & Elener; died Sept.28,1850-age 2yrs.
"	Maria Agor, wife Stephen Pinckney; 1832-1874.
"	Judson Pinckney; 1856-1880.
"	Thomas Pinckney; died Aug.10,1837-age 59 years.
"	Mary Pinckney; ----
"	Amanda, wife Israel; died May 20,1838-age 33yrs. 3mos.
"	Ivy Pinckney; died Mar.12,1870-age 56 years, 19 days.
Travis,	Sally Travis; died Dec.20,1880-age 82yrs. 8mos. 11days.

Bap. Mahopac

Pinckney, William Pinckney; died Nov.26,1863-age 46yrs. 9mos.
" Eliza J., wife Henry; died Mar.16,1856-age 46yrs. 21da.
" William H. son Henry & Eliza; d.Mar.20,1841-age 4mos.

Beyea, John Beyea; died Sept.12,1848-age 85 years, 8 months.
" Sally, wife John; died Nov.24,1833-age 66yrs. 8mos.
" James Beyea; Feb.21,1796--Feb.6,1835.
" Amy Carpenter, wife James Beyea; Dec.22,1803-Mar.28,1881
" Phebe Beyea; Dec.28,1830--Sept.9,1909.
" Ebenezer Beyea; died Aug.30,1848-age 43 years, 11 months
" John Beyea; died Dec.19,1864-age 74 years, 5 months.
" Elizabeth Beyea; died Feb.10,1866-age 58 years, 4 months
" Peter Beyea; died Nov.17,1873-age 79 years, 8 months.
" Mary Beyea; died Mar.28,1879-age 78 years, 7 months.

Kirkum, Zopher Kirkum; died Oct.20,1846-age 63 years, 9 months.
" Susan, wife Zopher; died Apr.6,1842-age 63 years.

Zemnen, Charles Zemnen; May 24,1865--Aug.24,1888.

Hadden, Celesta, dau.Hatvey & Charlotte; died April 18,1862-
age 2 years, 4 months, 3 days.

Barker, Jane, wife Michael; died Feb.15,1841-age 27yrs. 6mos.

Barrett, Daisy Leora,dau.Eli & Louisa M.; died Dec.8,1881-
age 1 year, 3 months, 17 days.
" Bertie M., son Eli & Louisa; d.Dec.21,1881-age 16 months

Willson, Rebecca, wife Jeremiah; died Oct.9,1864-age 48 years.
" Stone down;
" Gilbert, son Jeremiah & Rebecca; d.Sep.14,1839-age 18mos
" Martin, son Jeremiah & Rebecca; d.Jan.25,1860-age 9 year
" Charles, son Jeremiah & Rebecca A.; died Jan.30,1860-
age 11 years, 6 months, 27 days.
" Jerome, son Jeremiah & Rebecca; d.Feb.2,1860-age 7yr. 8mo

Bap. M.F.

Smith, Nancy, wife Cornelius; died Nov.20,1870-age 50yrs. 1mon.

" John, son Cornelius & Nancy; d.Feb.10,1862-age 7yrs. 6mos

Hill, Jackson Hill; June 7,1825--March 22,1914.

" Elizabeth A., wife Jackson; Mar.3,1831--Jan.24,1895.

" Hester T., dau.Jackson & Elizabeth; d.Nov.28,1869-age 9mo.

" Abraham, son Jackson & Elizabeth; d.May 7,1863-age 9yrs.

" Peter Pennington Sandford, son Jackson & Elizabeth A.; died Apr.13,1868-age 15yrs. 1mon.

" Esther, dau.Jackson & Elizabeth; d.Apr.3,1863-age 5yrs.

" Elizabeth, dau.Jackson & Elizabeth; died Apr.8,1863-age 1 year, 7 months, 15 days.

" Mary F. dau.Jackson & Elizabeth; died Mar.28,1863-age 11 years, 6 months, 7 days.

Depew, Mary, dau.Elijah & Bethier; d.Nov.20,1842-age 3yrs. 3mos.

Purcell, Platt Purcell; died Sept.2,1851-age 42 years.

" Arabella, wife Platt; died Jan.8,1870-age 58 years, 11 mos

" Lewis, son Platt & Arabella; died Aug.11,1851-age 12 years, 11 months, 23 days.

Banker, Silas Banker; Feb.8,1812--Apr.15,1875.

" Cornelia, wife Silas; died June 2,1871-age 58yrs. 3mos.

" Chloe, dau.Silas & Cornelia; died April 12,1856-age 16 years, 7 months, 25 days.

" Hosea, son Silas & Cornelia; died Aug.13,1845-age 7 years

Heroy, Alson Heroy; died July 11,1888-age 74 years, 10 months.

" Phebe, dau.Alson & Ruth; died Sept.14,1850-age 12yrs.10mo.

" Jane, dau.Alson & Ruth; d.July 15,1851-age 1 year, 11 mos.

" Harrison, son Alson & Ruth; d.Oct.15,1833-age 6mos. 13da.

Purcell, Selah, son Hosea & Sarah; d.Sept.13,1867-age 7mos. 15da.

" Charles, son Hosea & Sarah; d.Jan.31,1862-age 2mo. 15da.

" Ida A.Purcell; Feb.24,1864--May 21,1870.

Bap. M.F.

Butterfield,	Elizabeth J., wife Lott S., dau.Abraham & Mary Early; died Feb.10,1841-age 20yrs. 5mos.
Hitchcock,	Stephen Hitchcock; died Mar.3,1865-age 74yrs. 5mos.
Cavanaugh,	Susan R., wife John J.; died Dec.21,1898-age 61yrs.
Maynard,	William H. son Abram & Frances; Nov.1863-Mar.1866.
Agor,	Rebecca, wife Charles; died Apr.30,1834-age 91 years.
Simpkins,	Rachel, wife John; died Jan.4,1847-age 95yrs. 9mos.
Stokum,	Phebe, wife William; died July 31,1855-age 72yrs.10mo.
Agor,	Nicholas Agor; died Jan.12,1839-age 68 years, 22 days
"	Mary, wife Nicholas; died Mar.10,1837-age 72 years.
"	William Agor; died May 23,1863-age 55 years, 10 months
"	Irena, wife William; died Jan.22,1842-age 33yrs. 9mos.
"	George, son William & Irena; died Aug.23,1846- age 18 years, 3 months, 8 days.
"	Thaddeus M., son William & Irena; died May 3,1859- age 21 years, 19 days.
"	Mary E., dau.William & Irena; died Jan.5,1860- age 25 years, 2 months, 14 days.
Hill,	Lewis Hill; Nov.15,1830--Feb.18,1905.
"	Dorothy A., wife Lewis; Mar.8,1852-----
"	Eliza J., wife Lewis; died Mar.10,1868-age 39yrs. 9mo.
"	Imogene, dau.Lewis & Eliza; d.Oct.3,1854-age 1yr.11mo.
Austin,	Lena, dau.Smith S.& Mary J.; d.Nov.14,1861-age 5mos.
"	Sarah Libbey, dau.Smith & Mary; died Apr.26,1865- age 1 year, 8 months, 13 days.
Briggs,	Ferris Briggs; Mar.13,1829--Sept.28,1874.
Early,	Mary, wife Abraham; died Mar.15,1838-age 52yrs. 7mos.
Jenkin,	Jennie E.Jenkin; Apr.18,1872--Feb.3,1906.
Pinckney,	Israel Pinckney; ----------

Bap. M.F.

Travis,	Gilbert Travis; died Apr.27,1839-age 74yrs. 9mos.
Sackrider,	Sarah A. dau.George & Adelia; died Dec.19,1848-age 24da.
Horton,	Samuel Horton; died Apr.11,1866-age 77 years, 11 months
"	Sarah A. wife Samuel; died Aug.1,1845-age 55 years.
"	Samuel Washington, son Samuel & Sarah; died Aug.17,1845- age 21 years, 4 months, 30 days.
"	Phebe Horton; died Oct.23,1874-age 82 years, 3 months.
"	Louisa, wife John L.; died Sept.7,1872-age 42yrs. 5mos.
"	Mary F., dau.John & Louisa; died Jan.14,1878- age 15 years, 4 months, 14 days.
"	Sarah A. dau.John & Louisa; d.Mar.9,1865-age 2mo. 14da.
"	Infant dau.John & Louisa; died May 13,1853-age 16 days.
Carhart,	Mary, wife Alfred: Oct.3,1817--Aug.3,1884.
Smith,	Andrew Jackson Smith; 1828-1894.
"	Phebe Smith; Sept.4,1792-Mar.6,1871.
Hill,	Cornelius Hill; died Nov.22,1833-age 24 years, 2 months
"	Elizabeth, wife Cornelius; died Sept.4,1859-age 93 years
"	James Hill; Mar.9,1802-Nov.11,1887.
"	Sarah Pinckney, wife James Hill; May 12,1806-Oct.24,1891
"	Joseph Hill; died July 29,1884-age 43 years.
"	Melissa Warren, wife Joseph Hill; died July 7,1885-age 37 years.
"	Libbie, dau.Joseph & Melissa; d.Dec.4,1881-age 5 years.
Buckley,	Elizabeth, wife Sturges; died Sept.7,1873- age 32 years, 11 months, 6 days.
Hamilton,	Jemima Hamilton; died Nov.19,1832-age 43 years, 7 months
Conklin,	Ann, wife Nathan; died Feb.18,1848-age 79 years, 8 mos.
Colwell,	Alpha D., son Alvah & Catherine; d.Apr.16,1833-age 11mo.
Wardell,	Frederick J.Wardell; 1839-1916.
"	Hannah J.Wardell; 1837-----

Bap. M.F.

Pinckney, Maria, wife Frederick; died Apr.25,1877-age 55 years.

" Sarah A. wife Frederick; d.Jan.16,1856-age 33yrs. 3mos.

" Zelma, dau.Frederick & Sarah; died Dec.16,1866-
age 25 years, 8 months, 17 days.

Hall, Edmund Hall; died Aug.13,1850-age 37 years, 4 months.

--"---- Broken stone; ------- 1833-age 58yrs. 10mos. 27days.

Secor, Hannah, wife Isaac R.; died Jan.18,1849-age 45yrs.

Cronk, John H. Cronk; died Sept.17,1882-age 49yrs. 3mos. 10da.

" Nehemiah Cronk; died May 10,1867-age 65yrs. 11mos. 30da.

" Elizabeth, wife Nehemiah; died Mar.17,1870-
age 71 years, 2 months, 16 days.

Kemp, John A., son Jacob C.& Mary; d.July 22,1861-age 4mos.

" Anna Maria, dau.Jacob & Mary; d.Aug.15,1864-age 1mo.26da

" Jacob C. son Jacob & Mary; d.July 31,1870-age 1 month.

" Mary J. dau.Jacob & Mary; d.July 27,1873-age 9mos. 5days

" Florence, dau.Jacob & Mary; d.Aug.15,1875-age 8mos. 15da.

Munger, Nathaniel Munger; died Mar.30,1862-age 67 years, 3 month.

" Susan, wife Nathaniel; died Dec.10,1885-age 84 years.

" Mary F. Munger; died Apr.24,1883-age 49 years, 11 months.

Herrick, Tamar A., wife William; died Feb.5,1858-age 33yrs. 3mos.

Barrett, Elias Barrett; died Dec.8,1882-age 38 years, 4 months.

" Isaac Barrett; died May 4,1861-age 45 years.

" Mary Travis, wife Isaac Barrett; died Mar.3,1900-
age 77 years, 2 months, 21 days.

" Almira, dau.Isaac & Mary; died Nov.20,1877-age 16yrs.

" Franky Barrett; died Aug.30,1860-age 9 months, 6 days.

" Eddie Barrett; died Feb.17,1863-age 1 year, 7 months.

" Matty Barrett; -- -----

Travis, Jeremiah Travis; died Apr.3,1863-age 72 years, 4 months.

Bap. M.F.

Travis,   John W.Travis; "13th. Michigan Regt." died Apr.20,1862-
                    age 27 years, 2 months, 6 days.

"   Gould J., son John & Esther; died Apr.24,1863--age 7mos.

Odell,   Adolphus L.Odell; 1804-1881.

"   Susan Odell; 1808-1898.

"   Mary Ann Odell; 1810-1842.

Pinckney,   William E.Pinckney; died Nov.12,1884--age 69 years.

"   Mary, wife William; Aug.11,1813--Feb.18,1880.

"   Willett D., son William & Mary; d.Mar.2,1847-age 7yrs.

Carver,   James Carver; died July 2,1837-age 55yrs. 9mos. 6days.

"   Sarah Carver; died Dec.18,1854--age 66yrs. 7mos. 20days.

"   Hosea Carver; Sept.21,1812--Apr.25,1854.

"   Hannah J.Cole, wife Hosea Carver;
                    Nov.22,1815--Nov.27,1890.

"   James W., son Hosea & Hannah; d.May 31,1843-age 23mos.

"   Hannah A.Carver; May 2,1826--Apr.22,1900.

Smith,   Stephen Smith; July 27,1814--May 16,1894.

"   Jane R.Carver, wife Stephen Smith;
                    March 13,1818--May 9,1899.

Barrett,   Isaac D.Barrett; (stone broken) age 77yrs. 3mos. 4days.

"   Ida E.Barrett; died Dec.11,1879-age 22yrs. 4mos. 22days

"   Moseman Barrett; Sept.27,1826-May 4,1908.

"   Margaret M.Gay, wife Moseman Barrett;
                    Nov.18,1826--Mar.18,1856.

"   Maria A. dau.Moseman & Margaret; Mar.16,1856-Sep.14,1856

"   Cornelia Ludington, wife Moseman Barrett;
                    June 16,1832--April 11,1905.

"   Elon G.Barrett; Feb.21,1844--June 1,1911.

"   Mary A.Wixsom, wife Elon G.Barrett; -------

Bap. M.F.

Wixsom,	Drusilla Wixsom; died July 4,1896-age 83 years, 11 months
"	Rachel Wixsom; died Nov.8,1860-age 41yrs. 6mos. 24days
"	James T.Wixsom; died Mar.3,1853-age 46yrs. 8mos. 8days
"	Robert Wixsom; died Sept.19,1861-age 79yrs. 6mos.
"	Ann, wife Robert; died Aug.18,1864-age 78yrs. 4mos. 23da.
Wixson,	Alpheus T.Wixson; died Mar.26,1864-age 39 years, 7 months
"	Amy, wife Alpheus; died June 20,1863-age 35yrs. 5mos.
"	Robert, son Alpheus & Amy; died Aug.23,1871-age 10 years
"	Nathaniel Wixson; Aug.17,1814--Jan.3,1893.
"	Sarah Barrett, wife Nathaniel Wixson; Dec.18,1816--Feb.24,1890.
Cronk,	Abraham Cronk; Oct.29,1794--Apr.26,1871.
"	Billecha, wife Abram; Feb.20,1805--Mar.1,1884.
"	Joseph A.Cronk; Oct.3,1841--Aug.14,1866.
"	Susan E.Cronk; July 22,1833--Feb.16,1872.
"	Adolpheus Cronk; Oct.22,1827--Mar.21,1832.
Pearce,	Mary A.Pearce; Aug.11,1829--June 20,1881.
Hawkins,	Joseph B.Hawkins; Mar.3,1845--Jan.3,1915.
"	Naomi E.Ballard, wife Joseph B.Hawkins; June 9,1845-----
Ballard,	Jackson P.Ballard; Feb.9,1820--Apr.14,1890.
"	Sarah Hyatt, wife Jackson Ballard; July 8,1827--Oct.28,1900.
"	Mary Augusta, dau.Jackson & Sarah; died April 2,1851-age 3 years, 10 months, 7 days.
"	Rev.Enos H.Ballard; died Oct.25,1861-age 53 years.
"	Martha, wife Rev.Enos; died May 31,1873-age 64 years.
"	Amanda Ann, dau.Rev.Enos & Martha; died Jan.24,1835-age 3 years, 9 months, 18 days.
"	Naomi Jane Ballard; died Jan.30,1835-age 5yrs. 5mos.

Bap. M.F.

Curry,	Sarah K., wife Peter B.; died Apr.13,1866- age 28 years, 11 months, 11 days
"	Theron, son Peter & Sarah; died Mar.25,1866-age 4yrs.
Smith,	Abijah Smith; died Dec.3,1866-age 73 years, 10 months
"	Sena K., wife Abijah; died Sept.3,1881-age 78 years.
Agor,	Theron Agor; Nov.29,1880--Dec.8,1914.
"	Jessie Agor; Aug.5,1882--July 27,1888.
"	Kelsie Agor; Mar.29,1859--Mar.9,1889.
Sprague,	James Sprague; died Apr.14,1884-age 69yrs. 8mos. 19days.
"	Pamelia, wife James; died Sept.3,1882-age 79yrs. 10mos.
Hinds,	John F. Hinds; 1859-1910.
Hughes,	William Hyatt Hughes; July 11,1862--Oct.31,1907.
"	Elizabeth J., wife William H.; Jan.3,1873-------
"	William Hughes; Aug.14,1833--May 31,1906.
"	Sarah E. Hyatt, wife William Hughes; May 31,1834--Dec.29,1917.
"	Sarah E. Hughes; died Feb.20,1860-age 1yr. 5mo. 10da.
Hyatt,	Julia Ann Hyatt; Oct.6,1837--June 7,1866.
Horton,	William H. Horton; Oct.9,1841--July 4,1923.
"	Sarah Hart, wife William Horton; Mar.23,1830-Jan.8,1914.
"	Emma C. Horton; Mar.16,1893-----
"	Elijah Horton; died Dec.25,1883-age 76yrs. 7mos. 28days
"	Elizabeth A., wife Elijah; died Sept.2,1880- age 70 years, 4 months, 12 days.
"	Elias W., son Elijah & Elizabeth; died Dec.30,1855- age 16 years, 6 months, 30 days.
"	Ira T. Horton; Feb.4,1833--June 25,1909.
"	Adaline Cole, wife Ira Horton; Feb.6,1832-Oct.29,1877.
"	Rametta Horton; Apr.1,1858--Aug.29,1905.

Bap. M.F.

Cole, Levi H. Cole; died Oct.17,1860-age 69 years.
" Hannah, wife Levi H.; died Dec.16,1876-age 78yrs. 11mos.
" John B. Cole; April 10,1821--June 27,1893.
" Martha, wife John B.; died Sept.16,1881-age 56 years.
" Margaretta C., wife John B.; July 30,1850-Oct.13,1911.
" Daniel W. Cole; died July 20,1863-age 23 years.
" Alonzo O. Cole; Oct.8,1827--Mar.12,1899.
" Emily A., wife Alonzo O.; Apr.8,1834--Sept.14,1856.
" Emma M., wife Alonzo O.; Dec.27,1834--Nov.20,1873.
" Sarah C., wife Alonzo O.; Dec.7,1832--Nov.4,1885.
" Jennie A. Cole, dau. ------
" Fannie E. Cole; Sept.13,1870------
" Hattie I. Cole; Oct.10,1868--Mar.11,1892.
" Annie L. Cole; June 6,1865-------
" Edwin Cole; Aug.3,1863--Aug.23,1864.
" Sarah Browner Cole; died Apr.8,1862-age 2 years, 8 months.
" Carrie Adina Cole; died Apr.6,1862-age 3 years, 9 months.
" Joseph W. Cole; died Nov.30,1916-age 83 years.
" Mary E., wife Joseph W.; died Feb.15,1872-age 35 years.
" Ann W., wife Joseph W.; died June 15,1891-age 59 years.
" Antoinette C., wife Jasper F.; died Dec.22,1878-age 41yrs.
" Amanda, wife Theron; died Oct.6,1860-age 34 years.
" Laban Cole; died May 2,1848-age 49 years, 7 months, 15 days
" Esther, wife Laban; died Sept.10,1833-age 35 years, 5 month
" Ann, wife Laban; April 12,1800--August 20,1887
" Antha J. Barrett, wife Theron Cole;
                       Aug.21,1840--June 21,1914.

Bap. M.F.

Sackrider, George W. Sackrider;   Sept.20,1810--Mar.28,1885.
"   Adelia, wife George W.;   Sept.29,1808--Mar.11,1882.
"   Elias W. Sackrider;   Mar.5,1832--------
"   James J. Sackrider;   Jan.18,1833--------
"   Mary E. Sackrider;   Oct.5,1835--------
"   Susan A. Sackrider;   Apr.16,1837--------
"   Sarah A. Sackrider;   Nov.25,1848--Dec.11,1848.
"   George W. Sackrider;   Nov.25,1848-------
"   William J. Sackrider;   Dec.1,1846-------
"   Everett B., son William J.& E.;   Nov.29,1879-Apr.12,1882

Lockwood, Mahala Lockwood;   Apr.20,1844--Mar.2,1881.

Hunter,   David H. Hunter;   July 18,1894--------
"   Jacob C. Hunter;   died Oct.5,1880-age 54 years, 5 months
"   Hannah A. Hazelton, wife Jacob C. Hunter;   died Dec.15,1903
                                        age 81 years, 7 months, 16 days.
"   George H., son Jacob & Hannah;   died June 7,1851-age 3yrs
"   George, son Jacob & Hannah;   died Dec.12,1864-age 2 years

Agor,   Harrison Agor;   Feb.22,1818--Dec.4,1892.
"   Jane, wife Harrison;   Apr.7,1820--Dec.25,1891.
"   Mary E., dau. Harrison & Jane;   Dec.11,1856-Mar.14,1860.
"   Silas A. Agor;   Mar.2,1860--Apr.8,1898.
"   William Agor;   May 2,1853--April 15,1911.
"   S. Elizabeth Agor;   1851-1920.
"   Emeline Agor;   1854-------
"   Alanson Agor;   died Apr.17,1895-age 75 years, 8 months.
"   Lucinda, wife Alanson;   died Mar.31,1856-age 28yrs. 11mo.
"   Eliza, dau. Alanson & Lucinda;   age 1yr. 2mo. 12da.
"   Edson, son Wm.H.& Elizabeth;   Feb.26,1907-Aug.27,1907.

Bap. M.F.

Hyatt,	George W. Hyatt; Sept. 30, 1849--Nov. 1, 1883.
Ames,	Clarence N., son William Harvey & Minnie R.; died Jan. 30, 1888-age 2yrs. 7mos.
"	Infant son William H. & Minnie R.; --------
Hadden,	Azor B. Hadden; Aug. 9, 1865--Mar. 2, 1906.
Curry,	George Curry; died Oct. 1, 1875-age 71 years, 7 months.
"	Hannah Agor, wife George Curry; died Sept. 9, 1892- age 88 years, 21 days.
"	Melissa A., dau. George & Hannah; d. May 6, 1865-age 23yrs
"	Alfred Curry; died Jan. 15, 1915-age 77 years, 3 months.
Austin,	Amos L. Austin; June 10, 1827--April 21, 1897.
"	Cynthia J. Cole, wife Amos L. Austin; Nov. 6, 1829--Aug. 12, 1906.
"	Phebe E. Austin; July 15, 1825--Oct. 6, 1905.
Williams,	Frederick Williams; Mar. 27, 1884--June 8, 1907.
"	Charles Williams; Apr. 7, 1849------
"	Mary A. Jennings, wife Charles Williams; June 14, 1847---
Barrett,	Ebenezer Barrett; June 3, 1818--March 29, 1907.
"	Esther Barrett; May 20, 1836--June 27, 1908.
"	Mary E. Barrett; Aug. 17, 1858--Jan. 24, 1872.
"	Mary Barrett; May 15, 1816--May 15, 1882.
Young,	Dunbar H. Young; July 24, 1835--Sept. 4, 1898.
"	Susan R., wife Dunbar; Sept. 21, 1842--June 28, 1911.
"	Judson B., son Dunbar & Susan; Dec. 1, 1860-Oct. 17, 1895.
Sutton,	William Sutton; "Co. G. 1st. Regt. N.Y. H.A. Vol." died June 22, 1907-age 81 years.
"	Emma A. Sutton; April 2, 1840--June 8, 1910.
Wright,	Adelia, wife Alfred H.; Nov. 1, 1838--Oct. 28, 1900.
Retan,	Euphemia, wife Barnett L.; 1850-1922.

Bap. M.F.

Barrett,	Elbert Barrett;	Sept.8,1839--Mar.8,1894.
"	Marcus Barrett;	Aug.18,1810--Feb.25,1852.
"	Mary A., wife Marcus;	Sept.25,1814--Mar.18,1892.
"	Martha A. Barrett;	1852-------
"	Philena Barrett;	Dec.-- 1846-Jan.1,1891.
Cole,	Marie L. Guy, wife Frank J. Cole;	-------
"	Evangeline Guy, wife Frank J. Cole;	died Nov.7,1883- age 23 years, 2 days.
"	Margurite, dau. Frank;	died Aug.2,1883-age 1 year.
"	Ramah Cole;	Oct.1,1818--May 6,1892.
"	Charlotte L. Carver, wife Ramah Cole;	Dec.27,1821--Nov.30,1889.
"	Frank J., son Ramah & Charlotte;	-------
"	Abiather B., son Ramah & C;	July 30,1847-Feb.11,1851.
Cary,	Frank Cary;	Feb.11,1888--Jan.30,1910.
"	Mary Ethel Hulse, wife Frank Cary;	Jan.10,1890------
Sackrider,	James J. Sackrider;	1833-1916.
"	Sarah J. Tompkins, wife James Sackrider;	1841-1920.
Hulse,	Isaac Hulse;	Sept.28,1839--Feb.28,1911.
"	Mary A. Sackrider, wife Isaac Hulse;	Sept.20,1859--Mar.6,1909.
"	John H., son Isaac & Mary;	Apr.15,1894-Jan.27,1896.
"	Edson, son Isaac & Mary;	Apr.23,1886-May 31,1886.
"	Libbie, dau. Isaac & Mary;	Nov.19,1887-Jan.17,1888.
Hadden,	George L. Hadden;	Apr.29,1854--July 5,1921.
"	Phebe J., wife George L.;	Feb.15,1855-------
"	Pearle Esther Hadden;	Oct.26,1884-Sept.4,1900.
"	George Lewis Hadden;	Mar.9,1888--Mar.12,1888.
Post,	George L. Post;	died July 7,1896-age 40 years, 11 months

Bap. M.F.

Pratt,	Morris Pratt; Aug.25,1856-Dec.27,1921.
Agor,	Coleman Agor; 1859-1923.
"	Elsie Agor; 1899-1900.
"	Elisha Agor; 1884-1885.
Barrett,	Ottis H.Barrett; 1865------
"	Barbara, wife Ottis; 1879-1922.
"	Howard D.Barrett; died Sept.9,1881-age 43yrs. 10mos.
Curry,	Peter B.Curry; June 13,1837-Dec.26,1893.
"	Hannah J.Hill, wife Peter Curry; Apr.2,1849-Jan.23,1916.
"	James F.Curry; May 24,1884-June 13,1886.
"	Abraham H.Curry; July 1,1873-Sept.29,1873.
"	Bertha A.Curry; Aug.24,1881-Sept.11,1881.
Lockwood,	Smith Lockwood; died Aug.30,1866-age 42 years.
"	Caroline Hill, wife Smith Lockwood; died July 25,1892- age 68 years, 6 months.
"	Wallace Hill Lockwood; Mar.13,1865-Feb.8,1913.
"	Carrie, dau.Smith & Caroline; died Dec.25,1870-age 9yrs.
"	William H.Lockwood; June 8,1895-June 26,1915.
Hill,	Lorenzo D.Hill; died Feb.13,1889-age 68yrs. 9mos. 10da.
"	Emily Hill; died Jan.11,1888-age 74 years, 4 days.
Smith,	Adeline Hill, wife William C.Smith; Nov.22,1842--Mar.21,1916.
"	Edson L.Smith; Mar.12,1881--July 2,1909.
Moore,	William H.Moore; Jan.27,1872-Apr.5,1916.
"	---------, wife ------
Barrett,	Wright Barrett; Jan.16,1832--Jan.3,1912.
"	Rebecca Clauson, wife Wright Barrett; Aug.20,1833--Feb.28,1892.
"	Kelsie Barrett; Feb.13,1877--Nov.19,1900.

Bap. K.F.

Barrett, Earle Barrett; June 29,1898-Sept.24,1898.

Hill,   William Hill; July 4,1834--April 27,1888.

"   Cornelius Hill; Oct.20,1832--Jan.12,1913.

"   Harrietta Brush, wife Cornelius Hill;
                    May 20,1838--March 28,1892.

Austin, Smith A.Austin; 1830--------

"   Mary Jane, wife Smith A.Austin; 1835-1904.

"   Robert J.Austin; June 21,1866-------

"   Julia M.Dean, wife Robert Austin; Oct.17,1869------

"   Lily J.Austin; Oct.19,1892--Feb.15,1896.

Moore,   Julia Tompkins, wife John Moore; Dec.25,1828-May 16,1902

Griffin, Mary J.Hadden, wife Marcus Griffin;
                    Sept.26,1828--Oct.17,1903.

Austin, Carrie A.Cole, wife David C.Austin; d.Mar.13,1893-29yrs.

Williams,Moseman L.Williams; Feb.15,1858------

"   Rachel Ann, wife Moseman J.Williams;
                    Jan.12,1858--June 25,1906.

Pierce, Bessie Pierce; died Feb.9,1901-age 6 months, 23 days.

Barrett, Retta C., wife Joseph; Mar.9,1865--Oct.16,1885.

"   Lawrence Barrett; April 18,1825-June 28,1900.

"   Lucinda Post, wife Lawrence Barrett;
                    July 2,1834--May 23,1908.

Horton, Sarah E.Barrett, wife Frank Horton; died May 13,1894-
                    age 34 years, 1 month, 6 days.

Agor,   Orson Agor; 1810-1883.

"   Abigail Agor; 1807-1852.

"   Elnora Agor; 1839-1923.

Frost,   Georgiana, wife Edward I.; July 11,1879-Jan.7,1911.

"   Hazel Louise Frost; Oct.2,1908--Sept.19,1908.

"   Helen Lee Frost; July 23,1905-March 15,1909.

Bap. M.F.

Lounsbury, Hosea F. Lounsbury; Jan.5,1836-Oct.3,1913.

" Mary Elizabeth Agor, wife Hosea F. Lounsbury;
" Aug.23,1836-Mar.27,1874.

" Elizabeth Curry, wife Hosea F. Lounsbury;
June 12,1839-Jan.23,1904.

Barrett, Boyd K. Barrett; Nov.27,1887-Feb.16,1915.

" Sarah J., wife Boyd K.; -------

" Lorin Barrett; Apr.12,1845------

" Mary Boyd, wife Lorin Barrett; July 21,1846-Aug.13,1922

" Bertham, dau. Lorin & Mary; Jan.13,1878-Feb.7,1882.

Horton, Nelson S. Horton; Apr.20,1837-Sept.27,1886.

" Frances O., wife Nelson S.; May 29,1841-Nov.3,1917.

" A. Jackson Horton; March 7,1833-June 3,1905.

" Amanda J. Barrett, wife A.J. Horton;
March 23,1839--August 11,1901.

Barrett, Peter B. Barrett; Sept.26,1829-Apr.23,1904.

" Mary A. Hazen, wife P.B. Barrett; Aug.17,1829-Feb.19,1903

" Sarah J., dau. P.B. & M.A.; Nov.22,1854-Jan.16,1855.

" Emily J., dau. P.B. & M.A.; Nov.21,1862-------

" Theron Barrett; ----

" Isaac Barrett; died Nov.13,1869-age 81 years, 9 months.

" Rachel Barrett; died Dec.26,1871-age 79 years, 8 months

Odell, Irving R. Odell; died Mar.21,1900-age 17yrs. 1mon. 8days

Pinckney, Thaddeus Pinckney; May 28,1859-Feb.12,1918.

" Hubert, son Thaddeus & Jessie; died Mar.3,1885-age 14mos

Arnold, Stephen E. Arnold; died April 7,1896-age 75 years.

" Sarah J., wife Stephen E.; died Oct.9,1893-age 73 years

Lockwood, Mary A. Lockwood; died Dec.10,1840-age 25 years.

Bap. M.F.

Sackrider,	George W. Sackrider; died Jan.11,1900-age 51 years.
"	Caroline, wife George W.; died Jan.31,1885-age 38yrs.
Heroy,	Harrison Heroy; died Feb.19,1894-age 61 years.
"	Annie M., wife Harrison; died Jan.23,1881-age 59yrs.
Wilson,	Thomas B. Wilson; died June 19,1873-age 62yrs. 18days
"	Sally, wife Thomas; died Nov.14,1866-age 50yrs. 4mos.
Abberley,	Charles Abberley; Aug.14,1841--Dec.26,1910.
"	Zillah V., wife Charles; May 15,1842-Feb.14,1916.
Quillin,	Rev. Horace S. Quillin; Jan.16,1863-Apr.8,1916.
Agor,	Jesse Agor; died Feb.24,1910-age 78yrs. 7mos. 20days.
"	Mary E., wife Jesse; died May 29,1894-age 57yrs. 7mos.
"	Howard Agor; Aug.10,1905-------
"	Theda Agor; ---------
Riedl,	Otto Eugene Riedl; Oct.3,1910-July 20,1911.
"	Otto H. Riedl; 1846-1912.
"	Josephine S. Riedl; 1858-1921.
Denike,	Charles H. Denike; -------
"	Ella E. Crawford, wife Charles H. Denike; May 3,1849--Nov.18,1915.
"	Ella L. Denike; Feb.29,1876-Nov.27,1923.
Waite,	William A. Waite; Jan.21,1878----
"	Goldie I. Pierce, wife William A. Waite; June 11,1878---
DeForest,	Mary J. Pierce, wife ---- May 25,1834--Sept.20,1911.
Curry,	Ezra Curry; July 22,1849-Jan.25,1913.
Mead,	Lyman Mead; Dec.5,1852------
"	Hannah J., wife Lyman; Apr.5,1850-May 15,1923.
Hadden,	Charles A. Hadden; Sept.18,1866-Dec.29,1916.
"	Maud B. Hallock, wife Charles A. Hadden; Mar.12,1869----

Bap. M.F.

Benjamin,	William Benjamin; 1843-1912.
"	Eliza J. Smith, wife William Benjamin; 1845-1917.
McBride,	William McBride; July 25,1837-Dec.21,1909.
Mead,	Ira C. Mead; June 14,1877- ------
"	Henrietta S. Mead; Mar.9,1877-------
Tompkins,	Nathaniel C. Tompkins; Feb.26,1897-Dec.17,1916.
Oakley,	Therasa E. Smith, wife Nathaniel Oakley; Mar.8,1874-May 14,1916.
Pinckney,	Michael Pinckney; May 1,1826-June 18,1882.
"	Miranda E. Crawford, wife Michael Pinckney; Mar.17,1832-Sept.21,1916.
"	Zillah A., dau. Michael & Miranda; June 22,1858------
"	Wayne C., son Michael & Miranda; Oct.3,1856-Apr.28,1859.
"	Chauncey B., son Michael & Miranda; June 21,1860-May 22,1911.
Wixon,	John S. Wixon; Nov.5,1865-Aug.9,1923.
"	Wright, son John S. & Laura A.; Feb.24,1895-Aug.2,1905.
Pinckney;	Azor B. Pinckney; Oct.28,1865-Oct.24,1909.
Hadden,	Elon Hadden; -----
"	Julia L., wife Elon; Nov.18,1861-Jan.29,1911.
Post,	Marietta, dau. John H. & Mary H.; 1875-1924.
Barrett,	Harold Barrett; Jan.25,1903-Jan.25,1903.
"	Myrtle K. Barrett; May 2,1901-Apr.10,1914.
Smith,	Abel Smith; 1821-1868.
"	Amy Potter, wife Abel Smith; 1822-1899.
Arnold,	Antha J., wife John C.; May 15,1844-Mar.21,1866.
"	William E. Arnold; Sept.22,1864-Aug.5,1912.

Bap. M.F.

Barrett, Levi Barrett; 1829-1904.

"   Adah, wife Levi; 1827-1903.

"   Cynthia J., dau.Levi & Adah; Apr.1,1858-Mar.11,1881.

------- Paul William, grandson Stewart;
                    Nov.20,1921-June 21,1923.

Barrett, Isaac Barrett; died Feb.29,1880-age 71 years, 7 months.

"   Mary A.Cole, wife Isaac Barrett; died Aug.20,1895-
                    age 79 years, 11 months, 10 days.

Kinsman, William Ross Kinsman; 1858-1922.

"   Fannie E.Kinsman; 1870-1922.

Bray,   Thomas W.Bray; Mar.17,1830-Apr.3,1905.

"   Sarah A.Horton, wife Thomas Bray;
                    Oct.17,1831--Sept.23,1910.

"   Frank Bray; died July 29,1871-age 19yrs. 6mos. 12days.

Hunt,   Sally Ann, wife Joshua; died Mar.10,1843-
                    age 49 years, 3 months, 24 days.

Pinckney,Israel Pinckney; -------

Potter, Samuel Potter; died Dec.23,1873-age 79 years, 11 months

"   Malinda, wife Samuel; died Sept.27,1873-
                    age 72 years, 5 months, 23 days.

"   William Potter; died June 16,1880-age 47 years, 3 months

"   Fanny Potter; died Oct.17,1879-age 57 years, 11 months.

Presbyterian Ground

Mahopac Falls

Putnam County, N.Y.

Index Mahopac

Abbott, 18.	Ferguson, 16.	Magee, 14.
Abel, 5.	Fisher, 4,18.	Marshall, 13.
Aiken, 11.	Foster, 18.	Meyrick, 2,15.
Alley, 2.	Fowler, 11.	Miller, 1, 4. 8.
Anderson, 11,12,16.	Fox, 2.	Minthorne, 1.
Austin, 1, 5, 8,10, 16.	Frost, 18.	Mollenhauef, 13.
	Fuller, 11.	Moore, 3.
Badeau, 9,14,16,17.		Murden, 4.
Baker, 12.	Glover, 1,13.	
Banker, 5.	Gridley, 18.	Odell, 13,16.
Barger, 11.	Griffin, 15.	Owen, 8.
Barker, 8.		
Barmore, 18.	Hadden, 1,13,17.	
Benedict, 1.	Hagaman, 12.	Pierce, 3,18.
Benjamin, 6.	Haight, 18.	Pinckney, 1,12,16.
Beyea, 18,20.	Hart, 11.	Price, 5.
Biggs, 14.	Hazelton, 18.	
Boyd, 18.	Hazen, 17.	Rankine, 18.
Brown, 7,13.	Head, 13.	Robinson, 6.
Brundage, 4.	Heney, 13.	Rogers, 17.
Buckbee, 11.	Heroy, 2, 3.	Rorke, 14.
	Hill, 7.	
Campbell, 12.	Hoag, 17.	Sackrider, 11.
Card, 14.	Horton, 14.	Secor, 7,11.
Carman, 19.	Hull, 1.	Seeley, 13,14.
Carpenter, 6,16.	Hunt, 4.	Slawson, 15.
Carratt, 18.		Smith, 2,10,12,14,18
Cock, 3.	James 20.	Strang, 12.
Cornelius, 2.	Jenkins, 20.	Stuchfield, 16.
Cornell, 18.	Johnston, 9.	Sutton, 18.
Cowen, 2.		
Craft, 3,11.	Kennard, 20,	Thompson, 13.
Crookstone, 6.	Kirkham, 16.	Thorn, 12,13,14.
Crosby, 3.	Kniffin, 8.	Thorp, 11.
Currey, 9.	Knueppel, 16.	Tompkins, 2, 5,13,16.
Curry, 11,18.		Travis, 4, 6.
	Lane, 8.	Trowbridge, 6.
Dean, 8,17.	Lent, 15.	Turner, 13.
Dillingham, 6.	Lewis, 4.	
Downs, 7.	Lockwood, 11.	Valentine, 13.
	Lounsbury, 1,11, 16.	VanArsdale, 6.
Emigh, 12.		Vandevoort, 6.
		Vernol, 4.

Waters, 17.	
Waugh, 13.	
Webb, 3.	
Weeks, 3.	
Whiting, 7.	
Williams, 18.	
Winter, 3.	
Withers, 13.	
Wright, 7,12,14,17.	

Presb. Mahopac

Lounsbury, Robert W. Lounsbury; Nov.29,1817-Nov.17,1899.

" Mary J. Lounsbury; 1825-1911.

" Joshua Lounsbury; 1784-1833.

" Lydia Lounsbury; 1789-1866.

" Emmalinda, dau.Thomas & Jane; died Oct.5,1811-
        age 4 years, 3 months, 13 days.

" Emmalinda, dau.Alfred & Susan; died Nov.13,1827-
        age 4 months, 21 days.

Benedict, Sarah, dau.Joseph & Betsey; died Oct.12,1818-age 18mos.

Glover, Philip Glover; died Jan.5,1816-age 19 years.

" Catherine, wife Andrew; died May 20,1810-age 56 years.

Pinckney, William, son Lewis & Orphy; died Feb.27,1812-age 18yrs.

Minthorne, Sophia, wife William; died May 28,1807-age 31 years.

Hull, Eliphalet Hull; died July 19,1813-age 54 years.

" Eunice, wife Eliphalet; died Jan.5,1833-age 70 years.

" Happy, dau.Eliphalet & Eunice; died Oct.28,1823-age 35yr

" Julia, " " " " died Nov.3,1823-age 21yrs.

" Harriet, " " " " died May 31,1813-age 23yr.

" Thomas Hull; died Nov.5,1827-age 41 years.

" Walter B. Hull; died Feb.27,1850-age 23 years.

" Hezekiah Hull; died Nov.1,1823-age 69 years.

" Sarah, wife Hezekiah; died Apr.23,1850-age 89 years.

Miller, Gilbert, son Levi & Mary; died Mar.29,1830-
        age 5 years, 2 months, 4 days.

Hadden, Samuel Hadden; died Jan.13,1824-age 34 years.

" Anna, dau.Samuel & Libby; died Aug.8,1818-age 8 days.

" Jacob, son Samuel & Libby; died June 24,1820-
        age 8 months, 24 days.

Austin, Chloe, wife Elijah; died March 21,1832-age 20yrs. 8mos.

Presb. Mahopac

Cornelius,	Doct. Elias Cornelius; "A Soldier of the Revolution." died June 13, 1823-age 65 years.
"	Infant son Doct. Elias & Rachel; July 17, 1793-age 5wks.
"	Nancy Cornelius; died Mar. 22, 1823-age 19 years.
Tompkins,	Ira Tompkins; Oct. 2, 1799-June 29, 1889.
"	Betsey, wife Ira; died Sept. 28, 1852-age 55 years.
"	Henry Marlin, son Ira & Betsey; died June 10, 1838-
"	Emily, dau. Ira & Betsey; died May 16, 1839- age 7 years, 10 months, 18 days.
Meyrick,	Sarah Smith, wife Samuel S. Meyrick; 1784-1851.
"	Emily Meyrick; 1827-1832.
Fox,	Emily Syphia, dau. Moses & Saloma; died June 1, 1819-age 20 years.
Cowen,	Daniel R. Cowen; died Mar. 29, 1879-age 68yrs. 10mos.
"	Adah, wife Daniel; died Apr. 9, 1842-age 32yrs. 28days.
Heroy,	Solomon Heroy; died Jan. 22, 1858-age 78yrs. 11mos. 14da.
"	Margaret, wife Solomon; died Sept. 23, 1868-age 83 years.
"	Phebe, dau. Solomon & Margaret; died Feb. 21, 1815-age 7yr.
"	Charles Heroy; died Dec. 15, 1824-age 75 years.
"	Phebe, wife Charles; died Apr. 29, 1821-age 70 years.
"	Bethial, dau. Charles & Phebe; died Apr. 15, 1796- age 18 years, 7 months, 2 days.
"	Esther Heroy; died Jan. 11, 1849-age 77yrs. 2mos. 4days
"	Charles Heroy; died Dec. 4, 1852-age 76yrs. 2mos. 21days
"	Charles Heroy; died Dec. 28, 1785-age 66 years.
"	Esther, wife Charles; died Nov. 8, 1816-age 84 years.
"	Elizabeth, relict Isaac; died Jan. 12, 1856-age 88 years
Alley,	William Alley; died April 12, 1848-age 71 years.
"	Marian Alley; died Oct. 22, 1823-age 85 years.

Presb. Mahopac

Moore,	John Moore; Sept.1,1813-Feb.7,1893.
"	Freddie, son John & Julia; died Apr.22,1871-age 1yr. 2mo.
"	Lucie, dau. John & Julia; died Feb.3,1862-age 4yr. 1mo.
Pierce,	William Pierce; died Dec.13,1858-age 72 years.
"	Elizabeth, wife William; died Dec.17,1858-age 72 years.
"	Susannah, dau. William & Elizabeth; died Oct.5,1820-age 18mo.
Winter,	Mary Winter; April 10,1814-April 29,1869.
Webb,	William Webb; died May 20,1825-age 62yrs. 2mos. 29days.
"	2 infants William & Phebe; died Mar.23,1789-age 3 days.
"	Billy, son William & Phebe; died Aug.19,1791-age 5 months
Craft,	Adah Heroy, wife James Craft; died Dec.3,1865- age 55 years, 7 months, 18 days.
Heroy,	Jacob Heroy; died May 11,1835-age 55yrs. 10mos. 14days.
"	Elizabeth, wife Jacob; died Apr.19,1852-age 65yrs. 4mos.
"	Peter Heroy; died Feb.15,1795-age 39 years, 6 months.
"	Catherine, wife Peter; died July 22,1836- age 76 years, 11 months, 10 days.
"	Mary Ann, dau. Peter & Catherine; died Jan.15,1799- age 27 years, 6 months.
"	Jane Heroy; died Apr.15,1832-age 39 years, 6 days.
"	Jacob, son Melancthon & Eliza M.; d.Aug.8,1837-age 2mos.
Crosby,	Benjamin Crosby; died July 22,1797-age 53 years.
"	Rachel, wife Benjamin; died Feb.25,1791-age 43 years.
"	Rachel, dau. Benjamin & Rachel; d.Apr.13,1788-age 14 years
"	Benjamin, son Benjamin & Rachel; d.July 15,1791-age 12yrs.
"	Sarah, dau. Benjamin & Rachel; died June 14,1793-age 22yrs.
Weeks,	Hannah, wife D.M.Weeks, dau. Benjamin & Rachel Crosby; died July 18,1795-age 19 years.
Cock,	Patty, dau. James & Hannah; died Sept.4,1792-age 6 years.

Presb. Mahopac

Travis, William Travis; died Oct.30,1869-age 94yrs. 5mos. 26days

"   Charlotte, wife William; died Feb.25,1860-
               age 86 years, 2 months, 5 days.

"   Mary, dau.William & Charlotte; died Feb.19,1842-
               age 39 years, 4 months, 20 days.

"   Daniel Travis; died Aug.7,1844-age 65yrs. 3mos. 5days.

Miller, Hiram Miller; died Jan.15,1814-age 31 years.

"   Mary, dau.Hiram & Ruth; died July 13,1823-age 12yrs. 1mon.

"   Johnathan Miller; died Jan.1,1815-age 69 years.

"   Mary, wife Johnathan; died Aug.3,1808-age 55yrs. 7mos.

"   Hester, wife Johnathan; died Aug.24,1835-age 59yrs. 3mos.

"   Polly, dau.Johnathan & Mary; died Jan.14,1812-age 15yrs.

"   Henry, son Johnathan & Mary; died Feb.11,1812-age 12yrs.

"   Gilbert, son Johnathan & Esther; died Oct.18,1810-age 1yr.

Fisher, Charlotte, dau.John & Sally; died Dec.27,1833-age 11mos.

Lewis, David, son William & Mary; died Sept.14,1803-age 9yr. 11mo.

Hunt, Bishop Hunt; died July 22,1875-age 87 years.

"   Rebecca, wife Bishop; died April 14,1868-
               age 82 years, 8 months, 20 days.

Vernol, James Vernol; died Dec.16,1873-age 84yrs. 10mos. 14days.

"   Susan, wife James; died Apr.25,1866-age 73 years, 8 days.

"   Susan, dau.James & Susan; died May 5,1857-
               age 24 years, 11 months, 9 days.

"   Deborah, dau.James & Susan; died Feb.10,1832-age 11 years

"   William, son James & Susan; died Feb.20,1832-
               age 7 years, 7 months, 15 days.

"   James C., son James & Susan; died May 22,1835-
               age 7 years, 6 months, 29 days.

Murden, Schuyler Murden; died June 22,1870-age 65yrs. 7mos. 4days

"   Sarah J. Brundage, wife Schuyler Murden;
               Oct.29,1818-Oct.20,1877.

Presb. Mahopac

Vandevoort,	Cornelius Vandevoort; died May 8, 1807 - age 76 years.
"	Michael Vandevoort; died Apr. 11, 1812 - age 41 years.
"	Mary G., dau. Charles M. & Deborah G.; Sept. 18, 1853 - Jan. 10, 1855.
"	Charles I., son Charles M. & Deborah G.; Nov. 1, 1859 - Jan. 14, 1862.
"	Carrie C., dau. Charles & Deborah; July 11, 1857 - January 21, 1862.
Benjamin,	Charles Benjamin; died July 1, 1879 - age 32yrs. 6mos.
VanArsdale,	Margaret Adelina, dau. Elias & Margaret; died May 1, 1806 - age 8 months, 5 days.
Trowbridge,	Ephriam, son Billy & Rhoda; died May 8, 1791 - age 14yrs.
Dillingham,	Henry Dillingham; died Mar. 24, 1812 - age 54yrs. 10mos.
"	Mary, wife Henry; died May 1, 1797 - age 32 years.
"	Julia Dillingham; died Aug. 28, 1826 - age 61 years.
Crookstone,	John Crookstone; died Feb. 6, 1793 - age 36 years.
"	Elenor Crookstone; died Apr. 13, 1848 - age 88 years.
"	Jane, wife Morris Crookston; dau. Johnathan & Mary Owen; died Oct. 21, 1858 - age 50 years.
"	Sophia, dau. Morris & Jane; died Aug. 18, 1851 - age 14yrs
"	Eugene, son Morris & Jane; died May 28, 1851 - age 4 years, 5 months, 21 days.
"	James S., son Morris & Jane; d. May 2, 1850 - age 9 years
"	Elizabeth, dau. Morris & Jane; died Feb. 13, 1839 - age 6 years, 1 month, 28 days.
"	Ellen Maria, dau. Morris & Jane; died Jan. 31, 1828 - age 11 years, 7 months, 13 days.
Carpenter,	Caleb Carpenter; died Oct. 24, 1791 - age 25 years.
Robinson,	Ruhamah, wife Martin; died Feb. 10, 1848 - age 59 years, 9 months, 7 days.
Travis,	Daniel Travis; died August 7, 1844 - age 65 years, 3 months, 5 days.

Presb. Mahopac

Wright,   Elijah Wright; died July 17, 1815 - age 64 years.

"   Margaret, wife Elijah; died Mar. 12, 1825 - age 54 years.

"   Robert Wright; died May 19, 1818 - age 81 years.

"   Phebe, dau. Robert & Mary; died Aug. 9, 1812 - age 14 years.

"   Ebenezer Wright; died Mar. 9, 1806 - age 43yrs. 2mos. 6days.

"   Rachel, wife Ebenezer; died Oct. 27, 1829 -
         age 66 years, 7 months, 17 days.

"   Rachel Wright; died Dec. 31, 1879 - age 79yrs. 6mos. 25days.

"   Johannah, wife Robert; died Jan. 24, 1788 - age 43 years.

Whiting, Johnathan Whiting; died Nov. 6, 1869 -
         age 87 years, 6 months, 17 days.

"   Eunice, wife Johnathan; died Feb. 29, 1848 -
         age 61 years, 2 months, 25 days.

"   Johnathan Whiting; died Jan. 14, 1797 - age 59yrs. 8mos.

"   Rachel, wife Johnathan; died Jan. 10, 1830 - age 88 years.

"   Sally, dau. Johnathan & Rachel; died Dec. 25, 1796 -
         age 13 years, 6 months, 6 days.

Downs,   Samuel Downes; died May 12, 1812 - age 49 years.

"   Esther Downs; died Oct. 12, 1832 - age 43 years.

"   Elizabeth, wife Samuel; died Mar. 1, 1814 - age 49 years.

Hill,   Noah D. Hill; died Sept. 22, 1839 - age 24yrs. 2mos. 9days.

"   Sarah, dau. Uriah & Anna; died Dec. 1, 1843 - age 15yrs. 1mon.

"   Susan, dau. Uriah & Anna; died June 21, 1839 - age 2mos. 10da

Secor,   Gedney Secor; died Mar. 1, 1812 - age 37 years.

"   Catherine S. Hill, wife Gedney Secor;
         died Feb. 15, 1861 - age 80 years.

"   Isaac Secor; died May 1, 1810 - age 71 years.

"   Mary, wife Isaac; died Feb. 21, 1812 - age 68 years.

"   Elizabeth, wife John; died May 28, 1791 - age 52yrs. 4mos.

Presb. Mahopac

Dean, Richard Dean; died May 23, 1859-age 87yrs. 8mos. 13days.

" Alethea, wife Richard; died June 24, 1876-
age 99 years, 5 months, 11 days.

" Robert, son Richard & Alethia; died Apr.5, 1800-age 21yrs.

" William A. Dean; died July 12, 1854-age 35yrs. 6mos. 8days

" John Dean; died Nov.23, 1832-age 35yrs. 1mon. 6days.

" Adah Dean; died Nov.2, 1837-age 31 years, 7 months, 5 days.

" Edwin L., son Lewis A. & Clarissa; died May 20, 1846-
age 6 months, 17 days.

" Adah E., dau. Lewis A. & Clarissa; died Dec.28, 1852-
age 4 years, 1 month, 3 days.

" John H., son Lewis A. & Clarissa; died Jan.3, 1853-
age 8 years, 10 months, 20 days.

" Mary A., dau. Lewis A. & Clarissa; died Feb.7, 1853-
age 2 years, 10 months.

" Margaretta A., dau. Lewis A. & Clarissa; died Mar.24, 1843-
age 2 years, 16 days.

" Cornelius Dean; Jan.13, 1814-Mar.17, 1886.

" Andrew J. Dean; Mar.12, 1834-May 30, 1909.

" Marie Owen, wife Andrew Dean; Apr.7, 1838-Nov.30, 1879.

" Lillie, dau. Andrew & Marie; June 29, 1876-Dec.29, 1881.

Lane, Nathan Lane; died July 19, 1817-age 38 years.

" William, son Nathan & Hannah; died Feb.20, 1810-age 4 years

" Nathan Lane; died Nov.28, 1811-age 72yrs. 10mos. 12days.

" Elanor, wife Nathan; died March 4, 1815-age 74 years.

" George C., son Nathan & Elanor; died Aug.25, 1808-
age 25 years, 6 months, 2 days.

Kniffin, Nancy, wife Hiram Kniffin, dau. Robert & Elizabeth Austin;
died Feb.11, 1838-age 27 years.

Barker, James Barker; died Jan.12, 1842-age 64 years.

Miller, Salome, wife B.H.; died Oct.22, 1809-age 34yrs. 4mos. 3day.

Presb. Mahopac

Johnston, Robert Johnston; died Jan.19,1823-age 89 years.

" Elizabeth, wife Robert; died Sept.27,1832-age 82yrs.

" Mary Johnston; died Aug.7,1846-age 71 years.

" Ogden, son Robert & Elizabeth; died Feb.14,1792-
age 1 year, 4 months.

" William H. Johnston; died Jan.10,1828-age 49 years.

Badeau, Isaac Badeau; died Sept.7,1842-age 93 years.

" Deborah, wife Isaac; died Apr.5,1840-age 77 years.

" Susannah, wife Isaac; died Apr.6,1812-age 59 years.

" Fanny, dau.Isaac & Susan; died July 14,1840-age 49yrs.

" John, son Isaac & Susan; died Jan.27,1844-age 47 years.

" Elias, son Isaac; --------

" Isaac, son Isaac; --------

" Gilbert, son Isaac & Susannah; Mar.23,1785-May 5,1867.

" Eliza, grand-daughter Isaac; died Sept.19,1885-age 85yr.

" Johnathan Badeau; died Apr.3,1854-age 27yrs. 3mos. 24day

" Rebecca, wife Johnathan; died Aug.19,1854-age 25yr, 1mo.

" Sarah Badeau; died Sept.21,1849-age 47 years.

" Peter Badeau; died Aug.9,1816-age 88 years.

" Katherine, wife Peter; died Feb.-- 1790-age 64 years.

" Elizabeth, wife Peter; died Oct.29,1826-age 77 years.

" ----- son J.& E.; died Jan.6,1839-age 12 years.

Currey, Lewis Currey; died June 18,1840-age 68 years, 28 days.

" Mariam, wife Lewis; died Aug.5,1828-age 48yrs. 1mon.

" John A., son Lewis & Mariam; died May 6,1825-
age 10 years, 9 months, 3 days.

" Peter B., son Lewis & Mariam; died Dec.31,1809-
age 1 year, 2 months, 21 days.

Presb. Mahopac

Smith, Abraham Smith; 1769-1813.

" Mary Smith; 1764-1850.

" Eliza, dau. Abraham & Mary; died July 18, 1820-age 19 years.

" Allen B. Smith; died Apr. 7, 1834-age 37yrs. 10mos. 21days

" Jeremiah F. Smith; July 27, 1828-Oct. 24, 1882.

" Abraham Smith; died Apr. 23, 1854-age 65 years.

" Caty, dau. Abraham & Mary; died Sept. 6, 1813-age 19 years.

" Peggy, dau. Abraham & Mary; died June 18, 1812-age 13yrs.

" Charity, wife John; died Apr. 29, 1813-age 52yrs. 10mos.

" Abraham Smith; died July 20, 1807-age 21yrs. 10mos. 10days.

" William M., son William & Mary; died Aug. 25, 1819-
age 1 year, 5 months, 6 days.

Austin, Robert Austin; died May 3, 1834-age 74 years.

" Robert Austin; died Jan. 23, 1872-age 80 years.

" Betsey, wife Robert; died Dec. 27, 1830-age 37 years.

" Nathaniel L., son Robert & Elizabeth; died Aug. 15, 1813-
age 18 years, 1 month, 28 days.

" Mary, dau. Robert & Elizabeth; died Mar. 6, 1830-age 38yrs.

" Amos L. Austin; died Dec. 7, 1824-age 31 years.

" Phebe Austin; died Mar. 24, 1825-age 25 years.

" George L. Austin; died Sept. 19, 1827-age 30 years.

" Absalom R., son Robert & Elizabeth; died May 9, 1848-
age 47 years, 7 months, 3 days.

" Cornelia, wife Absalom; died May 21, 1887-age 84yrs. 7mos.

" Ann Victoria, dau. Absalom & Cornelia; died Oct. 24, 1845-
age 8 years, 2 months, 3 days.

" George L., son Absalom & Cornelia; died Feb. 28, 1832-21mos.

" Smith Austin; died Sept. 17, 1834-age 81 years.

" Martha, wid. Smith; died Apr. 11, 1854-age 100 years.

Presb. Mahopac

Lounsbury, Alfred Lounsbury; died May 23, 1848 - age 48 years.

" Susan, wife Alfred; died July 20, 1845 - age 38yrs. 11mos.

Curry, Peter B. Curry; died Oct. 28, 1886 - age 75yrs. 5mos.

" Elizabeth Hart, wife Peter B. Curry; died Apr. 1, 1896 - age 73 years, 11 months, 17 days.

" Wright H., son Peter & Elizabeth; died July 9, 1877 - age 11 years, 3 months, 15 days.

" Franklin, son Peter & Elizabeth; died Feb. 27, 1858 - age 1 year, 2 months, 4 days.

Anderson, Mila Anderson; died April 17, 1854 - age 45 years.

Aiken, Hannah J., wife John A.; died Apr. 4, 1855 - age 43 years.

Lockwood, Sophia, wife David; died Sept. 1, 1834 - age 30 years.

" James F., son David & Sophia; died Sept. 30, 1852 - age 20 years, 5 months, 22 days.

Fuller, Mary, wife John H.; died Dec. 30, 1848 - age 27 years.

" William Rufus, son John H. & Mary; died Apr. 8, 1847 - age 2 years, 10 months, 14 days.

Fowler, Ardilla, wife Josiah; died Feb. 16, 1833 - age 22 years, 3 months, 27 days.

Craft, Mary, wife Joseph; died June 7, 1831 - age 49 years.

Buckbee, Isaiah Buckbee; May 12, 1853 - Nov. 2, 1877.

" Sarah Esther, wife Francis; Oct. 7, 1825 - Dec. 19, 1909.

Barger, Isaiah Barger; died Aug. 10, 1844 - age 28 years, 7 months.

" Esther, wife John; Mar. 5, 1787 - Mar. 5, 1876.

Thorp, John Thorp; died Dec. 1, 1837 - age 76yrs. 2mos. 16days.

" Ruth, wife John; died Apr. 7, 1814 - age 56yrs. 9mos. 19da.

Secor, Zillah, wife Allen; died June 28, 1826 - age 33 years.

" Isaac C., son Allen & Zillah; died Feb. 12, 1815 - age 2mos.

Sackrider, Eliza, wife James; died Dec. 11, 1856 - age 40yrs. 2mos.

" James H., son James & Eliza; died July 3, 1850 - age 18mos.

Presb. Mahopac

Hagaman, Mary E., dau. Henry & Adah; died Sept.10,1851-age 9mos.

" William H., son Henry & Adah; died June 30,1859-
age 9 years, 8 months, 4 days.

Baker, Caroline, wife William T.; Nov.27,1808-Nov.20,1891.

Wright, Robert Wright; died Oct.9,1838-age 50yrs. 9mos.

" Esther, wife Robert; died Feb.12,1874-age 75 years.

Pinckney, Charles Pinckney; died Oct.16,1834-age 68yrs. 4mos. 17day

Campbell, William Campbell; died Dec.11,1869-age 63yrs. 5mos.

" Caroline, wife William; died Feb.2,1876-age 69yrs. 5days.

Smith, Elias Smith; died May 3,1851-age 42yrs. 8mos. 9days.

" Harriet, wife Elias; died Dec.9,1864-age 61yrs. 4mos.

" James, son Elias & Harriet; died Jan.26,1838-age 8 years.

" Nancy, dau. Elias & Harriet; died Jan.24,1838-
age 5 years, 7 months, 6 days.

" Elias A., son Elias & Harriet; died Mar.2,1855-age 7mos.

" Nancy A. dau. Elias & Harriet; died March 2,1855-
age 15 years, 3 months, 19 days.

Anderson, Silas A. Anderson; Feb.4,1850-July 30,1915.

" Mary Emigh, wife Silas Anderson; Apr.22,1854-Jan.2,1917.

" Peter Anderson; died Apr.2,1882-age 71yrs. 6mos. 9days.

" Mary, wife Peter; died Dec.23,1891-age 78yrs. 10mos. 15da

" Mila C., dau. Peter & Mary; died Mar.18,1863-age 19yrs.

Thorn, James Anderson Thorn; Oct.2,1825-June 5,1913.

" Matilda J. Strang, wife James A. Thorn;
Oct.3,1830-Oct.25,1890.

" Gerard Everett, son James & Matilda; died Jan.21,1870-
age 1 year, 8 months, 4 days.

" Green Thorn; died July 21,1878-age 79 years, 14 days.

" Sarah Anderson, wife Green Thorn; died Jan.2,1858-
age 53 years, 7 months, 25 days.

Presb. Mahopac

Thorn,	Emelinda Thorn; died Aug.23,1851-age 17yrs. 11mos.
Mollenhauef,	Frederic Mollenhauef; July 19,1899-
Brown,	Margaret, wife Samuel H.; died Nov.7,1851-age 53yrs.
Marshall,	Charles Marshall; died July 8,1881-age 82yrs. 4mos.
"	Mary, wife Charles; died Jan.22,1857-age 55 years.
Seeley,	James Seeley; died Oct.1,1852-age 39yrs. 7days.
"	Polly T., wife James; died Jan.15,1842-age 28yrs. 5mo
Glover,	Mary Glover; died Jan.6,1879-age 82 years, 7 months.
Hadden,	Charles Hadden; Feb.7,1870-July 8,1893.
"	William Hadden; Apr.16,1825-Dec.19,1891.
Valentine,	David T. Valentine; Nov.22,1823-Oct.7,1888.
Head,	Samuel Head; died Feb.22,1882-age 82yrs. 2mos. 11days
"	Hannah, wife Samuel; died May 23,1888-age 80 years.
"	Elijah Head; died Jan.29,1865-age 32yrs. 10mos.
"	Robert H., son Samuel & Hannah; died Dec.27,1864-age 8 years, 6 months, 9 days.
"	Elam, son Samuel & Hannah; died Sept.9,1852-age 9days
"	John J. Head; "Co.G. 6th.N.Y. H.A." died April 17,1913-age 73 years.
Odell,	Joseph Odell; died Dec.22,1864-age 77 years, 4 months
"	Clarissa, wife Joseph; died May 19,1857-age 69 years, 11 months, 16 days.
Withers,	Elizabeth Heney, wife John Withers; died Aug.16,1888-age 70 years.
Turner,	John Turner; died Nov.15,1883-age 79 years.
Thompson,	Nathan L. Thompson; Mar.17,1815-Dec.28,1884.
"	Hannah M., wife Nathan; May 13,1814-July 23,1891.
Tompkins,	Hannah, dau.Ananias & Fanny; Jan.28,1812-Nov.14,1876.
Waugh,	John A. Waugh; died Aug.6,1918-age 24 years.

Presb. Mahopac

Rorke, Frank Pryor Rorke; Feb.18,1864-Aug.31,1915.

" J. Pryor Rorke; Feb.19,1834-Sept.6,1903.

" ---------------- Feb.22,1836-Feb.29,1921.

Thorne, Green Thorne; Oct.12,1863-July 18,1898.

" Gilbert G. Thorne; Aug.28,1896-Feb.20,1898.

" Gilbert Thorne; Mar.25,1831-Sept.18,1882.

" Mary E., wife Gilbert; July 10,1838-March 23,1908.

" Gilbert, son Gilbert & Mary; May 12,1867-July 8,1867.

Smith, Bertha Smith; Oct.17,1831-Oct.30,1894.

Horton, Ebenezer Horton; Nov.30,1796-Jan.9,1864.

" Eunice Horton; March 16,1798-June 28,1881.

Seely, Cyrus J. Seely; Feb.17,1834-June 5,1907.

" Phebe J. Seely; Feb.3,1829-Apr.11,1901.

" Susie E. Seely; Mar.18,1862-June 20,1900.

Wright, Jackson Wright; Aug.21,1827-Mar.3,1905.

" Sarah C. Magee, wife Jackson Wright;
Sept.21,1827-July 26,1906.

" Louisa, dau. Jackson & Sarah; June 28,1876-age 16yrs. 11mos

Smith, Saxton Smith; 1802-1890.

" Phebe Smith; 1791-1868.

" Prudence Smith; 1786-1869.

Card, Edson Card, M.D. 1856-1917.

Badeau, Isaac Badeau; Feb.23,1822-Sept.24,1902.

" Lydia P., wife Isaac; Oct.29,1822-June 28,1870.

" Louise Badeau; Mar.12,1860-Oct.1,1912.

" Ruth, dau. Charles & Mary; May 25,1889-May 7,1890.

" Freddie, son Charles & Mary; July 5,1874-July 3,1877.

Biggs, Mary L., dau. Daniel & Mary H.; died Aug.26,1862-
age 7 years, 3 months, 21 days.

Presb. Mahopac

Slawson, Amzi Slawson; died Sept. 27, 1882-age 58yrs. 8mos. 18days.

" Elizabeth, wife Amzi; died May 21, 1893-
age 70 years, 7 months, 21 days.

" Abijah Slawson; Jan. 6, 1855-Oct. 21, 1918.

" Clara Slawson; --------

" Silas Slawson; June 23, 1848-Feb. 13, 1906.

" Silas Slawson; died Jan. 1, 1860-age 78 years.

" Clarissa, wife Silas; died Aug. 5, 1856-age 70 years.

" William, son Silas & Clarissa; died Dec. 21, 1837-
age 16 years, 6 months.

" Cornelia, dau. Silas & Clarissa; died Oct. 24, 1841-
age 14 years, 10 months, 5 days.

" Abraham Slawson; died July 23, 1825-age 40 years.

" Mercy Slawson; died Nov. 8, 1860-age 86yrs. 6mos. 23days.

" Abram Slawson; died May 10, 1829-age 92 years.

" Mary, wife Abram; died Sept. 3, 1826-age 87 years.

" Seeley Slawson; July 27, 1817-Jan. 5, 1882.

" Phebe Lent, wife Seeley Slawson; Apr. 6, 1818-Nov. 3, 1880.

" Mary C., dau. Seeley & Phebe; died Aug. 19, 1862-age 3yrs.

" Abbey Jane, wife Seeley; died Feb. 11, 1848-age 28yrs. 7mos

" Laura C., dau. Seeley & Abbey; died July 13, 1847-
age 6 months, 23 days.

" Martha Eva, dau. William & Mary; died March 24, 1863-
age 5 months, 15 days.

Meyrick, Caroline Meyrick; Jan. 8, 1811-Aug. 25, 1892.

" Margaret P. Meyrick; April 6, 1818-June 19, 1897.

Griffin, John Griffin; died Apr. 3, 1893-age 91yrs. 5mos. 15days.

" John Griffin; Jan. 10, 1863-May 20, 1897.

" Esther Griffin; ---------

Presb. Mahopac

Lounsbury,	Isaac Lounsbury; Dec.15,1815-Mar.16,1881.
"	Catherine S., wife Isaac; Mar.27,1815-May 30,1869.
Carpenter,	Caleb Carpenter; Mar.11,1811-Mar.1,1905.
"	Adelia Austin, wife Caleb Carpenter; Nov.20,1823-Oct.18,1898.
"	Robert, son Caleb & Adelia; Oct.2,1862-Sept.14,1883.
Austin,	Job C. Austin; died Jan.4,1862-age 83 years.
"	Hetty, wife Job; died Oct.1,1866-age 63 years.
"	Orpha J. dau. Job & Hetty; Apr.9,1840-July 17,1892.
"	Emma Odell, wife C.L.Austin; Aug.17,1845-Mar.14,1912.
"	J.Louise, dau.C.L.& E.; Aug.21,1873-Sept.26,1910.
Knueppel,	Mary Jane, wife Henry; July 30,1857-Oct.4,1911.
Tompkins,	Nathaniel Tompkins; Feb.11,1864-Dec.22,1911.
Pinckney,	Ira Pinckney; July 14,1792-July 9,1872.
"	Mary Anderson, wife Ira Pinckney; Dec.12,1801-Nov.7,1861.
"	Susan, dau. Ira & Mary; May 23,1832-Jan.21,1909.
Ferguson,	Thomas Ferguson; Feb.26,1838-Nov.22,1883.
"	Mary L. Kirkham, wife Thomas Ferguson; March 12,1847-November 26,1901.
Stuchfield,	Sells B. Stuchfield; July 4,1841- --------
"	Annie L. Austin, wife Sells B. Stuchfield; dau. Job C. & Hetty Austin; July 4,1843-March 24,1897.
"	Thomas Stuchfield; Junior; Feb.15,1837-Oct.17,1862.
"	Thomas Stuchfield; Jan.6,1809-Mar.11,1881.
"	Susan Badeau, wife Thomas Stuchfield; Apr.18,1815-Dec.30,1881.
"	Margaret A. Stuchfield; Nov.13,1820-Dec.25,1879.
"	Mary E. Stuchfield; Nov.26,1849-Aug.29,1850.

Presb. Mahopac

- **Dean,** Amzi L. Dean; Sept. 5, 1811 - Oct. 4, 1876.
- " Catherine, wife Amzi; Dec. 20, 1819 - Jan. 23, 1894.
- " Adrian H. Dean; --------
- " Flora Wright, wife Adrian Dean; Nov. 28, 1854 - Dec. 28, 1892.
- " William A., son Amzi & Catherine; Jan. 19, 1854 - Aug. 12, 1917.
- " Laura Jane, dau. Amzi & Catherine; died Feb. 19, 1844 - age 1 year, 9 months, 5 days.
- **Wright,** Joseph Sackett Wright; Mar. 9, 1817 - May 22, 1887.
- " Almira Waters, wife Joseph Wright; June 4, 1826 - Jan. 2, 1894
- " Josie, dau. Joseph & Almira; 13 months.
- " Edgar Wright; June 27, 1846 - May 22, 1897.
- " William H. Wright; June 16, 1853 - Feb. 22, 1919.
- " Annie S., wife William H.; Dec. 29, 1859 - June 14, 1888.
- **Hoag,** Isabel Wright, wife Seeley T. Hoag; Oct. 13, 1850 - Mar. 28, 1890.
- **Badeau,** John Henry Badeau; Feb. 29, 1808 - Nov. 8, 1893.
- " Cordelia R. wife John H. Badeau; Mar. 13, 1821 - May 2, 1899.
- **Rogers,** Edgar H. Rogers; May 17, 1864 - --------
- " Adeline Badeau, wife Edgar Rogers; Dec. 17, 1868 - -------
- " Sallie J., dau. Edgar & Adeline; Dec. 8, 1889 - ----
- " Gilbert Edgar, son Edgar & Adeline; died June 6, 1898 - age 37 years.
- " Adeline, dau. Edgar & Adeline; died Jan. 13, 1913 - buried at San Rafael, Calif.
- **Hadden,** William Hadden; died Aug. 10, 1871 - age 52 years.
- " Elizabeth, wife William; died Oct. 16, 1861 - age 42yrs. 3mos.
- " Alonzo W. Hadden; July 26, 1839 - Apr. 16, 1916.
- " Fannie A. Hazen, wife Alonzo W. Hadden; Sept. 25, 1843 - Feb. 14, 1920.

Presb. Mahopac

Fisher, James Fisher; Apr. 18, 1810 - Oct. 31, 1902.

" Almira Barmore, wife James Fisher;
Oct. 22, 1816 - May 17, 1896.

" Daniel O. Fisher; 1839 - 1903.

" Sarah Fisher; 1838 - 1916.

" Benjamin Fisher; 1872 - 1909.

" Henry C. Fisher; May 16, 1849 - Oct. 18, 1901.

" Benjamin Fisher; Nov. 13, 1836 - June 9, 1908.

" Louisa Williams, wife Benjamin Fisher;
May 7, 1839 - May 28, 1896.

" Benjamin Fisher; died Mar. 23, 1863 - age 82 years.

" Charlotte, wife Benjamin; died May 16, 1825 - age 40 years.

" Emily, dau. James & Almira; died July 27, 1865 -
age 18 years, 9 months, 8 days.

" William, son James & Almira; died May 20, 1831 - age 6 mos.

" Henrietta, dau. Daniel & Sarah; died Mar. 19, 1871 -
age 9 years, 6 months, 18 days.

" Joshua Fisher; July 1, 1835 - ------

" Clarissa, wife Joshua; Feb. 15, 1837 - Aug. 1, 1913.

" Emma Fisher; died Apr. 28, 1868 - age 1 year, 6 months.

" Libbie Fisher; died Oct. 2, 1882 - age 20 yrs. 3 mos. 26 days.

Foster, Rev. Joseph C. Foster; Interred at Carmel 1860.

" Hannah H., wife Rev. Joseph C.; 1823 - 1891.

Gridley, Christian Gridley; 1839 - 1915.

" Mary, wife Christian; 1835 - 1915.

Carratt, Henry M. Carrett; 1865 - 1912.

Sutton, John W. Sutton; "Co. M. 6th. Regt. N.Y. H.A."
Aug. 30, 1832 - Apr. 16, 1914.

Fisher, Anna May, dau. Henry & Jennie; died Sept. 23, 1884 -
age 2 years, 4 months, 16 days.

Presb. Mahopac

Cornell, Ira J. Cornell; May 30, 1874 - March 29, 1905.

Haight, George W. Haight; died Apr. 26, 1878 - age 44yrs. 1mon. 12da

Pierce, William H. Pierce; Dec. 8, 1813 - Mar. 6, 1863.

" Isaac B. Pierce; Apr. 29, 1816 - May 24, 1903.

" Mary J. Hazelton, wife Isaac B. Pierce;
    Feb. 4, 1820 - May 12, 1900.

Curry, Robert S. Curry; Aug. 30, 1802 - Jan. 14, 1879.

" Almira C. Abbott, wife Robert S. Curry;
    June 11, 1797 - Aug. 26, 1874.

" Also an infant daughter; ---

" Antha A. Curry; Jan. 4, 1833 - May 12, 1905.

" Almira C. Curry; Sept. 21, 1834 - Oct. 22, 1908.

Boyd, Stillman Boyd; Jan. 27, 1802 - Apr. 7, 1890.

" Mary E. Smith, wife Stillman Boyd;
    January 4, 1804 - June 27, 1884.

" Mary, dau. Stillman & Mary; Aug. 15, 1830 - Sept. 10, 1894.

" Ebenezer Boyd; "A Soldier of the Revolution."
    died Mar. 27, 1848 - age 82yrs. 8mos.

" Louisa, wife Ebenezer; died May 12, 1841 - age 81yrs. 6mos.

" Our little boys; -----

Rankine, Henry Rankine; Dec. 6, 1815 - Jan. 28, 1894.

" Mary Rankine; -------

" Ann Rankine; --------

Beyea, Ira Beyea; died Nov. 30, 1888 - age 79 years, 7 months.

" Eunice P., wife Ira; died Aug. 13, 1890 - age 73yrs. 10mos.

" Lewis Beyea; 1878 - ------

" M. Anna Frost, wife Lewis Beyea; 1878 - 1907.

Carman, Hannah, wife Doct. Aaron Carman; died Feb. 28, 1856 -
    age 59 years, 2 months, 8 days.

Presb. Mahopac

Kennard, James F. Kennard; 1832-1918.
" Arity P. Beyea, wife James F. Kennard; 1838-1904.
" Ira B. Kennard; 1863-1904.
Jenkin, Elijah Jenkin; Mar.23,1840-Nov.23,1882.
" Alice James, wife Elijah Jenkin;
          Aug.21,1839-Dec.29,1900.
" Elijah Jenkin, Jr.; Mar.20,1867-Apr.16,1896.

The Hill Plot

On German Flat Road

between Mahopac Falls & Mahopac Mines

Putnam County, N.Y.

Hill Plot

Curry, Leonard Curry; July 19,1843-Mar.22,1905.

" Tamelia Hill, wife Leonard Curry;
   Apr.25,1845-Mar.17,1914.

Gregory, Horace Gregory; died Dec.9,1863-age 71 years, 8 months.

" Betsey, wife Horace; died Mar.31,1885-age 86yrs. 3mos.

Hill, William Hill; died August 1796-age 70 years.

" Bethiah, wife William; died August 1798-age 60 years.

" Noah Hill; died Jan.3,1830-age 75 years, 9 months, 6 days

" William Hill; Dec.14,1760-Nov.29,1851.

" Nancy, wife William; died June 12,1831-age 65 years.

" William Hill,Jr.; died Mar.30,1842-age 48 years, 8 months

" Allen B.Hill; June 4,1835-Jan.19,1894.

" William, son Allen B.& Hattie; Oct.7,1887-Apr.10,1888.

" Abraham Hill; died Mar.7,1886-age 74 years, 10 months.

" Tamar Hill; died Nov.3,1851-age 36 years, 3 days.

" Solomon Hill; Apr.9,1805-June 8,1887.

" Thomas Hill; June 16,1809-April 19,1878.

" Addison Hill; died June 5,1863-age 60 years, 9 days.

" Abraham Hill; died Mar.25,1813-age 38 years, 8 months.

" Deborah, wife Abraham; died Sept.6,1849-age 69 years.

" Isaac L.Hill; 1801-1886.

" Mary Gregory, wife Isaac Hill; 1823-1907.

" Elizabeth G., dau.Isaac & Mary G.; 1846-1904.

" Abraham L., son Isaac & Mary G.; d.June 27,1840-age 19mos.

" Cornelius Hill; died Nov.12,1815-age 51 years.

" Celia Celeste, dau.Isaac & Mary; died Dec.31,1854-
   age 3 years, 1 month, 7 days.

Hill Plot

Hill,   Clorinda, wife Charles S.; Mar.11,1840-Jan.5,1884.

Heroy, Phebe Mary, dau. Solomon & Margaret; died May 18,1843-
         age 26 years, 1 month, 22 days.

Travis, Daniel Travis; died Sept.13,1846-age 36 years.

Halstead Ground

North of Meads Corners

Putnam County, N.Y.

Index

Adams,	2.	Lewis,	11.
Austin,	7.	Light,	3, 9, 10.
Ayres,	1.	Lockwood,	2.
		Losee,	11.
Barrett,	2, 3, 7, 9, 10.		
Beach,	3.	McCoy,	11.
Beacon,	1.	McDonald,	5, 7.
Bennett,	4, 5, 8, 9, 10.	McDowell,	1.
Booth,	2.	Mead,	2, 4.
Brewer,	7.	Merritt,	6.
Cargain,	2.	Owen,	6.
Cargan,	7.		
Clauson,	2.	Parker,	7, 9.
Cole,	3.	Perry,	11.
Conklin,	8.	Post,	8, 9.
Crosier,	11.	Prout,	4.
		Purdy,	7.
Dakin,	7.		
Denike,	7.	Reed,	4.
Drew,	6.	Rickey,	2, 10.
		Ridgeway,	8, 9.
Ferris,	7.	Rogers,	7.
Foshay,	6, 11.	Russell,	3, 8.
Gilbert,	5, 12.	Sarlls,	6.
Griffin,	6.	Schreder,	10.
		Smalley,	3, 4, 6, 8, 10.
Halstead,	1.	Smith,	2, 3, 7.
Hazen,	11.	Sprague,	4, 11.
Henion,	1, 4, 5.	Stephens,	9.
Hobard,	7.	Stevens,	9.
Hopkins,	9.	Sutton,	2.
Horton,	3, 5, 11.		
Hults,	1.	Tompkins,	1, 5, 8.
Hunt,	2, 7, 9.	Townsend,	1, 3, 5, 9.
Hyatt,	9.		
		VanBenschoten,	5.
Kernathan,	1.		
Knapp,	5, 7, 10, 11.	White,	5, 12.
Knox,	3.	Williams,	1, 4, 5, 7.
Kopp,	7.	Wixon,	1, 4, 10.
		Wright,	4, 5, 7, 9.

Halstead

Halstead,	Benjamin Halstead; died May 6, 1899-age 80yrs. 2mos.
"	Nancy, wife Benjamin; died Aug.30,1875- age 57 years, 6 months, 15 days.
"	Sarah, dau.Benjamin & Nancy; died Aug.4,1863-age 8yrs.
"	Henry, son Benjamin & Nancy; d. Apr.21,1850-age 17mos.
"	John Halstead; died Dec.21,1879-age 89 years.
"	Betsey, wife John; died Sept.19,1877-age 77yrs. 11mos.
Wixon,	Edward Wixon; died Nov.12,1868-age 22 years.
Ayres,	Deborah Ayers; died April 6,1849-age 83 years.
Tompkins,	George Tompkins; died June 10,1888-age 28yrs. 2mos.
"	Archibald Tompkins; -------
"	Maria, wife Archibald; died Feb.21,1890-age 63yrs. 9mos
Townsend,	Luly M. Townsend; 1882-1897.
Kernathan,	Mary Beacon, wife Thomas Kernathan; died May 30,1898- age 55 years, 11 months, 5 days.
Beacon,	William Beacon; died Oct.26,1886-age 68 years, 5 months
"	Jane, wife William; died Apr.29,1890-age 73 years.
"	William H. Beacon; Sept.20,1856-Mar.24,1917.
"	Anna A., wife William H.; Dec.5,1857-Apr.29,1917.
Williams,	John P. Williams; Oct.4,1847-----
"	Caroline E. McDowell, wife John P. Williams; Sept.7,1850-Nov.9,1917.
Hults,	Ira M. Hults; July 6,1863-Dec.21,1911.
"	Jennie Williams, wife Ira M. Hults; -------
"	Nellie L., dau.Ira & Jennie; Oct.3,1890-Nov.15,1890.
"	Gertrude, dau.Ira & Jennie; Jan.12,1894-Feb.2,1894.
Wixon,	Anna Wixon; died Dec.7,1885-age 98 years.
Henion,	Elias Henion; died Oct.16,1883-age 76 years.

Halstead

Cargain,	Susan Cargain; died May 8,1918-------
"	Joseph Cargain; Jan.10,1838-Jan.27,1900.
"	Sarah J., wife Joseph; -------
Barrett,	Solomon Barrett; died May 1,1883-age 71yrs. 6mos. 22da.
"	Lydia, wife Solomon; died Aug.14,1906-age 83yrs. 6mos.
"	Elmer S.Barrett; died Nov.15,1896-age 34yrs. 11mos.
"	Dennis Barrett; June 23,1841-June 17,1906.
"	Adeline Sutton, wife Dennis Barrett; Sept.14,1839-Nov.16,1910.
Adams,	Stephen D.Adams; 1853- ----
"	Harriet A.Hunt, wife Stephen Adams; 1857-1876.
"	Hester E.Barrett, wife Stephen Adams; 1860- ----
Lockwood,	Theodore Lockwood; Jan.3,1845-Sept.24,1894.
"	Emma C.Smith, wife Sylvester Lockwood; Aug.11,1843-Sept.8,1884.
"	Jennie Lockwood; Sept.9,1875-Aug.7,1894.
Rickey,	Peter C.Rickey; died Nov.25,1881-age 60 years.
"	Catherine S., wife Peter C.; died Dec.9,1902-age 75yrs.
"	Judson K., son Peter & Catherine; Aug.26,1867-Sept.17,1876.
Booth,	Gracie G., dau.George H.& Effie; died Aug.10,1880- age 2 years, 6 months, 26 days.
"	Frances W., dau.George & Effie; d.Aug.10,1880-age 6mos.
Mead,	Lot Mead; died Oct.5,1888-age 87 years.
"	Minerva, wife Lot; died Oct.7,1909-age 84 years.
Clauson,	Deborah F.Mead, wife Elim Clauson; died Mar.22,1889-age 33 years.
"	Minerva, dau.Elim & Deborah; died July 25,1909-age 23yrs
Mead,	Samuel P. son Lot & Minerva; d.May 4,1918-age 55 years.
"	Tunis Mead; -------

Halstead

Russell, Harriet Russell; Dec.4,1828-Jan.4,1873.

"   Morris Russell; died May 2,1874-age 72 years.

"   Mahala, wife Morris; died July 2,1866-age 65yrs. 7mos.

Light,   Percis, wife Isaac; Jan.4,1832-Oct.30,1914.

Smith,   Peter Holland Smith; Nov.1,1842-July 14,1898.

"   Julia Frances, wife Peter H.; Feb.14,1866-May 2,1897.

"   Ida May, dau.Peter & Julia; May 24,1884-Mar.5,1903.

Barrett,   Solomon Barrett; Mar.3,1836-Dec.26,1909.

"   Sarah Knox, wife Solomon Barrett; Oct.16,1835-Mar.2,1903

"   Hannah D. Barrett; Aug.10,1871-May 15,1889.

"   Laborn E. Barrett; June 25,1875-Mar.1,1878.

Beach,   Byronette, wife Frank; May 8,1859-May 28,1902.

Cole,   Phebe, wife Norman; June 20,1820-Feb.14,1904.

"   Eland G., son Norman & Phebe; d.Aug.29,1853-age 1 year.

Horton,   William R., son Richard & Addelaide E. died Feb.27,1864-
                     age 3 years, 11 months, 6 days.

"   Margaret, dau.Richard & Adelaide; d1Aug.23,1872-age 3mo.

"   Ida, dau.Richard & Adelaide; died Sep.8,1875-age 7mos.

"   Arthur, son Richard & Adelaide; died Jan.18,1879-
                     age 1 year, 2 months, 15 days.

"   Joseph L., son Richard & Adelaide E.; died Feb.19,1881-
                     age 15 years, 8 months, 15 days.

Smalley,   Rev.James G. Smalley; Oct.13,1813-June 11,1903.

"   Elizabeth, wife Rev.James G.; Apr.21,1817-Jan.13,1898.

"   Newman Smalley; 1853-1899.

"   Flora, wife Newman; 1859-1896.

"   Edie, son Newman & Flora; 1883-1895.

Townsend, John J. Townsend; Mar.22,1837-July 10,1913.

"   Sarah Smalley, wife John J. Townsend;
                 Aug.28,1840-Apr.8,1905.

Halstead

Sprague,   Palmer Sprague; Sept.11,1865-

"   Sarah E.Williams, wife Palmer Sprague;
                    Oct.6,1866-Mar.29,1919.

"   Charlie, son Palmer & Sarah; died Feb.21,1899-
                    age 11 years, 3 months, 6 days.

Williams,   Garry Williams; Oct.8,1820-Aug.13,1910.

"   Louisa S., wife Garry; died June 30,1899-age 70 years.

"   Leonard J.Williams; Jan.31,1856-

"   Emily R.Mead, wife Leonard Williams;
                    June 14,1853-Oct.27,1918.

"   Emma May, dau.Leonard & Emily; May 31,1886-Sep.1,1894.

"   Sarah, wife Garry; died June 3,1862-age 39 years.

"   Mary J, wife Valentine; died Aug.2,1862-age 34yrs. 8mos

"   Isaac, son Valentine & Mary; d.May 2,1862-age 11 months

Prout,   Anna L.Williams, wife Edward Prout; died Oct.31,1881-
                    age 30 years, 11 months.

Smalley,   Herbert L.Smalley; July 26,1871-

"   Clara E.Reed, wife Herbert L.Smalley;
                    Feb.6,1879-Apr.10,1903.

"   Leon R., son H.L.& Fanny; Dec.14,1910-May 23,1915.

"   Alice E., dau.James K.& Helen G.; died Dec.11,1878-
                    age 11 months, 2 days.

"   George M.Smalley; died Oct.13,1889-age 47yrs. 5mos.

"   Emeline, wife George M.; died Feb.9,1886-age 43yrs. 7mos

"   James Smalley; died Jan.7,1868-age 84 years, 3 months.

"   Phebe, wife James; died Apr.29,1880-age 67yrs. 2mos.

Wixon,   Phebe Wright, dau.Robert & Nancy; died Jan.2,1895-
                    age 87 years, 9 months, 23 days.

"   Ellen Bennett, wife John Wixon; 1849-1879.

Hanion,   John Hanion; died Feb.2,1848-age 86 years.

"   Mercy, wife John; died Mar.15,1839-age 56yrs. 4mos,15da

Halstead

VanBenschoten,	Catherine VanBenschoten; Oct.15,1825-Jan.2,1887.
Horton,	George F.Horton; 1848-
"	Addie VanBenschoten, wife George F.Horton; 1850-
"	Frederic D., son George & Addie; 1875-1899.
Bennett,	John Bennett; Mar.17,1798-Jan.21,1899.
"	Amelia, wife John; died May 2,1861-age 38 years.
"	Infant son John & Amelia; age 2 weeks.
"	Caroline, dau.John & Amelia; d.Mar,8,1860-age 8mos.
"	George Bennett; died Jan.15,1858-age 21 years.
"	James Bennett; -------
"	Eliza J.Williams, wife James Bennett; 1825-1902.
Gilbert,	Moses J.Gilbert; Apr.27,1857-Mar.19,1905.
"	Hattie VanBenschoten, wife Moses J.Gilbert; Feb.26,1858-
Knapp,	Dedrick H.Knapp;
"	Amelia Townsend, wife Dedrick Knapp; died May 22,1885 age 28 years, 2 months.
"	Ida J.White, wife Dedrick Knapp; Jan.30,1864-Jan.1,1912.
"	Holmes B.Knapp; Jan.7,1829-Dec.19,1863.
"	Uretta B.Wright, wife Holmes B.Knapp; Mar.26,1826-Dec.11,1886.
"	Geneva B., dau.Robert & Mallisa B.; died June 15,1877-age 7 months.
Tompkins,	Mary Tompkins; Jan.26,1820-Oct.3,1901.
Gilbert,	Daniel Gilbert; Feb.24,1820-Dec.3,1882.
"	Eliza, wife Daniel; Sept.2,1826-Dec.6,1897.
McDonald,	Lee McDonald; died May 27,1848-age 43yrs. 11mos.
"	Mary Hanion, wife Lee McDonald; died Jan.18,1879- age 73 years, 2 months, 9 days.
"	Jefferson McDonald; died Dec.27,1867-age 27 years.

Halstead

Sarlls,	Samuel Sarlls; died Apr.19,1869-age 72 years.
"	Annis, wife Samuel; died Jan.29,1871-age 74 years.
Drew,	Annis B., dau.Sarlls & Deborah A.; died Oct.29,1873-age 17 years, 7 months, 6 days.
"	Thomas E., son Sarlls & Fayette; died Mar.12,1869-age 3 years, 2 months, 28 days.
"	Josie B., dau.Sarlls & Fayette; died Mar.20,1869-age 1 year, 6 months, 19 days.
"	Lilly, dau.Sarlls & Fayette; d.Sept.16,1873-age 3mos.
Foshay,	Hattie L. dau.John W.& Matilda; died Mar.16,1875-age 4 years, 3 months, 2 days.
"	Lines Foshay; died Sept.23,1849-age 44 years, 5 months.
"	Ruhamy, wife Lines; died Feb.16,1886-age 80 years.
"	Andrew J.Foshay; Jan.21,1830-May 1,1900.
"	Emeline Griffin, wife Andrew Foshay; May 21,1829-april 9,1925.
"	John G., son Andrew & Emeline; died Apr.22,1863-age 1 year, 7 months, 22 days.
Merritt,	Ezekial Merritt; died Dec.12,1890-age 78 years, 5 months
"	Rebecca, wife Ezekial; died Sept.1,1875-age 11 mons.
"	Stephen H., son Ezekial & Rebecca; d.Aug.19,1863-26yrs.
"	Ann, dau.Ezekial & Rebecca; died Feb.22,1860-age 20 years, 3 months, 7 days.
"	George D., born Nov.19,1834-died July 31,1906.
Foshay,	James A.Foshay; Nov.25,1856-Jan.14,1914.
"	Andrew J.Foshay; Dec.19,1865-Feb.3,1892.
"	Grace, dau.Edward H.& Rosetta S.; July 16,1890-Sept.18,1891.
Smalley,	Joshua Smalley; Nov.6,1823-Aug.15,1899.
"	Caroline, wife Joshua; July 2,1829-Mar.19,1904.
Owen,	Lavinia, dau.Joseph & Fanny; died Feb.22,1866-age 10mos

Halstead

Barrett,	Truman Barrett; died Aug.10,1906-age 61yrs. 4mos.
"	Ella McDonald, wife Truman R.Barrett; died Mar.29,1905-age 57 years, 8 months, 29 days.
"	Charlesett, dau.Truman & Ella; died Feb.28,1876-age 6 years, 2 months, 28 days.
Denike,	Charles T.Denike; Feb.26,1865-Nov.24,1914.
Williams,	Abel Williams; 1834-1894.
"	Sarah J.Knapp, wife Abel Williams; 1838-
"	Jemima, wife Abram; died Sept.2,1911-age 52 years.
"	David S.Williams; died May 3,1880-age 35 years, 7 months
"	Warren G., son David & Kate; died Jan.30,1874-age 5da.
Parker,	Phebe Wright, wife A.T.Parker; Mar.19,1863-Dec.28,1902.
Wright,	Mary E.McDonald, wife Robert D.Wright; Aug.6,1844-Apr.27,1913.
Purdy,	Ethel J.Purdy; July 11,1889-Sept.6,1894.
"	Leslie S.Purdy; Feb.18,1891-Sept.3,1894.
Dakin,	James J.Dakin; Sheriff of Putnam County; died July 28,1883-age 34yrs. 1mon.
Austin,	Elizabeth Shaw, wife ---- May 7,1825-Feb.6,1902.
Kopp,	Charles Kopp; Dec.19,1850-
"	Ellen E.Hobard, wife Charles Kopp; Feb.22,1853-Oct.27,1911.
Ferris,	Byron J.Ferris; May 22,1863-Mar.12,1901.
"	Amanda Hunt, wife Byron Ferris;
Cargan,	Noah Cargan; died June 25,1891-------
Smith,	Joseph A., son Orlando & Sarah E.; April 28,1878-August 28,1883.
Brewer	Jeremiah Brewer; Oct.29,1827-June 21,1911.
"	Rachel Barrett, wife Jeremiah Brewer; Oct.28,1829-Mar.31,1899.
Rogers,	Jacob A.Rogers; died Jan.31,1879-age 40 years.

Halstead

Bennett, Edward Bennett; Apr.9,1851-Feb.21,1904.

" Roland S., son Edward & Georgetta;
Sept.3,1883-Feb.26,1901.

" Edith K., dau.Edward & Georgetta;
age 2 years, 3 months, 18 days.

" James D.Bennett; Sept.24,1822-Feb.20,1903.

" Jane A., wife James D.; Aug.25,1827-Nov.2,1896.

" Joseph Bennett; Dec.28,1849-Mar.4,1892.

" Mary J.Smalley, wife Joseph Bennett;
Aug.27,1852-May 7,1912.

" Frank Bennett; Aug.1,1891-Sept.9,1891.

" Charles W.Bennett; died June 16,1880-age 25 years.

" Sarah, wife Jacob D.; Apr.9,1855-Feb.22,1904.

" Ella, dau.Jacob & Sarah; June 20,1893-Dec.7,1911.

" David Bennett; Jan.20,1825-Oct.12,1887.

" Amanda Tompkins, wife David Bennett;
June 3,1827-Sept.2,1918.

" Bryant, son J.A.& Fannie; died Feb.2,1877-age 2yrs. 2mos

Ridgeway, Chester S., son Wilbur & Sarah; age 1 year.

" Olive E., dau.Wilbur & Sarah; Dec.5,1884-Apr.24,1898.

Post, Abram S.Post; died June 2,1884-age 69 years, 4 months.

" Emily A.Bennett, wife Lafayette Post; died Jan.22,1875-
age 25 years, 8 months, 19 days.

" Anna A., dau.Lafayette & Emily; died Feb.3,1867-
age 17 years, 3 months, 21 days.

Smalley, Isaac D.Smalley;

" Iva O.Conklin, wife Isaac Smalley;
March 29,1880-May 26,1909.

" Katurah Russell, wife Erastus Smalley;
Mar.15,1834-Mar.11,1919.

" Esther K., dau.Erastus & Katurah;
June 11,1861-Dec.19,1918.

Halstead

Townsend,	Lewis B. Townsend; Aug. 22, 1855-Mar. 31, 1911.
"	Jennie D. Hunt, wife Lewis Townsend; Nov. 3, 1859-----
Hyatt,	Ruhamy, wife James D.; Sept. 25, 1863-Mar. 14, 1895.
Ridgeway,	Wilbur A. Ridgeway; Nov. 26, 1863-Jan. 26, 1888.
"	Edward Ridgeway; 1822-1876.
"	Mary J. Post, wife Edward Ridgeway; 1833-1882.
Bennett,	William H. Bennett; died Feb. 28, 1896-age 70 years.
"	Susan Barrett, wife William Bennett; died April 25, 1892-age 64 years.
Wright,	Louis M. Wright; Sept. 8, 1865-Apr. 12, 1901.
Stephens,	David Stephens; died May 21, 1874-age 73 years, 2 months
"	Mary, wife David; died May 10, 1890-age 81yrs. 11mos.
Stevens,	Martin B. Stevens; Feb. 20, 1839-June 5, 1918.
"	Estella, dau. Martin & Sarah; Jan. 22, 1869-Sept. 13, 1891.
"	S. Bertha, dau. Martin & Sarah; July 24, 1870-Apr. 14, 1892
Hopkins,	Jemima, wife Lewis; died Jan. 1, 1872-age 73 years.
Light,	Mary H., wife Harvey; died Apr. 19, 1879-age 32yrs. 7mos.
"	Infant child; April 9, 1870-----
"	Night Light; died April 15, 1854-age 39 years.
"	Isaac Light; died May 13, 1884-age 41 years.
	Henry Light; died May 18, 1874-age 65yrs. 10mos. 21days.
"	Susan J., wife Henry; died Mar. 31, 1887-age 68yrs. 11da.
"	Charles H. son Henry & Susan; died Mar. 16, 1858- age 3 years, 9 months, 8 days.
"	Phebe J., dau. Henry & Susan; died June 1844-age 3mos.
"	Infant born 1848-----
Parker,	Sarah J., wife Isaac W.; died Apr. 3, 1886-age 36yrs. 6mos
"	Elmer F., son Isaac & Sarah; Jan. 21, 1868-June 9, 1891.

Halstead

Barrett,	Sarah E., dau. Samuel H. & Jennie; died Sept.8,1853- age 10 years, 5 months, 12 days.
"	Norman, son Samuel & Jennie; died Mar.31,1838-age 3yrs.
Knapp,	Angeline Barrett, wife Enoch Knapp; died Mar.10,1895- age 61 years, 3 months, 11 days.
Barrett,	Samuel H.Barrett; died Sept.16,1842-age 37yrs. 7mos.
"	Reuben R.Barrett; died Aug.17,1828-age 65yrs. 9mos.
"	Elizabeth, wife Reuben; died Apr.10,1853-age 83yrs. 5mo
"	Newman L.Barrett; Aug.5,1832-June 27,1892.
"	Adelia G., wife Newman; died July 19,1904-----
"	Samuel T.Barrett; died Oct.20,1879-age 59yrs. 7mos.
"	Arvilla C., wife Samuel; died Jan.5,1895-age 71yrs. 9mos
"	Smith T.Barrett; May 8,1844-Jan.1,1888.
Rickey,	Charles G.Rickey;
"	Estella G.Barrett, wife Charles G.Rickey;
Bennett,	Isaac Bennett; died Nov.11,1878-age 76 years.
"	Jemima, wife Isaac; died Feb.5,1889-age 81yrs. 1mon.
Smalley,	Isaac Smalley; 1836-1889.
"	Phebe A.Light, wife Isaac Smalley; 1844-
Wixon,	Elnathan Wixon; 1868-
"	Annie A.Smalley, wife Elnathan Wixon; 1869-
Schreder,	William S.Schreder; "5th.N.Y. Duryeas Zouaves" died July 3,1866-age 47 years.
"	Abby J., wife William S.; died Nov.21,1868- age 26 years, 11 months, 22 days.
"	Frederick J., son William & Abby; d.July 1,1868-8mos.
"	Infant son William & Abby; died Apr.21,1866-age 15days.
Light,	Henry C.Light; died July 1,1889-age 80 years, 3 months
"	William H., son Henry & Sarah; died Mar.30,1845-age 2mos

Halstead

Sprague, Rev. Samuel Sprague; Apr.10,1821-Feb.27,1892.

" Cordelia Knapp, wife Rev. Samuel Sprague;
Aug.7,1839-Apr.26,1893.

" Albert W. Sprague; June 23,1870-June 2,1890.

Lewis, Alosia M. Sprague, wife Freman Lewis;
Sept.16,1866-Aug.28,1887.

Losee, Abraham W. Losee; died Dec.8,1854-age 29 years.

" Area Losee; died Oct.8,1864-age 71 years, 5 months.

" Eliza Perry, wife Area Losee; died Dec.10,1881-age 80yrs.

Foshay, David Foshay; died Mar.18,1853-age 53yrs. 4mos. 5days.

" Margaret Horton, wife David Foshay; died Aug.16,1876-
age 80 years, 2 months.

" John Foshay; died Oct.24,1850-age 73 years.

" Esther, wife John; died Mar.5,1850-age 74 years, 8 months

Perry, Demmon R. Perry; died Sept.26,1857-age 45 years, 2 months.

" Jane, wife Demmon R.; died May 1,1853-age 42yrs. 5mos.

" Joseph, son Demmon & Jane; died Mar.26,1846-age 1yr. 1mo.

" Briggs, son Demmon & Jane; died Feb.4,1844-age 8 months.

" Rev. Briggs Perry; died Nov.19,1879-age 72 years.

" Nancy McCoy, wife Rev. Briggs Perry; died Feb.12,1899-
age 80 years, 2 months, 4 days.

Crosier, John B. Crosier; died May 12,1883-age 78 years.

" Mary, wife John; died July 1,1890-age 79 years.

" Edna J., dau. John & Mary; Feb.26,1841-Feb.21,1919.

Hazen, Joshua Hazen; died Apr.17,1840-age 68 years, 4 months.

" Elizabeth, wife Joshua; died Mar.2,1838-age 66 years.

" Mary B., dau. Joshua & Elizabeth; died Nov.14,1833-age 19yr

Knapp, Israel Knapp; Aug.9,1826-June 13,1902.

" Ann M. Smalley, wife Israel Knapp; June 14,1826-

Halstead

White, Charles H. White; died Mar.27,1887-age 51 years, 7 months.

" Mary A., wife Charles; died Mar.7,1908-age 79yrs. 7mos.

Gilbert, Moses Gilbert; died Dec.18,1873-age 55 years, 11 months.

" Emily, wife Moses; died Nov.9,1908-age 78yrs. 10mos. 8da.

" Albert Gilbert; died Aug.22,1920-age 66yrs. 10mos. 8days.

" Cordelia F. White, wife Albert Gilbert; died Apr.19,1909-
age 49 years, 8 months, 5 days.

" Mamie, dau. Albert & Cordelia; died Jan.28,1880-age 4days

" Alice, dau. Albert & Cordelia; died Oct.14,1886-age 1mon.

" Leslie G., son Albert & Cordelia; died Sept.4,1887-
age 9 months, 2 days.

Methodist Ground
at Mekeels Corners,
Putnam County, N.Y.

Mekeels Corners

Barnes,   Mary, dau. Joseph & Ann; died March 16, 1830-
                    age 4 years, 2 months, 18 days.

Barrett, Gideon, son Sarah; died Oct. 25, 1878-age 23yrs. 2mos. 14da

Bell,   Charlotte, wife Peter; died Nov. 26, 1856-
                    age 58 years, 11 months, 9 days.

Bunnell, Samuel W., son Joel & Britania; died Apr. 29, 1844-
                    age 2 years, 5 months, 15 days.

"   Dugles, son Joel & Britania; died May 14, 1832-
                    age 4 years, 11 months, 17 days.

Denna,   Seney, wife Schofield; died Mar. 18, 1845-age 32 years.

"   Harriet, wife Schofield; died Feb. 24, 1856-
                    age 39 years, 3 months.

"   Elizabeth, wife William A.; died May 19, 1898-age 47yrs.

"   Hannah, dau. Peter & Catherine; died Apr. 16, 1838-
                    age 4 years, 6 months.

Denney,   John Denney; 1809-1840.

"   Esther T., wife John; died May 1826-age 24 years.

"   Mahala J. Denney; Feb. 25, 1810-Feb. 27, 1889.

"   Jacob Denney; died Dec. 3, 1851-age 72yrs. 1mon. 3days.

Denny,   Schofield Denny; died Aug. 6, 1868-age 54yrs. 5mos. 11days

"   Richard Denny; died July 28, 1825-age 80 years.

Early,   Absalom Early; died May 23, 1825-age 97 years.

Ferris,   Elijah Ferris; died Aug. 25, 1842-age 26yrs. 6mos. 10days.

"   Joseph Ferris; died Dec. 3, 1851-age 77 years.

"   Mary, wife Joseph; died Jan. 22, 1850-age 72yrs. 4mos.

"   Perry Ferris; "Co. I. 6th. N.Y. H.A."
                    died Oct. 23, 1897-age 48 years.

Gilleo,   Senath Gilleo; died Apr. 10, 1829-age 30 years, 2 months.

Hults,   Elisha Hults; died Dec. 25, 1835-age 46 years, 5 months.

Mekeel Corners

Ireland,   Elizabeth, wife Abraham; died Oct.7,1826-age 76 years.

"   Ephriam, son Abraham & Martha; died Feb.7,1831-11wks.

"   Nathaniel, son Abraham & Martha;
           died May 19,1832-age 3 months.

"   Lydia Ann. dau.Abraham & Martha;
           died Nov.27,1836-age 17 months.

"   Mary Elizabeth, dau.James & Nancy; died Mar.15,1853-
           age 26 years, 7 months, 11 days.

Jaycox,   Eliza Jane Jaycox; diednJuly 25,1856-
           age 5 years, 4 months, 5 days.

"   George W., son William & Catherine; died Feb.28,1861-
           age 6 years, 2 months, 11 days.

"   Charles Henry Jaycox; died June 27,1848-
           age 2 years, 11 months, 16 days.

Lane,   Jemima, wife David; died Jan.19,1816-age 81 years.

Loveless,   Chloe, wife Harvey; died March 29,1836-
           age 24 years, 7 months, 21 days.

Mead,   Joshua Mead; died Aug.12,1820-age 77 years.

"   Phebe, wife Joshua; died July 14,1834-
           age 77 years, 7 months, 28 days.

"   Sarah, wife Jacob; died Jan.5,1843-age 32 years.

Meeker,   David Meeker; Jr. of Washington, Conn.;
           died Sept.23,1813-age 27 years.

Miller,   John Miller; died Dec.12,1841-age 60 years.

"   Susan Miller;   died Feb.15,1840-age 24 years.

"   John Miller,Jr.;   died Jan.7,1849-age 24 years.

"   Andrew Miller;   died Oct.24,1851-age 37 years.

Mosher,   Mary Jane, dau.Coles & Rachel;   died July 3,1831-
           age 3 years, 4 days.

"   Sally Ann, dau.Coles & Rachel; died May 29,1845-
           age 4 years, 1 month.

Nelson,   Mary Ann, dau.Justus & Mary; died Sept.24,1829-
           age 2 years, 2 months.

Mekeels Corners

Nelson,	James Nelson; died Nov.24,1815-age 73yrs. 5mos. 4days
"	Catherine, wife James; died Sept.3,1813-age 70 years.
Odell,	Gabriel Odell; died Feb.9,1835- age 70 years, 8 months, 25 days.
"	Jesse Odell; died Nov.22,1841-age 51 years.
Smith,	Benjamin Smith; died Aug.25,1841- age 74 years, 2 months, 18 days.
"	Hannah, wife Benjamin B.; died June 25,1827- age 29 years, 10 months, 10 days.
"	Phebe, wife William D.; died Nov.13,1803- age 34 years, 2 months, 3 days.
Sofield,	Clarkson, son Augustus & Phebe; died Sept.3,1834- age 1 year, 3 months. 17 days.
Townsend,	William, son Harrison & Harriet; died Sept.13,1838- age 5 months, 7 days.
"	Betsey, dau.James & Polly; died June 25,1828- age 1 year, 15 days.
Vredenburgh,	Clark H., son Daniel & Phebe; died Jan.12,1834- age 1 year, 7 months.
Wright,	Catherine Wright; died Apr.18,1839-age 25yrs. 4mos.
"	Milton H., son George & Catherine; died Feb.11,1838- age 4 years, 15 days.
"	Hannah Elizabeth, dau.George & Catherine; died Jan.7,1838-age 9 months, 13 days

Some old markers

in the Milltown grounds

Putnam County, N.Y.

Milltown

Baker,   Joseph Baker; died Apr.12,1847-age 81 years.

Baldwin, Thomas Baldwin; died Jan.28,1868-age 91 years.

"   Esther, wife Thomas; died Nov.3,1864-age 72 years.

Cole,   Heman H.Cole; died Aug.20,1864-age 40 years.

"   Timothy Cole; died 1866-age 82 years.

"   Eliza, wife Timothy; died 1867-age 76 years.

Couch,   Johnathan Couch; died July 4,1845-age 68 years.

"   Esther, wife Johnathan; died May 13,1819-age 43 years.

"   Betsey, wife Johnathan; died Nov.22,1861-age 73 years.

Crane,   Anson Crane; died June 7,1860-age 77 years.

"   Isaac Crane; died June 1,1853-age 72 years.

"   Mary, wife Isaac; died Mar.30,1868-age 84 years.

"   Johnathan Crane; died Sept.25,1878-age 92 years.

"   Orrin B.Crane; died Nov.7,1864-age 70 years.

"   Isaiah Crane; died Nov.28,1842-age 70 years.

"   Kezia, wife Isaiah; died Apr.20,1849-age 74 years.

"   Dr.Joseph Crane; died Aug.20,1825-age 76 years.

"   Anna, wife Dr.Joseph; died Apr.4,1807-age 48 years.

"   Johnathan Crane; died Aug.27,1834-age 88 years.

"   Bethia, wife Johnathan; died May 11,1839-age 88 years.

Crosby,   Sylvanus Crosby; died Apr.29,1814-age 45 years.

"   Stephen Crosby; died Apr.10,1851-age 73 years.

"   Lydia, wife Stephen; died July 3,1867-age 87 years.

"   Thomas Crosby; died Feb.16,1844-age 76 years.

"   Hannah, wife Thomas; died Feb.24,1855-age 83 years.

"   Col.Isaac Crosby; died Nov.22,1829-age 46 years.

Milltown

Crosby,	Solomon Crosby; died Mar.16,1816-age 66 years.
"	Elizabeth, wife Solomon; died May 3,1818-age 66 years.
"	Isaac Crosby; died Feb.17,1815-age 97 years.
"	Thankful, wife Isaac; died Feb.19,1815-age 87 years.
DeForest,	David L.DeForest; died Nov.26,1819-age 57 years.
"	Sarah, wife David; died July 28,1822-age 55 years.
"	Capt.Archibald DeForest; died May 13,1849-age 52 years
"	Sally, wife Capt.Archibald; died Aug.3,1867-age 68yrs.
Doolittle,	Phineas Doolittle; died July 25,1814-age 57 years.
"	Sarah, wife Phineas; died Dec.20,1817-age 55 years.
"	Capt.Ichabod Doolittle; died Dec.17,1806-age 76 years.
"	Deborah, wife Capt.Ichabod; died Apr.21,1820-age 93yrs.
Gage,	Elihu Gage; died June 6,1834-age 58 years.
"	Elizabeth, wife Elihu; died Apr.24,1838-age 64 years.
"	Sylvanus Gage; died Nov.13,1814-age 62 years.
"	Elizabeth, wife Sylvanus; died Mar.17,1814-age 62yrs.
Green,	Nathan Green; died Oct.22,1821-age 86 years.
Haines,	Joseph Haines; died Dec.17,1818-age 65 years.
Hall,	Samuel Hall; died Nov.13,1814-age 78 years.
"	Elizabeth, wife Samuel; died Mar.23,1832-age 82 years.
"	David Hall; died Nov.17,1850-age 75 years.
"	Lydia, wife David; died Mar.25,1856-age 93 years.
"	Morton Hall; died Feb.27,1818-age 75 years.
"	Patience, wife Morton; died Mar.11,1828-age 83 years.
Hine,	Charles Hine; died Dec.24,1846-age 88 years.
Hopkins,	Isaac Hopkins; died Mar.16,1853-age 71 years.

Milltown

Howes,	Moody Howes; died May 18,1827-age 75 years.
"	Esther, wife Moody; died Sept.26,1823-age 67 years.
Hoyt,	Asa Hoyt; died July 31,1831-age 60 years.
Hubbell,	Andrew Hubbell; died Dec.21,1843-age 63 years.
"	Sarah Hubbell; died Aug.1,1866-age 84 years.
Northrop,	James Northrop; died Oct.4,1855-age 73 years.
Penney,	David Penney; died Mar.23,1814-age 42 years.
Rice,	Edward Rice; died Nov.6,1826-age 61 years.
"	Lucy, wife Edward; died Mar.23,1826-age 55 years.
Richards,	Nathan Richards; died Feb.15,1839-age 62 years.
"	Cynthia, wife Nathan; died Apr.20,1848-age 72 years.
"	Ezra Richards; died Apr.25,1819-age 68 years.
Sandford,	Zalmond Sandford,Esq.; died Apr.30,1809-age 41 years.
Sears,	Samuel Sears; died Oct.10,1830-age 57 years.
"	Benjamin Sears; died Mar.12,1827-age 90 years.
"	Mary, wife Benjamin; died May 26,1814-age 78 years.
"	Seth Sears; died Apr.2,1809-age 73 years.
"	Capt.Knowles Sears; died June 10,1817-age 79 years.
Waring,	Peter Waring; died June 27,1849-age 67 years.
"	Esther, wife Peter; died July 16,1831-age 49 years.

Episcopal & Presbyterian

Church Grounds

Patterson, Putnam County, N.Y.

Patterson

Abbott,	Jesse Abbott; died Mar.7,1863-age 62 years.
"	Enoch Abbott; died Sept.10,1823-age 71 years.
"	Molly, wife Enoch; died Sept.18,1853-age 95 years.
Beach,	J.Sterling Beach; died 1874-age 73 years.
Benedict,	Comfort Benedict; died 1835-age 86 years.
"	Benjamin Benedict; died 1832-age 88 years.
"	Elizabeth, wife Benjamin; died 1839-age 80 years.
Birdsall,	Abraham Birdsall; died 1856-age 60 years.
Bowne,	Benjamin Bowne; died 1873-age 74 years.
Boyd,	Cyrus Boyd; died Jan.29,1879-age 64 years.
Brush,	Eli Brush; died 1835-age 79 years.
Burch,	Samuel Burch; died 1845-age 78 years.
"	Mary, wife Samuel; died 1841-age 67 years.
"	Samuel Burch; died 1853-age 68 years.
Bush,	Eli Bush; died Nov.11,1835-age 79 years.
Clinton,	Levi Clinton; died 1860-age 68 years.
"	Susannah, wife Levi; died 1865-age 69 years.
Coe,	Aaron Coe; died 1812-age 87 years.
"	Ruth A., wife Aaron; died 1836-age 78 years.
"	Austin B.Coe; died Jan.26,1836-age 52 years.
"	Susan, wife Austin; died Mar.14,1870-age 75 years.
Cook,	Eunice, wife Daniel; died 1830-age 61 years.
Cornwall,	Samuel Cornwall; died July 17,1801-age 42 years.
"	Martha, wife Samuel; died Feb.26,1846-age 81 years.
Couch,	Hezekiah Couch; died 1864-age 74 years.
Cowl,	William Cowl; died 1852-age 70 years.
"	Lydia, wife William; died 1864-age 70 years.

Patterson

Cowl,	Benjamin Cowl; died 1851-age 68 years.
"	Elizabeth, wife Benjamin; died 1843-age 71 years.
Dean,	Elijah Dean; died 1836-age 80 years.
"	Ann, wife Elijah; died 1855-age 93 years.
Delavan,	Dr.James Delavan; died Nov.10,1823-age 57 years.
"	Mercy, wife Dr.James; died Dec.18,1857-age 91 years.
"	Nathaniel Delavan; died Aug.9,1798-age 52 years.
"	Electa H.Delavan; died Apr.27,1877-age 82 years.
"	Timothy Delavan; died Jan.19,1813-age 71 years.
"	David C.Delavan; died 1883-age 81 years.
Eastwood,	Elkanah Eastwood; age 75 years.
Ellsworth,	Alfred Ellsworth; died 1879-age 72 years.
Ferguson,	Alson Ferguson; died 1879-age 83 years.
Fleming,	Thomas Fleming; died Oct.22,1792-age 47 years.
"	Helen, wife Thomas; died Oct.11,1830-age 83 years.
Fletcher,	Dr.Ebenezer Fletcher; died 1852-age 72 years.
"	Mary, wife Dr.Ebenezer; died 1851-age 74 years.
Frase,	Andrew Frase; died Jan.7,1835-age 85 years.
"	Grace A., wife Andrew; died Nov.14,1847-age 72 years.
Gibson,	Thomas Gibson; died 1858-age 93 years.
"	Margaret, wife Thomas; ------ age 88 years.
Grant,	James Grant; died Apr.25,1796-age 69 years.
"	Christina, wife James; died May 4,1838-age 76 years.
"	Robert Grant; died Apr.27,1830-age 40 years.
Haight,	Elizabeth Haight; died Jan.25,1848-age 68 years.
Haines,	Daniel Haines; died 1854-age 84 years.
"	Ada, wife Daniel; died 1857-age 69 years.

Patterson

Hayt,	John Hayt; died July 18,1835-age 75 years.
"	Elizabeth, wife John; died Oct.6,1845-age 73 years.
"	Thankful Hayt; died 1881-age 86 years.
"	David Hayt; died Apr.2,1849-age 53 years.
"	Mary Hayt; died Apr.27,1849-age 53 years.
"	Stephen Hayt; died Sept.17,1834-age 75 years.
"	Hannah, wife Stephen; died Jan.23,1843-age 80 years.
"	Samuel Hayt; died July 30,1850-age 84 years.
"	Sarah, wife Samuel; died Jan.2,1829-age 59 years.
"	Rebecca, wife Samuel; died Apr.18,1843-age 61 years.
"	Elizabeth Hayt; died Sept.22,1835-age 96 years.
"	Heman Hayt; died Feb.11,1852-age 93 years.
"	Sarah Hayt; died Sept.3,1852-age 56 years.
Hoag,	Asa Hoag; died Aug.10,1828-age 63 years.
Holmes,	John Holmes; died 1839-age 86 years.
"	Catherine, wife John; died 1840-age 90 years.
"	John Holmes, Jr.; died 1862-age 79 years.
"	Rachel Holmes; died 1862-age 70 years.
Hurlburt,	Sarah, wife Stephen; died 1797-age 43 years.
Jennings,	John Jennings; died 1796-age 80 years.
"	Ezra Jennings; died 1802-age 56 years.
"	John Jennings; died 1869-age 86 years.
Kidd,	Capt.Alexander Kidd; died 1806-age 78 years.
"	Sophia, wife Capt.Alexander; died 1802-age 70 years.
Lawrence,	John B.Lawrence; died 1809-age 26 years.
"	David H.Lawrence; died 1872-age 68 years.
"	---------

Patterson

Ludington,	Henry Ludington; died 1817-age 78 years.
"	Abigail, wife Henry; died 1825-age 80 years.
"	Derick Ludington; died 1840-age 69 years.
McLean,	John McLean; died 1819-age 90 years.
"	Margaret, wife John; died 1816-age 77 years.
"	Lockland McLean; died 1850-age 76 years.
Merritt,	Joseph Merritt; died 1851-age 68 years.
"	Esther, wife Joseph; died 1879-age 80 years.
Mitchell,	Ruth, wife Thomas; died 1853-age 35 years.
Mooney,	Rhoda Mooney; died Sept.1862-age 67 years.
Morrison,	Violet Morrison; died 1812-age 66 years.
Newman,	Nathaniel Newman; died 1794-age 71 years.
"	Martha, wife Nathaniel; died 1811-age 75 years.
Nickerson,	Albert Nickerson; died 1852-age 54 years.
Ogden,	Sibbell Edward Ogden; died 1839-age 77 years.
Osborn,	Abner Osborn; died 1811-age 82 years.
"	Rebbecca, wife Abner; died 1804-age 64 years.
Palmer,	Nathan Palmer; died 1828-age 78 years.
"	Deborah, wife Nathan; died 1829-age 78 years.
"	Ebenezer Palmer; died 1813-age 70 years.
"	Elizabeth, wife Ebenezer; died ---- age 104yrs. 7mos.
Patrick,	Lewis Patrick; died 1871-age 72 years.
Patterson,	Matthew Patterson; died Oct.9,1799-age 23 years.
"	Matthew C.G.Patterson; died Nov.23,1809-age 18 years.
"	John Patterson; died Nov.21,1821-age 58 years.
"	Matthew Patterson; died 1817-age 85 years.
"	Elizabeth, wife Alexander K.; died 1815-age 40 years.

Patterson

Peet,	Stiles Peet; died 1832-age 68 years.
"	Lydia, wife Stiles; died 1817-age 51 years.
Pugsley,	Benjamin Pugsley; died 1864-age 80 years.
"	Polly, wife Benjamin; died 1843-age 56 years.
St.John,	William St.John; died ---- age 78 years.
Smith,	Horace Smith; died 1846-age 48 years.
Starr,	Abijah Starr; died 1839-age 95 years.
"	Mindwell Starr; died 1846-age 88 years.
"	Josiah Starr; died 1875-age 88 years.
Stebbins,	Samuel Stebbins; died 1828-age 66 years.
Stephens,	Samuel Stephens; died 1850-age 88 years.
Stone,	Darius Stone; died 1819-age 70 years.
"	Elijah Stone; died 1812-age 58 years.
"	Frederick Stone; died 1857-age 72 years.
Thorpe,	Abigail Thorpe; died Mar.8,1816-age 70 years.
Turner,	John Turner; died 1814-age 68 years.
"	Abigail, wife John; died 1836-age 83 years.
"	Edward Turner; died May 12,1872-age 82 years.
"	Edward Turner, Jr.; -------
Vail,	John N.Vail; died Dec.21,1816-age 31 years.
Warden,	Nathaniel Warden; died 1807-age 72 years.
"	Sarah, wife Nathaniel; died 1826-age 92 years.
"	Dr.Stephen Warden; died 1848-age 68 years.
Weed,	Justus Weed; died 1819-age 77 years.
"	Sarah, wife Justus; died 1831-age 86 years.
"	Ebenezer Weed; died 1845-age 68 years.
"	Sarah Weed; died 1864-age 71 years.

Two Plots
The Cole farm ground
located near Secords Corners

The Bolding plot on the
North side of Lake Mahopac.

Cole farm plot

Cole, Elisha Cole; died Feb.3,1826-age 83 years, 5 months.
" Joseph Cole; died Feb.9,1811-age 68 years.
" Rebeccah, wife Joseph; died Feb.15,1801-age 49 years.
" John Cole; died Feb.3,1822-age 39 years.
" George E. Cole; died Dec.1,1826-age 28yrs. 11mos. 11days.
" Infant George & Elizabeth; buried Oct.5,1822---
" George, son Nancy; died June 12,1827-age 2 months, 3 days.
" Susan, wife Charles G.; died Feb.9,1827-age 24yrs. 1mon.
" William E., son Charles & Susan; died July 21,1827-
    age 11 months, 21 days.

Bolding Plot

Bolding, Elisha Bolding; died Oct.19,1816-age 65yrs. 8mos. 12days
" Elizabeth, wife Elisha; died June 2,1831-age 76 years.
" Letitia, dau. Elisha & Elizabeth; died Oct.26,1787-
    age 1 year, 3 months, 10 days.
" J.B.; died April 24,1783-age 87 years.
Griffin, John Griffin; born 1788-died April 16,1855.
" Benjamin Griffin; died May 26,1825-age 78 years.
" Phebe, wife Benjamin; died Dec.11,1849-age 92 years.
Wright, E. Wright; died Nov.11,1827-age 45 years.

Crane Ground

near Secords Corners

Putnam County, N.Y.

Crane ground

Baldwin, Henry Baldwin; died Apr.19,1825-age 72 years.
- "   Nancy, wife Henry; died Mar.28,1812-age 53 years.
- "   Hannah Baldwin; died Feb.25,1827-age 30 years.
- "   Rachel, wife John; died Sept.17,1833-age 38yrs. 3mos.
- "   James Baldwin; died Sept.13,1858-age 70 years.
- "   Adah, wife James; died Sept.9,1855-age 68yrs. 4mos. 25days
- "   William W., son Sears & Catherine; January 21,1857-June 6,1858.
- "   Jane Baldwin; 1816-1888.
- "   Ancel C.Baldwin; died Nov.18,1850-age 38yrs. 9mos. 18days
- "   Ancel C.Baldwin; died Dec.26,1850-age 10 months, 4 days.
- "   Rachel Jane Baldwin; died Apr.17,1854-age 17yrs. 3mos.
- "   Daniel, son Isaac & Jeannet; died May 1,1823-age 3yrs. 5mo

Carpenter, Tamer Carpenter-Crane;

Crane, Elizabeth, dau.Clorinda; died Apr.8,1827-age 5 years.
- "   Benjamin Townsend Crane; Jan.24,1824-Mar.11,1901.
- "   Emma Augusta Washburn, wife Benjamin T.Crane; May 10,1837-Dec.21,1883.
- "   Laura, dau.Benjamin & Emma; d.Feb.20,1865-age 19 months.
- "   John, son Benj.& Emma; died Dec.9,1865-age 1 month.
- "   Roland, son Samuel B.& Gertrude T.; May 8,1903-
- "   Tamar, dau.Stephen & Sally; d.July 13,1799-age 17 months.
- "   Aninniant, son Samuel & Betsey; born & died Jan.30,1827.
- "   Infant Samuel & Betsey; born & died Dec.23,1824.
- "   Bessie, dau.Ira & Louisa; died Nov.10,1888-age 2yrs. 7mos.
- "   John J., son Ira & Hannah; died Mar.29,1825-age 11yrs.5mos
- "   John Crane; Nov.24,1742-June 9,1827.
- "   Tamar Carpenter, wife John Crane; Dec.1,1747-May 19,1823.

Crane Ground

Crane, Nathaniel Crane; died Sept.27,1855-age 78 years, 7 months.
" Sally Ann, wife Nathaniel; died May 1,1825-age 41 years.
" Lydia, wife Nathaniel; died Dec.25,1841-age 62 years.
" John A., son Nathaniel & Sally; died Sept.9,1801- age 4 years, 2 months, 4 days.
" Tamar A., dau.Nathaniel & Sally; died Dec.17,1825- age 23 years, 11 months.
" James T., son Nathaniel & Sally; d.Dec.14,1826-age 23yrs.
" Frederick, son Nathaniel & Sally; d.Dec.11,1826-age 19yrs.
" Nathaniel Morton Crane; Feb.23,1816-Dec.25,1891.
" Amelia P.Taber, wife Nathaniel M.Crane; Nov.6,1822-Aug.16,1897.
" Elijah Crane; died Apr.25,1856-age 54 years, 6 months.
" Noah H.Crane; died May 24,1836-age 50 years.
" Joseph Crane; died Dec.26,1835-age 70 years.
" Chloe, wife Joseph; died Mar.12,1836-age 69 years.
" Charles L., son Joseph & Chloe; died Apr.26,1808-age 4yrs.
" John Crane,Jr.; died June 1,1825-age 52 years.
" Hannah, wife John Jr.; died Aug.1,1853-age 76 years.
" Alson B.Crane; Dec.30,1810-Nov.7,1888.
" Jerusha, wife Alson B.; died Jan.20,1842-age 25yrs. 6mos.
" Ira S., son Alson & Jerusha; died May 27,1847- age 5 years, 5 months, 12 days.
" Azor B.Crane; May 25,1801-Oct.14,1864.
" Aurelia Doane, wife Azor Crane; Feb.21,1814-Oct.22,1859.
" Azor B.Crane, Jr.; May 15,1838-Sept.9,1841.
" George T., son Azor & Aurelia; Feb.28,1840-Mar.2,1841.
" George B., son Azor & Aurelia; Aug.3,1845-June 19,1848.
" Ira, son Azor & Aurelia; Aug.13,1834-Mar.12,1915.

Crane ground

Doane,   Aurelia Doane-Crane;

Fowler,   Adah Crane, wife Moses Fowler, Jr.; died Dec.10, 1854-
            age 86 years, 6 months, 4 days.

"   James G. Fowler; died Jan.21, 1861-age 25 years, 4 months.

"   Charlotte L., wife Ammon M.; died Oct.5, 1867-
            age 56 years, 9 months, 8 days.

Hutchings, Samuel Lewis Hutchings; died Jan.21, 1864-
            age 46 years, 4 months, 21 days.

"   Susan Amelia, wife Samuel; died July 27, 1858-age 38yrs.

"   Helen W., dau. Samuel & Susan; died Apr.17, 1851-age 7yrs.

"   A. Bleecker, son Samuel & Susan; died May 22, 1851-
            age 3 years, 4 months.

"   S. Lewis, son Samuel & Susan; died Dec.20, 1846-age 10mos.

Lee,   James H. Lee; died Nov.3, 1869-age 52 years, 7 months,

"   Mary, wife James; died March 24, 1869-age 54yrs. 5mos.

"   Maria Frances, dau. James & Mary; died Oct.6, 1858-
            age 6 years, 9 months, 2 days.

"   James B., son James & Mary; died Mar.27, 1858-
            age 3 years, 2 months, 11 days.

"   Catherine Ann, dau. James & Mary; died Oct.10, 1848-
            age 1 year, 6 months, 7 days.

"   Mary Agness, dau. James & Mary; died June 7, 1845-
            age 2 years, 4 months, 25 days.

"   Rachel, dau. James & Mary; 1859-1914.

Monk,   William Monk; died Mar.25, 1888-age 77 years.

"   Mary A., wife William; died Apr.20, 1871-age 64 years.

"   Stephen Monk; died Mar.15, 1850-age 56 years.

"   Clorinda C., dau. Stephen & Clorinda;
            died Dec.18, 1853-age 13 years.

"   Annis N., wife John; died Mar.17, 1843-
            age 26 years, 10 months, 15 days.

Newman,   Nancy, wife Elias; died Aug.31, 1835-age 30yrs. 3mos.

Crane ground

Newman,	John C., son Elias & Nancy; died Apr.4,1826-age 5mo. 5da
"	Infant Elias & Nancy; born & died Apr.27,1827.
Pinckney,	Caroline T., wife Pierce Pinckney, dau.N.& S.A.Crane; died Feb.16,1839-age 33 years.
"	Granvil, son Pierce & Caroline; died June 22,1841-age 3 months, 16 days.
"	Nathaniel, son Pierce & Caroline; died Aug.15,1842-age 8 years.
Pratt,	Emeline Crane, wife Reynolds Pratt; May 3,1807-April 1,1889.
Reed,	Lydia J., wife Lewis; died Oct.14,1845-age 30yrs. 4mos.
"	Samuel J., son Lewis & Lydia; died Sept.18,1863-age 18 years, 9 months, 28 days.
Storms,	George Woodward, son William & Josephine; died Apr.9,1862-age 1 year, 2 months.
Taber,	Amelia P.Taber-Crane;
Townsend,	Benjamin Townsend; died May 2,1838-age 79 years.
"	Anna, wife Benjamin; died Apr.1,1825-age 61 years.
Washburn,	Emma Augusta Washburn-Crane;

Burial Ground

Up on hill back of Church

at Tilly Foster

Putnam County, N.Y.

Old Church at
Tilley Foster, New York.

View opposite Old Church at
Tilley Foster, New York.

Church Ground
Tilly Foster, New York

Ellis,	Josiah F. Ellis; died Aug. 18, 1842 - age 75 years.
"	Elizabeth, wife Josiah F.; died Nov. 30, 1835 - age 65 years.
"	Jacob, son Josiah F. & Elizabeth; died Nov. 20, 1829 - age 34 years.
Gay,	Daniel Gay; died June 20, 1812 - age 63 years.
"	Sarah, wife Daniel; died Oct. 22, 1847 - age 93 years, 6 months, 22 days.
Hartwill,	Peter Hartwill; died Dec. 16, 1760 - age 48 years.
"	Mary, wife Peter; died July 15, 1758 - age 41 years.
Kelley,	Johnathan Kelley; died July 8, 1805 - age 44 years, 10 months, 10 days.
"	Grace, wife Johnathan; died Sept. 12, 1826 - age 64 years.
King,	Heman King; died Jan. 21, 1812 - age 85 years.
"	Elizabeth, wife Heman; died Aug. 30, 1811 - age 81 years.
"	Jedudinum King; died Aug. 6, 1789 - age 21 years.
Wright,	Joseph C. Wright; Mar. 3, 1846 - Jan. 23, 1872.

Many field stones as grave markers - and some carved by amateurs but illegible.

Fowler Ground

On the Schiber Farm

Near Tilly Foster

Putnam County, New York

Fowler Plot

Cole,   Esther, wife Laban; died Sept.10,1833-age 35yrs. 5mos.

Fowler, William Fowler; died Apr.12,1842-
                        age 81 years, 2 months, 28 days.

"   Esther, wife William; died Apr.16,1798-age 30 years.

"   Elizabeth, wife William; died May 12,1838-age 81 years.

"   Daniel Fowler; died Oct.15,1813-age 26 years.

"   Moses Fowler; died Sept.1,1821-age 92 years.

"   Elijah Fowler; died Dec.5,1825-age 19 years.

Strang, Jane, wife John; died June 7,1830-age 73 years.

"   Abigail, wife Seth; died Jan.25,1836-
                        age 46 years, 8 days.

Several common field stones.

Church ground
at Towners Corners
Putnam Co. N.Y.

Towners Corners

Baldwin,	Daniel Baldwin; died Jan.25,1874-age 90 years.
"	James Baldwin; died Sept.5,1827-age 67 years.
"	James Baldwin; died Apr.13,1865-age 71 years.
Brown,	Elisha Brown; died July 14,1854-age 91 years.
Crosby,	Abigail D.Crosby; died Sept.28,1869-age 80 years.
Dykman,	Elisha Dykman; died Aug.4,1871-age 75 years.
"	Peter Dykman; died May 16,1840-age 71 years.
"	Tanny, wife Peter; died Jan.8,1856-age 71 years.
"	Elisha Dykman; died May 20,1881-age 82 years.
"	Joseph Dykman;
"	Elizabeth, wife Joseph; died 1831-age 87 years.
"	Isaac Dykman; died Jan.16,1872-age 83 years.
Haines,	Edmund Haines; died June 28,1872-age 87 years.
Haviland,	Benjamin Haviland; died May 20,1882-age 70 years.
Howland,	Nathaniel Howland; died Jan.2,1840-age 82 years.
"	Margaret, wife Nathaniel; died Sept.24,1838-age 70 year
Kent,	Sarah Kent-Knapp;
"	Elihu Kent; died Sept.17,1807-age 58 years.
"	Abigail, wife Elihu; died May 21,1821-age 82 years
"	Peter S.Kent; died May 24,1857-age 81 years.
"	Margaret Kent; died June 4,1869-age 77 years.
"	Daniel Kent; died June 1,1860-age 77 years.
"	Sarah Kent; died Feb.9,1871-age 84 years.
"	Laura Kent; died Mar.11,1871-age 63 years.
"	Samuel Kent; died Oct.9,1875-age 64 years.
"	David Kent; died Apr.9,1870-age 77 years.

Towners

Knapp,	Hiram Knapp; died Dec.23,1871-age 63 years.
"	Sarah Kent, wife Hiram Knapp; died Mar.10,1879-age 74yr.
Lee,	Chapman Lee; 1788-1876.
"	Laura, wife Chapman; 1800-1869.
Mabie,	Joshua Mabie; died May 30,1854-age 84 years.
"	Elizabeth, wife Joshua; died May 7,1836-age 60 years.
"	Dr.Elisha G.Mabie; died Apr.19,1836-age 28 years.
"	Samuel Mabie; died Dec.13,1851-age 53 years.
"	Samuel Mabie; died Oct.14,1856-age 84 years.
"	Ruth, wife Samuel; died Nov.9,1868-age 84 years.
Robinson,	Moses C.Robinson; died June 8,1847-age 63 years.
Sunderlin,	John Sunderlin; died Aug.30,1817-age 45 years.
Towner,	James Towner; died Sept.14,1870-age 87 years.
"	Mary, wife James; died Sept.1,1849-age 65 years.
"	Samuel Towner; died Apr.1,1814-age 70 years.
"	Mary, wife Samuel; died Oct.8,1827-age 80 years.
"	John Towner; died Oct.9,1865-age 86 years.
"	Jane, wife John; died Apr.22,1852-age 68 years.
"	Samuel Towner; died Aug.29,1884-age 78 years.
Yale,	Benjamin Yale; died Oct.25,1854-age 71 years.

Cemetery

at Union Valley

Putnam County, N.Y.

South Of Lake Mahopac

Index

Adams,	1.	Gaibel,	8.
Agor,	2.	Ganong,	3, 4, 6, 7, 9, 10.
Angevine,	4.	Ganun,	5, 10.
Anderson,	14.	Ganung,	9, 10, 11, 13, 14, 15.
Archer,	6.	Gray,	7.
Austin,	11.	Gregory,	11, 13.
Bailey,	13, 14	Gumpert,	8.
Baker,	7.	Haines,	14.
Banker,	13, 15, 16.	Higgins,	3.
Barker,	3.	Hitt,	5, 11.
Barrett,	10.	Horton,	14.
Bates,	6.	Hudson,	9.
Benda,	14.	Hults,	9, 16.
Bennett,	12, 16.	Hyatt,	3.
Bittner,	9.	Inslee,	6.
Boker,	8.	Jelliff,	4.
Brady,	15.	Kenney,	6.
Braithwaite,	1.	Knapp,	4, 8.
Brewer,	9.	Kniffin,	5, 8.
Brien,	11.	Knox,	11.
Brundage,	8.	Laraway,	5.
Church,	15.	Lent,	8, 15.
Clark,	15.	Light,	14.
Coons,	9.	Lounsbury,	14.
Corsa,	4.	Matthews,	9.
Cowan,	14.	Mead,	8, 9, 12, 15.
Craft,	2.	Merrick,	15.
Croft,	14.	MCaull,	2.
Cullen,	12.	McCollum,	3, 7, 8.
Curry,	13, 16.	McKeel,	15.
Dayton,	12.	Odell,	5.
Deats,	4.	Ostrander,	1.
Delavan,	8, 11.	Palmer,	13, 15.
D'Orchimont,	1.	Phillips,	7.
Drew,	1.	Pinckney,	4.
Dunning,	15.	Potter,	14.
Dyke,	8.	Pottow,	1.
Ellis,	7.	Powers,	8.
Ferguson,	14.	Prendergast,	13.
Fisher,	1.	Purdy,	15.
Fosdick,	3.	Quick,	1, 5.
Fowler,	8, 12.	Ritchie,	12.
Frost,	16.	Romanowsky,	1.
Fuller,	12.	Roussin,	6.
		Rusky,	12.
		Ryder,	11.

Index

Scofield,	7.
Seaman,	6.
Selfe,	9.
Shear,	6.
Shenton,	12.
Sloat,	4, 5, 6, 7,10,12,14,15.
Smalley,	5.
Smith,	1, 2, 8, 9,16.
Sprague,	9.
Springsteel,	1.
Stanton,	4.
Stevens,	9.
Swanson,	9.
Taylor,	2, 8.
Tilford,	12.
Tompkins,	1, 3, 5, 9.
Townsend,	5.
Travis,	1, 3, 4, 5, 7.
Turrell,	2.
Vail,	10,11,13.
Vermilyea,	5.
Vores,	2,10.
Vredenburg,	6.
Warren,	5, 6, 7,10.
Weeks,	13,14.
Westcott,	6.
Wheeler,	2,15.
Whitney,	9.
Wiley,	12.
Wilson,	8.
Wolf,	8.
Wright,	1, 5, 6, 7,11,12,13,14.
Yeamans,	1.

Union Valley

Fisher,	Adelaide, dau. Edwin & Mary E.; died Aug.3,1881-age 6mo.
Travis,	Lewis Travis; Apr.28,1811-Nov.20,1866.
"	Elizabeth, wife Lewis; Jan.29,1822-Apr.14,1893.
Adams,	Fletcher Adams; Jan.9,1847-
"	Amanda, wife Fletcher; Feb.8,1843-May 20,1892.
Wright,	David Wright; died Nov.14,1872-age 46yrs. 2mos. 8days.
"	Gilbert Wright; died May 28,1869-age 70yrs. 8mos. 15da.
"	Eliza, wife Gilbert Wright; died May 6,1892- age 87 years, 8 months, 15 days.
"	Lewis, son James H. & Mary; d. June 9,1872-age 7mo. 20da.
Springsteel,	Theda Wright, wife Matthew; Nov.4,1840-Mar.4,1907.
Yeamans,	Susan, wife Amplias Yeamans, dau. Gilbert & Eliza Wright died Oct.20,1877-age 47 years.
Braithwaite,	George H. Braithwaite; Feb.20,1875-June 14,1908.
Romanowski,	Frederick H. Romanowski; Dec.30,1858-Sept.13,1908.
D'Orchimont,	Estelle Y. D'Orchimont; 1860- (wife Arthur Pottow?)
Pottow,	Arthur Pottow; 1859-1914.
Vredenburgh	Clarissa Vredenburg; Dec.6,1815-July 21,1895.
Ostrander,	Isabella Ostrander; 1806-1887.
"	James R. Ostrander; 1843-1914.
"	Laura Drew, wife James R. Ostrander; 1849-
"	Susie D., dau. James & Laura; 1873-1897.
"	Walton Drew, son James & Laura; July 19,1893-Nov.6,1893
Quick,	Thomas H. Quick; 1852-1919.
"	Kate Tompkins, wife Thomas Quick; 1856-1915.
Tompkins.	Dilazon Tompkins; died Feb.8,1867-age 47 years.
"	Jane Smith, wife Dilazon Tompkins; died April 12,1901-age 86 years.

Union Val.

Smith,   John J. Smith; 1811-1897.

"   Elizabeth A., wife John J.; 1808-1861.

Vores,   Charles Vores; "Ord.Sergt.Co.E. 95th.Regt.N.Y.S.Vol."
                        son David & Rachel; born Oct.3,1844-
                        killed Gettysburg battle July 1,1863.

"   David Vores; died Feb.23,1883-age 84 years, 13 days.

"   Laura, wife David; died May 26,1870-age 53yrs. 2mos. 23days

"   James Henry Vores; Mar.8,1830-Jan.2,1910.

"   Hettie E., wife James Henry; died May 28,1870-age 24yrs. 5mo.

"   Roberta C., dau.M.F.& Hattie; died Sept.20,1877-
                        age 8 months, 16 days.

"   Margery, dau.M.F.& Hattie; died May 7,1887-age 8mos. 21days

"   Stephen Vores; Nov.12,1812-Aug.27,1893.

"   Nettie, wife Stephen; July 16,1812-Feb.9,1865.

Craft,   George A.Craft; died Apr.13,1871-age 34yrs. 7mos. 14days.

McCaull,   Thomas McCaull; Oct.14,1825-Nov.16,1881.

"   Esther, wife Thomas; Feb.13,1827-Oct.6,1903.

"   John C.McCaull; Sept.5,1855-May 23,1892.

"   Esther, dau.Thomas & Esther; Nov.20,1871-Jan.23,1872.

Agor,   Everett Agor; July 16,1856-Oct.31,1909.

"   Eliza G.Taylor, wife Everett Agor; Apr.5,1858-

"   Anderson, son Everett & Eliza; died Mar.13,1883-age 1mo. 9da.

Taylor,   William Taylor; died Feb.17,1887-age 58yrs. 10mos. 21days.

"   Sarah Elizabeth, wife William Taylor; died June 19,1894-
                        age 63 years, 10 months, 27 days.

Wheeler,   Phebe Jane, wife Stephen; died Dec.27,1873-age 33 years.

"   Willie, son Stephen & Phebe;- Oct.22,1871-Dec.8,1871.

"   Frank A., son Stephen & Phebe; died Oct.17,1870-age 2mo.19da.

Turrell,   Phebe Ann, wife Ephriam; Apr.6,1817-Mar.26,1895.

Union Val.

Tompkins,	James P. Tompkins; 1841-1908.
"	Harriet J., wife James; 1847-
"	Jared W., son James & Harriet; ----
"	Thadius, son James & Harriet; ----
"	Judith, dau. James & Harriet; ----
"	Thomas W. Tompkins; 1790-1865.
"	Judith L., wife Thomas; 1801-1891.
Ganong,	Abel W. Ganong; died June 14, 1879-age 82yrs. 2mos. 9days
"	Eliza, wife Abel; died Mar. 24, 1857-age 54yrs. 7mos. 29da.
"	Thomas F. Ganong; May 20, 1839-Feb. 28, 1895.
"	Frank E. Ganong; Mar. 7, 1910-
"	George W. Ganong; ----
"	William H. Ganong; died Sept. 16, 1873-age 52yrs. 8mos. 24da.
"	Josephine M., dau. William & Josephine; died June 28, 1858- age 6 years, 19 days.
Hyatt,	Alvah Hyatt; Oct. 26, 1828-June 14, 1897.
"	Catherine, wife Alvah; May 1, 1833-July 11, 1920.
"	Sarah M., wife Alvah; died Mar. 5, 1863-age 27yrs. 5mos.
"	Lucy Ann, wife Alvah; died Apr. 14, 1857-age 26yrs. 4mos.
"	Maggie, dau. Alvah & Catherine; died Apr. 23, 1869-age 2mo.
Barker,	William A. Barker; May 18, 1859-Jan. 12, 1892.
"	Frank C. Barker; July 1, 1861-May 6, 1901.
"	William Barker; died Mar. 3, 1874-age 38yrs. 3mos. 23days.
Higgins,	Lewis Higgins; died Sept. 10, 1874-age 63 years.
"	Salinnia, wife Lewis; died June 4, 1862-age 56yrs. 9mos.
McCollum,	Benjamin McCollum; 1819-1901.
"	Polly J. Fosdick, wife Benjamin McCollum; 1841-1911.
"	Catherine C. wife Benjamin; died May 24, 1874-age 55yr. 1mo.

Union Val.

Ganong, Jackson Ganong; Jan. 12, 1832 – June 13, 1898.

" Cecelia Travis, wife Jackson Ganong;
    June 17, 1831 – January 2, 1911.

" Ralph M., son E.C. & H.G.; died Oct. 2, 1884 – age 2 months.

" Chauncey, son Oscar & Deborah; ----

" Jonet Ganong; died Oct. 3, 1888 – age 81yrs. 3mos. 27days.

" Clarinda, wife Jonet; died May 19, 1885 – age 76yrs. 4mos.

" Clarence L. Ganong; Aug. 2, 1870 – Dec. 14, 1895.

" Infant dau. Chester C. & Sarah M.; dec. 2, 1876 ----

Jelliff, John B. Jelliff; Nov. 7, 1825 – Jan. 29, 1875.

" Jemima J., wife John B.; Nov. 14, 1829 – Mar. 26, 1900.

" Preston J. Jelliff; 1860 – 1909.

Deats, Cecilia Travis, wife William Deats; Nov. 8, 1868 – Mar. 14, 1896.

Travis, Joseph H. Travis; 1839 – 1909.

" Mary Sloat, wife Joseph Travis; 1839 –

" Samuel W. Travis; died Dec. 15, 1888 – age 84yrs. 11mos. 17days

" Hannah Pinckney, wife Samuel W. Travis; died Feb. 8, 1897 –
    age 90 years, 8 months, 9 days.

Smith, James Smith; June 11, 1801 – Jan. 6, 1888.

" Emma Angevine, wife James Smith; Mar. 5, 1808 – Apr. 16, 1896.

Corsa, William H. Corsa; 1844 – 1895.

" Charlie, son William H. & Josie E.; d. Mar. 12, 1878 – age 7yrs.

Sloat, Bud F. Sloat; Sept. 12, 1802 – May 1, 1873.

" Mary, wife Bud; June 19, 1808 – April 26, 1879.

Knapp, Robert L., son Drake C. & Heater K.; died Dec. 28, 1865 –
    age 13 years, 5 months, 2 days.

" Sanford C. son Drake & Hester; died Aug. 27, 1879 – age 13y. 9m.

Stanton, Eddie L., son Edward F. & Annie T.; died Nov. 10, 1879 –
    age 5 years, 2 months, 29 days.

Union Val.

Tompkins,	Dennie J. son Jacob C.& Augusta; Jan.23,1881-Dec.7,1881.
Quick,	Albert Quick; 1846-
"	Phebe A.Townsend, wife Albert Quick; 1847-
"	Augustus B.Quick; died Dec.25,1885-age 61yrs. 8mos. 11da.
"	Mary Hitt, wife Augustus Quick; 1827-1910.
Ganun,	Jackson P.Ganun; Aug.11,1823-Sept.9,1890.
"	Sarah Vermilyea, wife Jackson Ganun; June 5,1902 ---
"	Ashbel G.Ganun; Apr.25,1853-Feb.6,1882.
Laraway,	Saidee Urania Ganun Laraway; Sept.25,1866-Apr.27,1910.
Odell,	Ella Kniffin, wife Hezekiah Odell; Jan.15,1858-July 3,1892.
"	Curtis, son Hezekiah & Ella; Sept.22,1877-Nov.18,1899.
Kniffin,	Silvenus Kniffin; Aug.22,1835-Jan.6,1917.
"	Susan Travis, wife Silvenus Kniffin; Dec.8,1828-Dec.13,1907.
"	David, son Silvenus & Susan; Jan.10,1866-Dec.16,1869.
"	Robert, son Silvenus & Susan; Feb.26,1868-Dec.24,1869.
"	Sarah Travis, wife David Kniffin; died Sept.30,1862- age 66 years, 8 months, 1 day
"	Claude S., son Emmalinda; died July 31,1886-age 6yr. 7mo.
Smalley,	Phebe J.Smalley, dau.Bud & Mary Sloat; June 11,1837-March 29,1908.
Wright,	Platt S.Wright; Aug.17,1821-May 21,1883.
"	Sarah Sloat, wife Platt Wright; Feb.19,1834-June 10,1908.
"	Platt S.Sloat,Jr.; Apr.19,1861-Sept.4,1871.
Warren,	Melvin C.Warren; 1841-1905.
"	Sarah E.Wright, wife Melvin Warren; died Oct.20,1868- age 26 years, 2 months, 20 days.
"	Henry C., son Melvin & Sarah; died Jan.30,1867-age 2mo.25d.
"	Hamilton, son Melvin & Sarah; d.Aug.1,1868-age 4mo. 5da.

Union Val.

Warren,   Ettie, dau.Melvin & Sarah; died Apr.8,1870-age 5yrs. 10da.

Wright,   Father & Mother; ------

Bates,   Eulia Anna Wright, wife Joseph T.Bates; died Feb.12,1866-
           age 20 years, 8 months, 19 days.

Wright,   Lewis Wright; died Aug.30,1873-age 76yrs. 3mos. 14days.

"   Martha Ganong, wife Lewis Wright; died Oct.9,1880-age 79yr.

Westcott, William Westcott; ----

"   Carrie E.Sloat, wife William Westcott;
                       May 28,1859-June 23,1901.

Warren,   Enos Warren; died May 13,1878-age 68 years.

"   Eliza, wife Enos; died July 2,1888-age 77 years.

"   Euphemia, dau.Enos & Eliza; died Jan.25,1857-age 23yr. 9mo.

"   James Kendree, son Enos & Eliza; 6 years.

"   Jane Chambers, dau.Enos & Eliza; 2 years.

"   James Washington, son Enos & Eliza; 16mos.

"   Amelia Cook, dau.Enos & Eliza; 4 mos.

"   John Sloat Warren; 1841-897.

Inslee,   Nettie, wife Edwin W.; dau.Enos & Eliza Warren;
                       died May 1,1866-age 18 years.

"   Henry Edwin, son Edwin & Nettie; died Sept.4,1866-age 4mo.

Wright,   Susan E.Shear, wife Elbert Wright; Sep.17,1855-Feb.1,1914.

Shear,   Daniel B.Shear; died June 22,1892-age 70yrs. 4mos. 6days

"   Martha A., wife Daniel; died Mar.4,1897-age 67yrs. 3mos.

Seaman,   Emma Jane Seaman; 27 years.

"   Lydia A.Seaman; 75 years.

Roussin,   Carrie E.Roussin; 37 years.

Archer,   Edgar A.Archer; June 10,1853-Aug.10,1904.

"   Elizabeth, wife Edgar; Mar.27,1853-Jan.13,1918.

Kenney,   William N. son Robert & Josephine; 1920-1920.

Union Val.

McCollum,	Perry McCollum;	June 9,1822-Apr.10,1907.
"	Nancy Ganong, wife Perry McCollum; Aug.27,1827-Nov.8,1909	
Scofield,	Freddie, son George & Anna; died Mar.14,1865-age 2yr. 8mo	
"	Laura L.Gray, wife John J.Scofield; Sep.-1816-Nov.1,1903.	
Sloat,	Warren Sloat; Sept.30,1808-Jan.5,1876.	
"	Rachel Travis, wife Warren Sloat; June 7,1807-Mar.10,1899	
"	James Sloat; Nov.21,1786-Apr.23,1874.	
"	Hettie Sloat; Feb.21,1788-Mar.4,1872.	
"	Orman Sloat; June 27,1823-Mar.29,1902.	
"	Naomi Wright, wife Orman Sloat; Aug.19,1821-Mar.20,1895.	
"	Leonard G.Sloat; 1854-1919.	
"	Lucy Phillips, wife Leonard Sloat; 1857-	
"	Edson Sloat; Dec.20,1812-Mar.27,1876.	
"	Jane Wright, wife Edson Sloat; Jan.14,1820-July 21,1886.	
"	James Stanley, son Edson & Jane; died Nov.30,1861- age 19 years, 5 months, 21 days.	
"	Charley L., son Edson & Jane; died Oct.30,1861-age 5yr,3mo.	
"	Byron, son Edson & Jane; died Dec.6,1861-age 2yr. 8mo. 23d.	
"	Elbert Sloat; died Feb.12,1910-age 82 years.	
"	Mary E., wife Elbert; died Oct.11,1891-age 62 years.	
"	Benson, son Elbert & Mary; died Jan.12,1862-age 7mo. 14da	
"	David S.Sloat; died Oct.3,1834-age 1yr. 10mo. 18da.	
"	Henry Sloat; Nov.15,1799-Apr.1,1873.	
"	Annis Warren, wife Henry Sloat; June 1805-Mar.30,1890.	
Baker,	Howard E.Baker; son Leander & Annie; died Sept.22,1866- age 1 year, 5 months, 22 days.	
Ellis,	G.Edward Ellis; July 22,1866-Oct.4,1910.	
"	Nancy L.Ellis; June 3,1837-May 20,1904.	

Union Val.

Geibel,	George Geibel; 1835-1913.
"	Catherine Wolf, wife George Geibel;
Gumpert,	Otto Augustus Gumpert; July 2,1867-Feb.6,1912.
"	Laura S.C.Boker, wife Otto A.Gumpert; Dec.17,1867-Sept.19,1907.
Lent,	James Lent; Aug.3,1831-Feb.10,1916.
"	Lydia Delavan, wife James Lent; Apr.15,1842-Aug.26,1898.
"	Calvin C.Lent; Nov.14,1861-Dec.22,1883.
Wilson,	Henry M.Wilson; Mar.14,1846-Apr.19,1901.
"	Wendell W., son Clayton G.& Laura A.; Aug.20,1899-Mar.26,1900.
Fowler,	Thomas B.Fowler; Sept.18,1848-Sept.24,1886.
"	Frances O.Taylor, wife Thomas B.Fowler; April 8,1850-October 4,1906.
Kniffin,	Kelleb Kniffin; died May 15,1889-age 76 years.
Mead,	Ferris D.Mead; Jan.20,1823-Dec.28,1896.
"	Mary A.McCollum, wife Ferris D.Mead; Jan.24,1841-
Knapp,	Carrie F., dau.Elias & Frances E. died Sept.27,1880- age 18 years, 9 months, 12 days.
Smith,	George W.Smith; died June 4,1894-age 50yrs. 7mos. 26days.
"	Florence Jessie, dau.George W.& Jessie A.; Sept.29,1891-Aug.31,1909.
Dyke,	Susan Dyke; died Feb.1,1903-age 78yrs. 8mos. 2days.
Powers,	Samuel J.Powers; Jan.27,1830-Dec.27,1909.
"	Caroline M.Brundage, wife Samuel J.Powers; July 30,1827-Dec.2,1912.
"	Daniel T.Powers; Feb.15,1855-Feb.9,1863.
"	Oscar B.Powers; Jan.24,1859-June 21,1862.
"	Freddie E.Powers; Aug.4,1857-Feb.1,1858.
"	Samuel J. son Joseph T.& Beryl S; May 6,1893-Sep.24,1895.

Union Val.

Ganung,	Annie E., wife Thomas Ganung, dau. Stephen & Roxana Knox; April 26, 1843-
Bittner,	John Bittner; Feb. 4, 1879-
"	Lulu A. Coons, wife John Bittner; Nov. 9, 1889-Apr. 5, 1919.
Ganong,	Earle G. Ganong; Jan. 12, 1889-July 13, 1919.
"	Wallace O. Ganong; -----
"	Mabel A. Swanson, wife Wallace O. Ganong; 1896-1919.
"	Kenneth W., son Wallace & Mabel; 1915-1919.
Swanson,	Hilda, dau. Archie & Belle; Feb. 5, 1910-Feb. 12, 1910.
Selfe,	Jesse Selfe; born in England Jan. 18, 1812-died June 14, 1896
"	Elizabeth, wife Jesse; born in Wales Sept. 9, 1830-a died Nov. 16, 1908.
Whitney,	Ephriam Whitney; Aug. 4, 1827-Oct. 25, 1909.
"	Susan Brewer, wife Ephriam Whitney; Feb. 22, 1827-Nov. 22, 1904.
Smith,	William W. Smith; 1859-1915.
"	Mary Tompkins, wife William Smith; 1860-
"	James L. Smith; 1859-1916.
"	Melissa Sprague, wife James L. Smith; 1860-
Hudson,	Harriet Hudson; born in England; Nov. 14, 1807-June 24, 1890.
Matthews,	George W. Matthews; died June 21, 1909-age 75 years.
"	Susan L., wife George W.; died June 24, 1890-age 54 years.
"	John H. Matthews; died Dec. 8, 1862-age 68yrs. 10mos. 22days
"	Nancy, wife John H.; died Apr. 14, 1853-age 57yrs. 4mos.
Mead,	William E. Mead; 1861-1897.
Smith,	Leonard M. Smith;
"	Laura A. Hults, wife Leonard Smith; July 16, 1859-Nov. 16, 1912
Hults,	Henry A. Hults; May 15, 1865-Jan. 3, 1907.
Stevens,	Frederick, son James & Susan; Apr. 22, 1914-Feb. 12, 1916.

Union Val.

Ganung, Marcus Ganung; Nov. 22, 1804-Jan. 6, 1877.

" Ann Sloat, wife Marcus Ganung; Apr. 14, 1806-Nov. 2, 1864.

" Mary E., wife Thaddeus R.; died Oct. 9, 1854-age 24 years.

" Thomas Ganung; 1822-1899.

" Esther Sloat, wife Thomas Ganung; 1826-1873.

" Alonzo S., son Thomas & Esther; died Harpers Ferry, Va. Feb. 17, 1863-age 17 years, 6 months

" Willie, son Thomas & Esther; died Mar. 6,---- age 2 years.

" Tommie, son Bailey & Euphemia; Dec. 27, 1872-Jan. 12, 1874.

" Mattie, wife John; ----

" Lownie, son John & Mattie; ----

" Nellie, dau. John & Mattie; ----

" Abie A., son Theodore & E.W.; died Apr. 29, 1870-age 17mos.

Sloat, Charles Sloat; Nov. 12, 1811-Jan. 15, 1904.

" Rachel Ganung, wife Charles Sloat; Mar. 11, 1816-July 1, 1900

" Charles M. Sloat; ----

" Carrie M. Ganung, wife Charles M. Sloat; 1848-1919.

" Emma Florence, dau. Charles & Carrie; 1870-1875.

Ganong, Thomas W. Ganong; June 27, 1839-Dec. 14, 1903.

" Euphemia W., wife Thomas; Jan. 15, 1849-Apr. 12, 1906.

Sloat, Edson M. Sloat; 1870-

" Emma J. Vores, wife Edson Sloat; 1869-

Ganun, Thomas Ganun; died Apr. 6, 1876-age 92yrs. 7mos. 12days.

" Jane, wife Thomas; died June 5, 1869-age 76yrs. 11mos. 25da

" Elbert N. Ganun; Oct. 5, 1828-Nov. 1, 1895.

" Nancy J. Vail, wife Elbert N. Ganun; Aug. 28, 1831-Apr. 17, 1900

Warren, Benson Warren; Sept. 10, 1839-July 4, 1899.

Barrett, Clarissa J. Barrett; 1850-1916.

Union Val.

Austin,	Samuel Austin; 1797-1869.
"	Amy Hitt, wife Samuel Austin; 1804-1882.
Ganung,	James B. Ganung; died June 1,1873-age 54yrs. 9mos. 26days
"	Rebecca Austin, wife James Ganung; June 28,1819-June 27,1900.
"	Leonard Ganung; May 8,1823-June 5,1901.
"	Abigail Wright, wife Leonard Ganung; May 13,1823-May 2,1894.
"	Phebe A., wife Leonard; Mar.8,1820-Aug.19,1865.
"	Infant dau. Leonard & Phebe; Nov.6,1857---
"	Bailey Ganung; died Sept.13,1885-age 77 years, 6 months.
"	Malinda, wife Bailey; Dec.6,1877-age 66yrs. 3mos. 18days
"	Abraham Ganung; died June 27,1858-age 78yrs. 2mos.
"	Nancy, wife Abraham; died Mar.4,1872-age 86yrs. 3mos. 28da
Vail,	Frederick A. Vail; died Sept.18,1875-age 48yrs. 8mos. 13da.
"	Susan R., wife Fredk.A.; died July 30,1857-age 28yr. 10mo.
"	Infant dau. Fredk. & Susan; 7 weeks.
"	John Henry, son John T. & Mary A.; died May 14,1877- age 15 years, 2 months.
Knox,	William F. Knox; Jan.1,1837-Aug.16,1902.
"	Hattie A. Ganung, wife William F. Knox; Jan.17,1844-Sept.27,1913.
"	Stephen Knox; June 14,1798-Sept.10,1888.
"	Roxana Delavan, wife Stephen Knox; Sep.15,1810-June 23,1892
"	George H. Knox; Oct.16,1840-Sept.25,1908.
Ryder,	Jacob S. Ryder; Aug.28,1835-Sept.15,1907.
"	Eliza G., wife Jacob S.; Sept.6,1837-
Gregory,	George Melvin, son James & Susan; died Nov.19,1855- age 2 years, 9 months, 27 days.
Brien,	Jane, dau. James; died Aug.11,1889-age 75 years.

Union Val.

Wiley,	James Wiley; died Sept.13,1864-age 37yrs. 1mon. 13days.
"	Rebecca Richie, wife James Wiley; died Dec.17,1893-age 69yr
"	James Wiley,Jr.; died Aug.21,1862-age 4yrs. 9mos. 8days
"	Baby son Charles & Margaret; Nov.2,1879---
Ritchie,	Adam Ritchie; 1839-1908.
"	Elizabeth Shenton, wife Adam Ritchie; 1846-1912.
"	Mamie, dau.Adam & Elizabeth; died Sept.10,1869-age 10mos.
Cullen,	Elizabeth A., wife Thomas; died Aug.14,1871-age 26yrs. 2mo
Fowler,	William H.Fowler; May 17,1868-
"	Esther M.Sloat, wife William Fowler; Oct.12,1868-May 23,1910.
"	Carrie B. dau.William & Esther; Feb.22,1894-Feb.24,1894.
Rusky,	Noah Rusky; Dec.9,1809-Oct.4,1885.
"	Ellen, wife Noah; Feb.19,1811-July 15,1882.
Fuller,	Martha M., wife Elbert; Feb.14,1837-May 26,1897.
Wright,	Samuel V.Wright; May 5,1821-Mar.14,1900.
"	Oscar J.Wright; July 27,1847-Aug.19,1907.
"	Stephen Wright; ----
"	Ezra Wright; ----
"	Maria Wright; ----
Bennett,	Hazel K., dau.William B.& Kassie W.; died Aug.29,1894- age 8 years, 9 months, 11 days.
Dayton,	Benjamin F.Dayton; "Co.D. 1st.N.Y.Cav.Vol." May 6,1848-May 11,1918.
"	Emeline Mead, wife Benjamin Dayton; March 24,1849-August 14,1908.
Tilford,	Charles W.Tilford; Feb.26,1870-Sept.23,1911.
"	Edith May Dayton, wife Charles Tilford; Apr.23,1874-----
"	Gertrude, dau.Charles W.& Edith May; born & died November 6,1898.

Union Val.

Banker,	Stephen Banker; 1852-
"	Jane Curry, wife Stephen Banker; 1853-1914.
"	Irving Banker· 1878-
Ganung,	Jeremiah Ganung; died Aug.21,1863-age 84yrs. 5mos. 13days
"	Hannah, wife Jeremiah; died Aug.30,1869- age 84 years, 3 months, 22 days.
"	Marandah, dau.Jeremiah & Hannah; died Aug.8,1838- age 10 years, 6 months, 7 days.
Gregory,	Erastus R.Gregory; Feb.11,1825-Dec.6,1901.
"	Delia A.Vail, wife Erastus R.Gregory; June 8,1824-Mar. 29,1889.
"	Clara T.Gregory; Sept.16,1849-Dec.14,1891.
"	Alven Gregory; died Aug.12,1864-age 36 years.
"	Mary, wife Alven; died 1873----
Weeks,	Edward Weeks; ----
"	Lulu Weeks; ----
"	Mary Weeks; ----
"	Charles Weeks; ----
Wright,	Stephen T.Wright; Jan.19,1811-Apr.27,1873.
"	Dorinda, wife Stephen; Mar.7,1809-Dec.22,1897.
"	Augusta M.Bailey, wife Stephen T.Wright; Aug.23,1839-Nov.27,1907.
"	James Wright; Feb.20,1814-Aug.31,1887.
"	Mary Ann, wife James; Jan.1,1817-May 31,1893.
"	Fannie, wife Charles; dau.Philander & Mary Palmer; died June 13,1865-age 25yr. 8mo.
Palmer,	Benjamin Wright Palmer; died June 26,1893----
"	Philander Palmer; Dec.27,1802-Feb.26,1889.
"	Mary Prendergast Palmer; Mar.17,1815-July 22,1895.
"	Fannie W., dau.B.W.& S.E.; died Oct.18,1865-age 1mo. 5da.

Union Val.

Ferguson,	Elbert Ferguson; died Dec.9,1886-age 69 years.
"	Augusta, wife Elbert; died Jan.25,1894-age 72yrs. 5mos.
Bailey,	Ira Bailey; June 13,1835-June 13,1908.
"	Eliza J.Horton, wife Ira Bailey; Sept.20,1835-May 26,1913
"	Samuel E., son Ira & Eliza; died Oct.26,1866-age 1yr.9mo.
"	Grant, son Ira & Eliza; died June 19,1869-age 5 months.
"	Horace Bailey; Sept.4,1861-Aug.13,1907.
"	Juliaetta Lounsbury, wife Horace Bailey; June 11,1851---
"	Sarah Bailey; Feb.20,1814-Aug.31,1887.
Light,	William W.Light; Dec.12,1860-Mar.10,1888.
"	George E., son William W. & Mary E.; July 30,1887-November 2,1887.
Weeks,	Dorinda Wright, wife Jacob C.Weeks; April 30,1865-July 23,1899.
Anderson,	G.H.Anderson; Oct.19,1824-June 22,1904.
"	Tamer A.Ganung, wife G.H.Anderson; Nov.3,1827-Nov.14,1909
Ganung,	Rozana Ganung; died Feb.8,1887-age 75 years, 10 months.
Benda,	Frank Benda; died Dec.11,1878-age 22yrs. 6mos. 26days.
Potter,	George W.Potter; Dec.1,1823-Jan.27,1890.
"	Adah C.Cowan, wife George W.Potter; Nov.29,1833-Sept.21,1899.
Sloat,	Oliver M.Sloat; July 19,1840-Aug.27,1896.
"	Martha, wife Oliver; Mar.28,1845-Dec.12,1917.
"	Sammie, son Oliver & Martha; Mar.1,1868-Nov.30,1869.
"	Jessie, dau.Oliver & Martha; Apr.25,1874-Oct.15,1874.
"	Minnie, dau.Oliver & Martha; Sept.29,1866-Dec.5,1869.
"	Gracie, dau.Oliver & Martha; Aug.18,1871-Dec.21,1872.
Haines,	Francis Haines; June 28,1830-Jan.5,1899.
"	Laura J.Croft, wife Francis Haines; Apr.14,1831-Apr.8,1895

Union Val.

Merrick, George Clarence, son Charles C.& Carrie B.;
Oct.2,1895-July 28,1896.

McKeel, James McKeel; died May 10,1854-age 46 years, 9 months.

" Maria McKeel; died Oct.4,1871-age 64 years, 2 months.

" James M.McKeel; "Capt.4th.Artillery N.Y.Vol."
died Aug.25,1864-age 26yrs. 7mos.

" William O.McKeel; died June 15,1869-age 27yrs. 6mos.

" Sarah McKeel; died Dec.17,1870-age 23yrs. 1mon. 4days.

Purdy, Norman B.Purdy; died Nov.3,1864-age 20yrs. 11mos. 21days.

" Susie J., dau.A.B.& Julia; died Apr.13,1872-age 20yrs. 9mo

" James A. son A.B.& J.A.; died Oct.7,1859-age 21yr. 8mo.

Sloat, George F.Sloat; Aug.22,1848-July 4,1907.

" Levina C.Lent, wife George F.Sloat;
Feb.13,1850-Oct.19,1901.

Church, Frederick L.Church; died Nov.16,1870-age 20yrs. 8mos.

Ganung, Alfred & Phebe, children Isaac & Mary; ------

Clark, Henry D.Clark; Sept.5,1828-Sept.18,1910.

" Eliza Palmer, wife Henry D.Clark; May 31,1833-----

Dunning, Bennie, son Edward & Amanda P.; died Dec.5,1871-
age 2 years, 2 months, 10 days.

Wheeler, Emily Wheeler; died June 4,1889-age 72 years.

Mead, Jane, wife William O.; Dec.25,1831-Nov.24,1889.

Brady, Henrietta, wife Benjamin R.; Jan.13,1845-Jan.19,1896.

" Chester, son Benj.& Etta; June 19,1869-Dec.28,1885.

" Mattie H., dau.Benjamin & Henrietta;
died July 26,1868-age 6 months.

" Willie J., son Benjamin & Henrietta;
died Aug.10,1866-age 2 weeks.

" Cornelius T.Brady; 1871-

" Emma Banker, wife Cornelius Brady; 1870-1907.

Union Val.

Bennett,	Claude Bennett;	1899-1899.
"	Delia Bennett;	1895-1918.
"	Lydia Bennett;	1866-1869.
Frost,	James A. Frost;	Apr. 26, 1843-Nov. 1, 1907.
"	Hester A. Smith, wife James A. Frost;	July 28, 1849-January 25, 1890.
Smith,	Charles G. Smith;	Sept. 25, 1854- ----
"	Mary Elizabeth Hults, wife Charles G. Smith;	Sept. 2, 1853-June 6, 1905.
Banker,	Daniel Banker;	1835-1895.
"	Sarah Curry, wife Daniel Banker;	1847-1911.